BY WIND AND IRON

Commodore Thomas Macdonough at the Battle of Cumberland Bay by Alonzo Chappel, 1866.

BY WIND
AND IRON

NAVAL CAMPAIGNS IN THE
CHAMPLAIN VALLEY, 1665-1815

MICHAEL G. LARAMIE

WESTHOLME
Yardley

Westholme Publishing, LLC
904 Edgewood Road
Yardley, Pennsylvania 19067
Visit our Web site at www.westholmepublishing.com

First Printing June 2015
10 9 8 7 6 5 4 3 2 1
ISBN: 978-1-59416-198-8
Also available as an eBook.

Printed in the United States of America.

For Ryan, Andrew, Brittany, and Nathanael

CONTENTS

List of Maps and Plans ix
Foreword by Art Cohn xi

1. The Champlain Waterway 1

2. The First Fleets 7

3. The Destruction of the French Lake Champlain Fleet 25

4. Valcour Island 52

5. The Masters of the Lake 86

6. The Battle of Cumberland Bay 104

7. A New Lake 146

Appendix A: Maps 155
Appendix B: After Action Reports 170
Appendix C: Ship Types 185
Appendix D: The Fleets 186
Glossary 238
Notes 245
Bibliography 259
Acknowledgments 268
Index 269

Maps and Plans

Portion of a French Map showing Tracy's march to the Mohawk Villages	3
Plan of Fort St. Frédéric	9
Principal waterways in the Champlain Basin	13
Plan of Fort William Henry	17
A Plan of the fort and fortress at Crown Point, 1759	27
The Scuttling of the French Fleet Oct 11 and 12, 1759	37
The Destruction of the French Fleet at Ile aux Noix	49
A Plan of the Battle of Valcour Island	78
Plan of Carillon or Ticonderoga	88
A portion of a 1779 map of Lake Champlain	110–111
Plan of the Ile aux Noix	121
The Battle of Cumberland Bay	131
William Brasier's map of Lakes Champlain and George	156–157
Detail of Brasier's map showing the British victory on Lake Champlain	158
Detail of Brasier's map showing the flight of Arnold's fleet	159
Detail of an anonymous 1779 map showing the Battle of Valcour Island	160
Detail an anonymous 1779 map showing the flight of Arnold's fleet	161
A Sketch of the Battle of Valcour Island	162
Macdonough's Sketch of the Battle of Cumberland Bay	164
Plan of the Naval Action on Lake Champlain	165
The Battle of Cumberland Bay	166
Mahan's Map of teh Battle of Cumberland Bay	167
Manuscript Plan of the Battle of Plattsburgh	168–169

FOREWORD

Art Cohn, Senior Scientist, Lake Champlain Maritime Museum

F OR MOST OF MY ADULT LIFE, I HAVE BEEN A STUDENT OF THE military campaigns that took place in the Champlain Valley. I have focused on the naval aspects of this period and was surprised to learn the ways that French and British warships sailing on this inland lake helped tip the Old World balance of power and control. The revelation that the most powerful European nations of their day had waged warfare in this remote mountain lake before the American colonies had even dreamed of revolution is testimony to the significance of this water highway. While today we celebrate the beauty of Lake Champlain and the valley that surrounds it, in the world of Samuel de Champlain, Benedict Arnold, and Thomas Macdonough, the great value of the region lay in the north-south oriented 120 miles of navigable water and its ability to move ships, cannon, supplies, and fighting men.

The water highway was so significant that it figures large during three distinct military eras, all subjects masterfully chronicled in Michael Laramie's new book. France and Great Britain recognized the strategic transportation value of Lake Champlain and also the value of the raw materials for shipbuilding growing in the vast forests surrounding it. Following Great Britain's successful military mastery over France by 1760, the stage was set for the next military episode, the American struggle for independence. Just three weeks after the clash at Concord and Lexington, Ethan Allen and the Green Mountain Boys, with Benedict Arnold, surprised the British garrison at Fort Ticonderoga. Arnold, already an experienced mariner, recognized the strategic value of Lake Champlain and in short order had captured the lake's only large vessels.

For the next three years, from 1775 to 1777, events on the northern lake that reached into British Canada played a pivotal role in American history. Warships with names like *Liberty*, *Revenge*, and *Royal Savage* reflected the Americans' determination and mindset. In my work as a nautical archaeologist and historian, the vessels of the American and British fleets became my passion and the center of my research. It became clear to me that the invasion of Canada, the Battle of Valcour Island, and the American victory at Saratoga were all connected events that had a profound impact on the outcome of the war.

Thirty-five years later, the War of 1812 would engulf the Champlain Valley in its third and final military contest. During that conflict, the naval efforts of young Thomas Macdonough presented a true American hero to compare and contrast with the richly controversial Benedict Arnold. The 1812 and 1813 campaigns provided two years of sparring on the lake with naval superiority shifting between the combatants. These early struggles culminated in 1814 with the construction of the largest wooden warships on the lake and climaxed in the American land and naval victory on Lake Champlain on September 11, 1814. Macdonough's victory not only secured the Lake Champlain invasion route for the remainder of the war but also impacted the wider war and helped lead to a negotiated peace. These events and the role that Lake Champlain played in them were better understood and more widely known in the aftermath of the war than they are now. By the time the War of 1812 reached its two hundredth anniversary, it was sandwiched between the American Revolution and the Civil War and has become one of the world's forgotten wars.

The bygone era of wooden warships, driven by wind and fastened by iron, has left us with a tangible legacy of three-dimensional archaeological touchstones. These unique relics provide an extraordinary connection to their times and the men who fought aboard them for King and country. In my career I have been privileged to locate vessels from all the fleets that once sailed the lake. No discovery has been more exciting than locating, in 1997, the 1776 gunboat *Spitfire*. This gunboat, once part of Benedict Arnold's fleet, was abandoned in the dark of night on October 12, 1776, when Arnold and his men fled from a stronger British force toward the safety of their fortifications at Fort Ticonderoga after a five-hour battle at Valcour Island. We have also located the remnants of the 1777 "Great Bridge" which spanned Lake Champlain between Mount Independence and Fort Ticonderoga. While not a shipwreck, this amazing structure was built just months before Burgoyne's invasion by American forces using the winter's ice as a construction platform. This chapter in the story culminates in one of the profound events of the American Revolution, the British army's shocking defeat at Saratoga.

Today these archaeological treasures rest in the lake's cold, fresh water on the bottom of Lake Champlain. Some are partially buried while some remain remarkably intact, but all serve as time machines to another era and the events that helped define a Continent. During my career I have tried to better understand the nature of this collection and develop ways to preserve them and share their importance with the public. This has not always been easy, and the recently discovered infestation of zebra mussels has added a new layer of complexity to the work, an urgency driven in part by the discovery of the *Spitfire*. However, I am pleased to say that the military collection contained within Lake Champlain has helped push the boundaries in the development of a public policy framework to better preserve, protect, and share these fragile, finite, and powerful sites.

I have often stated that finding shipwrecks is the easiest part of my job, but that managing them for their intrinsic humanities value and preserving them for future generations is much more difficult. For this effort to result in good outcomes it is essential for the public to understand and appreciate the context and values involved. With this new book, Michael Laramie provides a crisp, new, and comprehensive context for the naval history and the shipwrecks left behind. His work will greatly help to raise public awareness and interest and assist in these noble efforts.

ONE

The Champlain Waterway

O N A GRAY AUTUMN DAY IN 1666 THE FIRST COLONIAL FLEET appeared on Lake Champlain, navigating its waters to the rhythm of oars and the occasional spread of sail. The fleet departed the recently built fort on Isle La Motte on October 1, and by the fifth, a flotilla of three hundred boats and canoes was working its way up the rain-swept length of the lake. At the head of this fleet was Louis XIV's acting viceroy in North America, Alexandre de Prouville, the Marquis de Tracy. Tracy had been given a French regiment of the line, orders to sail for Canada, and explicit instructions to remove the threat the Iroquois Confederacy posed to the French colony. The marquis, backed by a display of strength in the form of some 1,300 French regulars, had successfully negotiated a truce with four of the five tribes of the Iroquois Confederacy. The Mohawk, however, with villages in the upper Hudson Valley, proved determined to carry on the war against the colony. Rightly guessing that the Mohawk were the driving force behind the ongoing conflicts between the Iroquois and the French, Tracy decided on a military expedition against the tribe, not only to punish the Mohawk, but to also demonstrate to the other tribes of the confederacy that strength backed his words.

The French, Canadian, and native force of some 1,300 men dragged their boats out of the water at the Ticonderoga Peninsula and carried them around the cascading waterfalls to the outlet of Lake George. Here the army reembarked and traced its way up the length of Lake George, pulling ashore at the head of the lake a few days later. A detachment was left here to guard the vessels, while the army pushed southwest toward the Mohawk homelands. Although the marquis managed to burn down several hastily abandoned villages, in the end he failed to engage the elusive Mohawks, who wisely chose not to fight and simply disappeared into the forests.[1]

This left Tracy with a difficult decision. France and England were at war in Europe, and now as he looked south, he saw a lightly guarded New York, and a recently subjected Dutch populace who were allies of his king's cause. It was a golden opportunity, or an inviting disaster. Uncertain, the marquis summoned a council of war to discuss the army's next move.

The debate raged around a crackling bonfire as the king's viceroy listened to his senior officers. The arguments for invading New York were enticing. The English were known to be weak, a potential source of aid could be found in the Dutch populace, and the French army, thanks to the Iroquois, were well supplied and had suffered nothing in the way of casualties. New York, with its fertile lands and fine ice-free port, lay before them. And if they secured the Hudson Valley the Iroquois would have no choice but to deal with the French for their European goods—a condition which would significantly alter the confederacy's policy toward New France.

The counterarguments were rooted in the uncertainties. Advancing meant leaving perhaps a thousand Mohawk warriors in their rear, it was late autumn, and there were no guarantees that

Portion of a 1688 French Map of North America showing the route taken by Tracy and his men on their march to the four Mohawk villages (or Anniez as they were referred to by the French). Note the towns of Corlar (Schenectady) and Canastigaone (Saratoga) just north of Orange, both of which were destined to become frequent targets of French and Indian war parties.

the Dutch populace would welcome the French. Any of these matters, as well as a dozen others, could lead to a catastrophe.

In the end the risk to his army and the colony as a whole was too great, and with nothing else to be accomplished the French army retraced its steps back to the Richelieu River forts. By mid-November the lakes were quiet again, and the first naval expedition on Lake Champlain and Lake George was over.[2]

The next year a treaty was signed at Quebec between the Iroquois and the French that brought a generation of peace and growth to Canada.[3] During this time the importance of the water conduit formed by the Richelieu River, Lake Champlain, and Lake George became apparent to both the French and their English rivals in New York and New England. During King William's War in the 1690s English expeditions under Johannes and Peter Schuyler descended Lake Champlain and the Richelieu River to launch a pair of attacks on La Prairie, and an English expedition under General Fitz-John Winthrop targeting Montreal assembled at Wood Creek near the southern end of Lake Champlain, before eventually abandoning the effort. The French in turn launched raids up the waterways, burning down Schenectady in one instance, and successfully targeting the Mohawk villages in another. Throughout the conflict both sides considered erecting posts at Crown Point and Chimney Point to restrict enemy access to the lake, but nothing material came of such thoughts beyond a crude redoubt constructed at Chimney Point by Captain Abraham Schuyler in 1690.

Queen Anne's War, which occupied the English and French colonies in North America from 1702 to 1713, presented further challenges for both sides along the waterways. The number of small-scale raiders using this corridor decreased from King William's War, but this was in good part due to the peace treaty signed in Montreal between the Iroquois and the French in 1701. Larger scale threats, however, did emerge. English armies gathered at the base of Lake Champlain in 1709, and again in 1711, with intentions to strike at Montreal, but in both cases the expeditions were called off. French governor-general Philippe Vaudreuil responded to the growing threats posed by the waterways by rebuilding Fort Chambly in stone. Finished in 1712 and heavily modified half a dozen years later, the new fort was a welcome addition to the security of the Champlain-Richelieu corridor, but situated on the north side of the St. Jean rapids, it failed to address the issue at point: control over the waterways.[4]

Matters changed in 1731 when the French ministry, looking to reinforce their claim to Lake Champlain, authorized the construction of a small wooden fort at Chimney Point. The resulting hundred-by-hundred-foot wooden structure that sheltered a garrison of some twenty men was hardly an overwhelming statement, but it signaled a change in French attitudes toward the waterway. It was not only the reinforcement of an established territorial claim that propelled the project, but also sincere security concerns.

A subtle shift of the northern winds had placed the colony of New France to the north of its English neighbors along what is now the Maritime Provinces of Canada and down the length of the St. Lawrence Valley. The arrangement created a buffer zone of some two hundred miles of virgin forest that extended from northern Maine to the New York frontier. This wooded belt, although porous to small-scale raiders, all but ruled out large-scale threats by enemy armies. Without roads and in most cases even simple trails, moving an army, and the artillery required to seize a fortified position, was out of the question—not to mention the logistical nightmares and the threats posed by enemy ambuscades that such an approach risked.

There was, however, one exception, one fracture in the wooded barrier between the belligerents; the thin waterway consisting of the Richelieu River, Lake Champlain, and Lake George. By a twist of geography this string of waterways came to within a dozen miles of the Hudson River, a navigable body of water that ultimately led south to New York City, while to the north, the Richelieu

River at the upper end of this string passed within a dozen miles of Montreal before emptying into the St. Lawrence. Although armies and their guns could not penetrate the intervening forests, they could move by small boats along this water corridor, which was broken to waterborne transport in only a handful of places. Thus, Montreal on the north end, and Albany and New York City on the south end, faced the very real possibilities of having to repel an invading army, and given the speed in which vessels could move down the waterway there would be little time to organize one's defenses.

Thus far New France had been fortunate. Three British expeditions had attempted to exploit the undefended Champlain corridor to strike at Montreal, and although each had failed, the implications that these waterways posed to the safety of New France were clear. Soon the small fort at Chimney Point gave way to a more secure structure, Fort St. Frédéric at Crown Point on the west side of the lake. The fort was small by the standards of its day, but it was a remarkable achievement nonetheless. Built in the middle of the wilderness from limestone quarried at a nearby site, the fortification boasted twenty-foot-high and two-foot-thick outer walls, which encircled a four-story-tall battlement that bristled with cannon, firing ports, and bombproof arches. The strategic value of Fort St. Frédéric lay in the fact that its guns dominated a three-hundred-yard section of Lake Champlain, effectively barring all water traffic north with the exception of the occasional raiding party. And as it was made of stone, it would require heavy cannons and a siege on the part of the English to capture.[5]

It is with this fort that the naval story of Lake George and Lake Champlain rightly begins.

TWO

The First Fleets

G OVERNOR CHARLES BEAUHARNOIS GAZED OUT THE WINDOW at the bleak October rain. From his office in the Chateau Saint-Louis in upper Quebec he had a superb view of the capital of New France. The weather had discouraged most activity, but along the waterfront crews ignored the wet winds as they worked to prepare their ships for the return voyage to France. Winter would soon be upon Canada, and ice upon the St. Lawrence River. All involved wanted to be well on their way by then. Beauharnois watched for a time until his focus eventually landed on a French sloop-of-war riding at anchor. There was no flurry of activity surrounding this vessel. It was a dispatch ship, ready and waiting. The governor muttered to himself and returned to the letter on his desk.

Beauharnois was happy to inform the minister of the marine that the fort started at Crown Point on Lake Champlain in the spring of 1735 was now capable of taking on a garrison. Although there was still a good deal of work to do, his chief engineer

Chaussegros de Léry had reported that illness among the work-force had halted all efforts for the year. Construction on the black limestone structure would resume in the spring. With an eye toward the future and the ever-present task of wisely spending the king's money, the governor suggested that a ship be built which would "greatly facilitate the transport of provisions and munitions necessary for the garrison." Such a vessel could replace the numerous flotillas of bateaux that now supported the stronghold, deferring the cost of these vessels' upkeep, and the cost of their expensive crews.

Beauharnois found the minister of the marine receptive to the idea and the costs involved, but at the moment there was a major roadblock. The Richelieu River from St. Jean to Lake Champlain had not been sounded. For all the governor knew, the river might not be capable of taking on larger vessels. Until this matter was resolved the project was laid aside.[1]

It would be six years before reports reached Beauharnois that the Richelieu River above the St. Jean's rapids was capable of bearing heavy vessels. With the information in hand he directed the intendant of Canada, Gilles Hocquart, to contract local shipbuilder David Corbin to build a small *barque* at Fort St. Frédéric. Corbin and a dozen of his men spent the winter and spring of 1742 building and outfitting the vessel. The result turned out to be a forty-ton two-masted schooner some forty-eight feet long and fifteen feet abeam. It carried a crew of six to ten men, was likely equipped with oars to help handle the tricky confines of the Richelieu River, and was armed with four *pierriers*, small swivel guns initially designed to fire stone projectiles or musket balls. As with many of the details surrounding this vessel, its actual name has become clouded with the passage of time. Records shortly after her commissioning refer to her as the *Goélette du Roy*, the *Barque du Roy*, or the *Barque de Saintonge*. This last title was in clear reference to her master, Joseph Payant *dit* St. Onge, whom Swedish naturalist Peter Kalm in his travels through the region in 1749 had the opportunity to speak

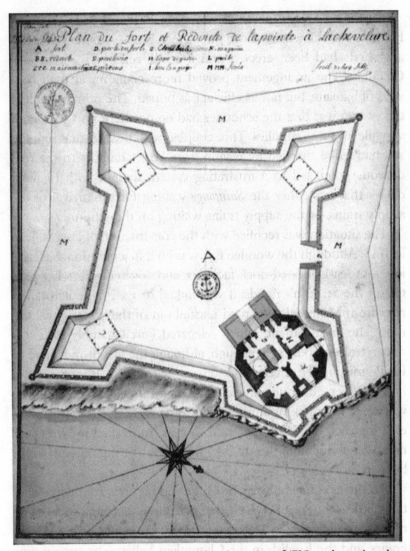

Fort St. Frédéric at Crown Point. Started in the spring of 1735 work continued on this stone structure for almost a decade, but when it was finished it was one of the strongest frontier forts in North America. In 1742 a dockyard was added to accommodate a barque as well as works to defend the landing area.

with, and who later claimed was one of the carpenters who built the vessel.[2]

For the next few years the *Saintonge* made runs between Fort St. Frédéric and the waters above the St. Jean rapids, where a few storage sheds had been erected and a crude road laid out to Fort Chambly. The arrangement proved more economical than convoys of bateaux, but not as efficient as hoped. The primary fault in the system was that the schooner had no northern port to anchor at while awaiting supplies. This, coupled with the fact that supplies still had to be shuttled by wagon from Fort Chambly to the rendezvous point, led to a frustrating system fraught with frequent delays that left either the *Saintonge* waiting for the arrival of the supply trains, or the supply trains waiting on the schooner.

The situation was rectified with the construction of Fort St. Jean in 1748. Although the wooden fort was built in a questionable fashion, it at least boasted dock facilities, and, located at the headwaters of the St. Jean's rapids, it was linked to La Prairie across the river from Montreal via a road hacked out of the swampy wilderness. The arrangement, which relegated Fort Chambly to a secondary role, worked well enough, although the fifteen-mile road to La Prairie proved a constant source of irritation. Runoff ditches had not been constructed, leaving the path a sea of mud and mire whenever it rained for any period of time. When Peter Kalm traveled the road in 1749 he referred to it as "unrivalled in wretchedness, wet and winding so that my horse sank in the mire up to his belly in most places."[3]

For the next several years St. Onge and his crew routinely sailed their little schooner between the two forts. The matter became more sensitive when in 1755 open warfare broke out between New France and the English in the Champlain Valley. The supply runs now became more critical, and the voyage's fraught with more perils. The schooner was fortunate and had avoided trouble, but on the morning of August 13, 1756, its luck changed. The *Saintonge*, a dozen or so miles from Fort St. Jean, stopped for some reason to put three of its crew ashore at the northern end of Ile aux Têtes. The vessel's progress had been monitored by an Iroquois war party, who by chance lay in wait near the landing site. The three crewmen were immediately ambushed and killed, at which point "the barque made such a great fire with her pierriers" that the Iroquois retreated without taking any scalps. The loss of three crewmen on such a small vessel weighed heavily on Captain Payant, but in reality he was more fortunate than he might have imagined. The indefatigable Captain Robert Rogers had come across the schooner a month before and formulated a plan to seize it while it lay at anchor in Basin Harbor. Only the untimely appearance of a pair of French bateaux upset Rogers's plan and saved the *Saintonge* from capture or destruction.[4]

For the moment the little schooner held a tentative control over the lake given that the English did not have a base on the waterway to build anything to compete with it. Her age and size however, was starting to become an issue, particularly given that another defensive position, Fort Vaudreuil (or Fort Carillon as it was later known) had been constructed on the Ticonderoga Peninsula a dozen miles up the lake from Fort St. Frédéric. It was clear that another vessel would be required to support both strongholds. To supplement the *Saintonge* Governor Pierre Vaudreuil ordered colonial shipbuilder Pierre Levasseur to proceed to Fort St. Jean in October 1756 with twenty carpenters and begin work on a new ship. Pierre was joined shortly thereafter by his father, New France's most prominent shipbuilder, René-Nicolas Levasseur, who oversaw the construction of the vessel over the course of the winter. Finished early the following summer and christened the *Vigilante*, it was a sixty-ton topsail schooner armed with ten four-pound cannon. After a quick shakedown cruise, the ship was handed over to the lake's most experienced mariner, Joseph Payant, and was soon on its way to Fort Carillon, arriving there on May 27, 1757.[5]

Although the *Saintonge*, the *Vigilante*, and a *gabare*, or sailing barge, launched at St. Jean the following spring were enough of a force to prevent a flotilla of British bateaux carrying an invasion army and their artillery from moving down the lake, they hardly sealed off the waterway. British raiders, primarily in the form of Robert Rogers and his Rangers, frequented the waterway in their canoes and small craft with near impunity. On numerous occasions Rogers and his men snuck past Forts Carillon and St. Frédéric on dark nights, their oars muffled with cloth to keep their presence concealed, passing close enough on some occasions that they could hear the sentries calling out their watchwords as the made their rounds along the forts' walls. Once past these outposts Rogers would prey on smaller French supply boats, which sent waves of alarms through the garrisons of the forts. In one instance Rogers attacked and seized a pair of French bateaux several miles below Crown Point. After sending the French vessels to the bottom the Ranger captain hid his boats and returned with his prisoners back to Fort Edward by foot, leaving the French convinced that the English had found a passage into the lake by means of Otter Creek.[6]

Traffic moved the other way as well. In fact, it was southbound raiders that dominated the lake's waters. Long strings of canoes and bateaux navigated the waterway from St. Jean to the southern forts, and from there they pushed south onto South Bay, or carried their vessels over to Lake George to continue their trek. The period is replete with accounts of dozens of canoes carrying hundreds of French and Indian raiders moving south along these passages. These war parties would conceal their vessels at South Bay or along the shores of Lake George and continue on by foot attacking towns, homesteads, and military posts as far south as New Jersey, and as far east as the outskirts of Boston.

In response to the enemy's use of Lake George, Royal Navy commander Joshua Loring was assigned to Lake George in 1756

Opposite: A map of the lakes and principal waterways in the Champlain Basin from Fort Edward on the Hudson River to Fort Sorel at the outlet of the Richelieu River. Note that directions on Lake Champlain and the Richelieu River are based on how both drain. Thus "down the lake/river" would be moving north and "up the lake/river" would be moving south.

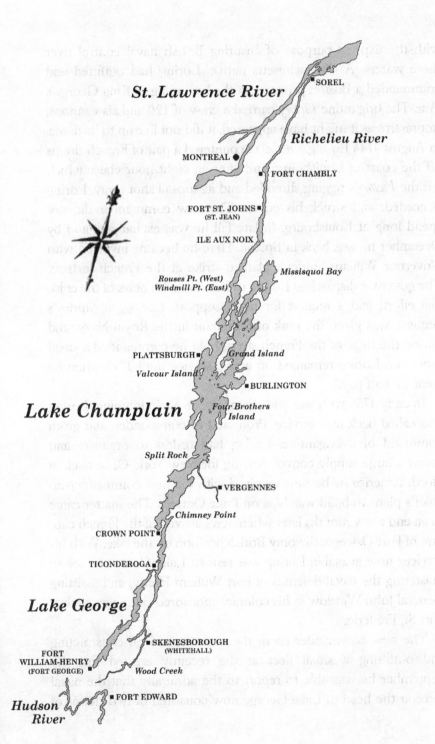

St. Lawrence River

■ SOREL

Richelieu River

MONTREAL ●

■ FORT CHAMBLY

FORT ST. JOHNS ■
(ST. JEAN)

ILE AUX NOIX

Rouses Pt. (West)
Windmill Pt. (East)

Missisquoi Bay

PLATTSBURGH ■ ■   Grand Island

Valcour Island

■ BURLINGTON

Lake Champlain   Four Brothers
Island

Split Rock

■ VERGENNES

Chimney Point

CROWN POINT ■

TICONDEROGA ■

Lake George

■ SKENESBOROUGH
(WHITEHALL)

FORT
WILLIAM-HENRY
(FORT GEORGE)   Wood Creek

■ FORT EDWARD

Hudson
River

with the express purpose of ensuring British naval control over these waters. A Massachusetts native, Loring had outfitted and commanded a Boston privateer at the beginning of King George's War. The brigantine *Victory* carried a crew of 120 and six cannons. Impressive as it might have appeared, it did not live up to its name. In August 1744 Loring's vessel encountered a pair of French sloops off the coast of Louisbourg, and after an eight-hour chase which left the *Victory*'s rigging shredded and its topsail shot away, Loring conceded, and struck his colors. The new commander did not spend long at Louisbourg. In late fall he was exchanged, and by December he was back in Boston. Here he became involved with Governor William Shirley's plan to strike at the French fortress. The governor dispatched Loring to London with news of the colonial effort, and a request for naval support. Loring, at Shirley's bequest, was given the rank of lieutenant in the Royal Navy, and during the siege of the French stronghold he commanded a small schooner. Loring remained on active service until 1749 when he went on half pay.[7]

In early 1756 with war with France once again looming, Loring was called back into service. Promoted to commander, and given command of a brigantine, Loring had orders to organize and escort a large supply convoy leaving for New York. Once back in North America he became involved with the new commander-in-chief's plans to build warships on Lake Ontario. The matter came to an end a few months later when news arrived of the French capture of Fort Oswego, the only British position on the lake. With his services now available Loring was sent to Lake George to see to bolstering the naval defenses of Fort William Henry, and assisting General John Winslow in his colonial-sponsored campaign against Fort St. Frédéric.

The new commander spent the summer of 1756 constructing and outfitting a small fleet at the recently erected fort. By September he was able to report to the admiralty that the naval force at the head of Lake George now consisted of two sloops of

38 tons each, two sloops of 24 tons each, one bay boat of 20 tons, four bay boats ranging from 12 to 15 tons each, three scows of 4 tons each, nine whaleboats, and 226 bateaux. As impressive as it sounded, this little fleet was something of a paper navy. Several of the larger vessels were without their cannons or were partially rigged, while many of the smaller craft required constant attention simply to stay seaworthy. On the night of September 2 Loring announced his navy's presence as a pair of English sloops and a number of bateaux appeared out of the fog near the French advanced post at the outlet of Lake George. The English however, did not press their advantage and instead satisfied themselves with lobbing a few cannonballs at the French positions before making their way home.[8]

Although it was too late in the year for the English to mount an assault on Fort Carillon, their increased naval presence on Lake George alarmed the governor of New France, Pierre de Rigaud, the Marquis de Vaudreuil. With such an array of naval might already in place at Fort William Henry, Vaudreuil was concerned that the English might launch an attack on Fort Carillon in the early spring when the ice on Lake George had broken but that along the northern portion of Lake Champlain was still intact. Should this happen the governor would be unable to reinforce the fort which, already low on supplies after a long winter, would certainly fall.

To avert this scenario Vaudreuil planned a winter expedition against Fort William Henry with the aim of burning the vessels huddled along the shoreline. The raid led by Vaudreuil's brother Rigaud proved a success. Although the British claimed victory given that the fort was successfully defended, they did so as a good part of the bateaux, all four sloops, and a new one on the stocks lay charred beneath a blanket of fresh snow. Rigaud's efforts had dealt a serious blow to Loring's naval force. But even so, a good number of vessels, such as the whaleboats, had avoided destruction, and two of the sloops, initially thought lost, proved not to be seriously damaged.[9]

British plans for 1757 did not call for an attack on Fort Carillon, the French stronghold on the Ticonderoga Peninsula. Instead, most of the regulars and a sizable number of colonials would rendezvous with a fleet sent from England, and together, this force would lay siege to the French fortress of Louisbourg which guarded the entrance to the St. Lawrence River. While General Loudoun was away with the bulk of the British army, General Daniel Webb was left in charge of defending the New York frontier with a force of 7,500 colonial and regular troops. Loudoun warned Webb before departing that the French would be likely to pay him a visit once it was clear that the bulk of the British army was occupied elsewhere. He recommended that Webb concentrate on building more ships to maintain his naval control over Lake George. With the British in control of the waterway the French commander, Louis-Joseph, the Marquis de Montcalm, would not dare advance up the lake with his vulnerable artillery barges.

Webb, who had an outstanding record but proved to be a jittery officer in North America, put a half-hearted effort into constructing two large row galleys, while a number of whaleboats were forwarded to Fort William Henry to augment those already on hand. In all, it left the fort with a respectable fleet of two sloops, two galleys, two bay boats, twenty-five whaleboats, and a handful of bateaux. The sloops however, had not been fully repaired, and the galleys were neither armed nor rigged. Still, even with just the services of the whaleboats and bay boats it was a substantial force to be reckoned with, considering each of these vessels was large enough to carry swivel guns and a few dozen men.[10]

On the afternoon of July 22, however, Lt. Colonel George Monro in command at Fort William Henry, reached a fateful decision that would eliminate any threat the British might pose to Montcalm on Lake George. Monro was frustrated with the lack of intelligence reaching him. The English Rangers, short the experienced companies of Rogers's corps and crippled by the untimely death of Richard Rogers, found the woods about the northern end

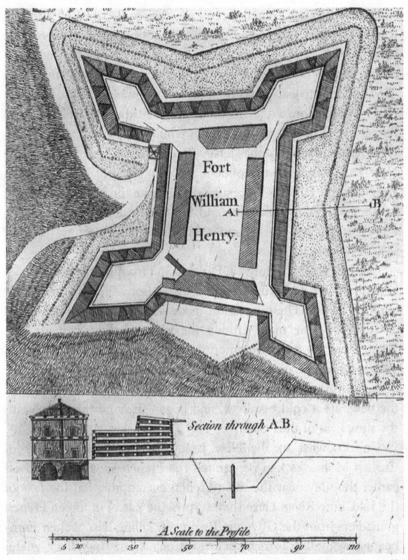

A 1755 layout of Fort William Henry by the fort's architect Captain William Eyre.

of Lake George teeming with French and Indian scouting parties. The screen all but cloaked French efforts in the area. A handful of Mohawks, acting as scouts for the English, had some success in picking off a few wayward sentries, but in general they had not shed any light on French intentions. A recent patrol by Richard Rogers's company fared no better. They managed to ambush a small French patrol just south of Sabbath Day Point, but although outnumbering the French by more than five to one they had allowed them to escape without securing a prisoner. Desperate for information, Monro and his officers agreed that Lt. Colonel John Parker of the New Jersey Regiment would depart the next evening with five companies of the "Jersey Blues" and two companies of the New York Regiment to conduct a reconnaissance in force down Lake George. Parker's force would sail down the length of the lake in the garrison's whaleboats and bay boats, attack and burn the French advanced posts, and then immediately return to Fort William Henry.[11]

On the evening of July 23, Parker's 350 troops in twenty whaleboats and two bay boats pushed away from the wharfs at Fort William Henry. The procession made its way down the lake and anchored for the night among the islands below Sabbath Day Point. Here the men attempted to get some sleep in the crowded vessels while Parker outlined his plan to advance under the cover of the morning mists to his officers. At daybreak, his men shook off the dew, ate a cold breakfast, and began their northward trek to the slow beat of their oars.

Unbeknownst to the New Jersey colonel, a detachment of English Mohawks had penetrated the French screen and arrived earlier that day near the main French encampment at the falls of the La Chute River. Here they surprised a patrol of fifteen French grenadiers from the Guyenne Regiment, killing two of their number and wounding as many before retiring south. Brigadier General François Levis, in command at the falls, immediately organized a pursuit. He ordered Rigaud at the advanced camps to organize two detachments to cut off the enemy's retreat. The first was sent toward the outlet of the Mohawk trail on the western side of the lake, while the second and larger party under Marine ensign Corbière was dispatched along the western shore of the lake toward Sabbath Day Point to cut off any possible retreat by water. Neither party encountered the retreating Mohawks, but in the evening twilight Corbière's scouts detected Parker's vessels lying at anchor above the Sabbath Day Point. Runners were immediately sent to the advanced camps with the news and a request for reinforcements. The response was immediate. Almost five hundred Ottawa, Chippewa, Potawatomi, and Menominee warriors along with fifty Canadians under the leadership of veteran partisans Charles Langdale and Joseph Hertel launched their canoes into the dark mountain waters and paddled to Corbière's assistance.[12]

With their forces in place, Corbière, Langdale, and the native chieftains formulated a plan. The canoes were dragged ashore and covered, and the warriors concealed within the western tree line. Here they would wait for the English, who would no doubt resume their trek at daybreak. It was agreed that everyone was to hold their fire until the flotilla had rounded Sabbath Day Point. At that point the attack would be launched, trapping the English between the attackers and the advanced posts to the north. It was a simple plan, executed to near perfection.

At daybreak the French and Indians crouching along the shoreline watched as a trio of boats emerged out of the fog. The word was given and the boats were allowed to pass. Soon three others appeared, and as before, they were allowed to pass unmolested. Clearly they were the main body's advance guard. Thus far everything had gone according to plan, but tensions were running high, and as so often the case in such situations, could not be held in check. When the main body of Parker's flotilla appeared out of the mist, emotions overcame planning. A hundred shrieks shattered the gray calm as the French and their allies darted from their concealment and threw their canoes into the water. Along the shore a tattered volley reached out toward the English, bringing Parker's vessels to a stop. There was a scattered response from the English as some switched from their oars to their muskets, but most had time to do neither. The surprise was near total, as was the resulting panic. Within minutes the more maneuverable birchbark canoes were among them, discharging muskets into the packed whaleboats, boarding those they could reach and capsizing others. The English flotilla soon lost cohesion. Some vessels made for shore, some foundered, a few managed to turn back, and a number attempted to surrender to an enemy not interested in taking prisoners. In desperation, many of the English abandoned their vessels for the safety of the water, only to find themselves speared from canoes as they swam for shore, or dragged down under the weight of their equipment. Those who were fortunate enough to reach the shore found it no safer than the water. Bands of warriors pursued the hapless English through the forest, which echoed with screams and bursts of gunfire. The six vessels in the advanced guard were taken without a shot, while four boats, including the one holding Parker, were far enough back to break free of the carnage and make their way back to Fort William Henry with news of the disaster.[13]

When it became apparent that the English were offering no resistance, the attack transformed into a collection of prisoners. Of the 350 men in Parker's command, 100 or so were killed or drowned, and another 150 were taken prisoner. A little over 100 made their way back to Fort William Henry, half of these in the four boats that managed to escape. All this at the cost of one French Indian who had his wrist dislocated by a musketball.[14]

As the dazed prisoners were led back into the French camps, Levis and Montcalm were stunned and at the same time delighted by the level of English folly. In a single blow the French had decimated the New Jersey Regiment and, more importantly, had achieved naval superiority on Lake George. It was the latter that both pleased and relieved Montcalm, who had been apprehensive of moving his artillery up the lake in the face of a sizable English naval force. For the defenders of Fort William Henry it was nothing less than a catastrophe, "a piece of stupidity" that almost guaranteed a siege. When Webb learned of the incident, he wrote

Loudoun that Parker had departed "without my knowing anything of the matter until too late to prevent it" and "to what purpose I really cannot tell." He was also quick to see the consequences. "Your Lordship will perceive the enemy have at the present the superiority on the lake, we having now but two old sloops and five whaleboats remaining." Upon receiving this news, Loudoun passed his opinion on to the secretary of state Holdernesse: "From their having permitted the enemy to get superiority of the lake, without which they could not have got up artillery, I look upon that place and garrison, as lost, with the whole troops there."[15]

Loudoun proved correct. Montcalm at the head of 7,900 Canadians, French regulars, and native warriors captured the fort and its garrison of some 2,300 after a five-day siege. The marquis had no intentions of occupying the fort, and after leveling its works retreated back down the lake to Fort Carillon. Neither the French nor the English were interested in another major engagement, and winter was soon upon the Champlain Valley, locking both Lake George and Lake Champlain in a familiar sheet of ice.[16]

Along with the fresh winter snows came new directives from London. One of the largest deployments of British troops outside of the British Isles was planned for the North American campaign of 1758. To the north, the first target was to be Louisbourg, which had escaped attack the previous year when weather and indecision caused the abandonment of the effort against the French fortress. Fourteen thousand regulars and a sizable portion of the British navy would strike at the maritime fortress in the spring. To the south an Anglo-Indian force of some 5,000 men would march along Braddock's old path to Fort Duquesne and strike at the French position at the forks of the Ohio. And in the center, General James Abercromby, who had replaced the Earl of Loudoun as British commander-in-chief in North America, would personally lead some 20,000 British regulars and colonial militia against the French fortifications of the Champlain Valley, starting with Fort Carillon.

Under the plan newly promoted Captain Loring once again found himself on Lake George building warships to assert naval control over the lake. Loring's task was far from ideal. A shortage of skilled manpower, naval supplies, and tools haunted the construction process. The late arrival of Abercromby's army at the head of Lake George created yet another complication. The captain had planned on building a sloop once he arrived, but the demands involved in transporting 16,000 men and their artillery down Lake George put the project on hold. As it turned out Abercromby's army, which extended down the lake for miles, would not require a naval escort. Nor was their visit to Ticonderoga to be long. Three days later, the army, having battered itself against the prepared French field works outside the fort, returned to Fort William Henry in a state of near panic.[17]

It would be two more weeks, and fears that Montcalm might attack, before Loring directed Captain Samuel Cobb, a Maine shipbuilder who had organized a company of ships carpenters, to cut the timber for a sloop. On July 27 Cobb raised the frame of the vessel. Loring pressed Cobb as to the launch of the vessel a few weeks later, but it would only be a few more days until it slid into the water. A week later, while a portion of his carpenters rigged and fitted out the vessel, Cobb landed twelve miles down the lake, and under heavy escort, felled the timber he needed for oars and for a large row galley that Loring had ordered him to build.

On September 2 the new addition to his majesty's navy on Lake George, the *Earl of Halifax* cast off its lines and proceeded down the lake for a shakedown cruise. It was a classic sloop, some 60 feet long, and 100 tons in burthen. Almost 90 sailors and marines were required to defend the decks and man the fourteen six- and four-pound cannons it carried. The vessel was also equipped with oars, or sweeps as they were called, which allowed it to make way when the lake winds proved contrary.[18]

To support the *Halifax* Loring had directed Cobb to build a trio of radeau—broad flat-bottomed vessels that could be either rowed

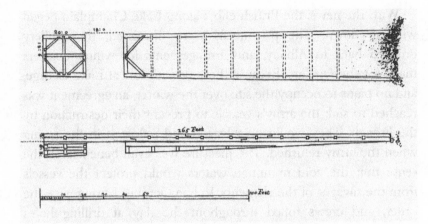

A sketch of a 165 foot pier built at Fort William Henry in 1756.

or rigged as ketches. The first of these was a 36 by 9 foot unnamed vessel launched without much fanfare on September 9. The other two craft were both launched a little over a month later, and after taking them out onto the lake Cobb was pleased with how well both vessels handled. The first was a small 30-foot craft while the second, known as the *Land Tortoise*, was slightly over 50 feet in length and 18 feet in beam. Its sides, which had provisions for 26 oars, were angled outward giving the seven-sided vessel the appearance of an ancient ark. Three gun ports were cut along the starboard side and two along the port side in an offset arrangement so all the guns could be pulled back at the same time. Another smaller gun port was placed on the starboard bow, and a last on the starboard quarter.[19]

By early October, Cobb and an anxious army awaited a meeting between General Abercromby and General Jeffery Amherst, who had just arrived from the capture of Louisbourg with seven regiments of regulars. Although their numbers and resources were sufficient to launch a second attack on Fort Carillon, after little in the way of debate both generals agreed that the season was too advanced to make an attempt.

With the news, the British effort along Lake Champlain began winding down. The provincials were dismissed, the artillery dragged back to Albany, and arrangements for winter quarters made for the regulars. Because there was no fort at Lake George, and no plans to occupy the site over the winter, an agreement was reached to sink the army's vessels to prevent their destruction by the French. They would be salvaged and refloated in the spring when the army returned. The measure was even beneficial in the sense that the cold mountain waters would protect the vessels from the ravages of the elements. In late October Loring gave the order, and crews toiled throughout the day at drilling holes through the vessels' hulls. Heavy rope was inserted through these openings, and when the crafts were in position, nets filled with heavy stones were attached to the ropes; dragging their charges to the bottom in a cauldron of bubbles.[20]

Although British plans in the Champlain Valley for 1758 had failed, with the launching of the *Halifax* and the *Land Tortoise* shortly thereafter, there was no question as to who possessed naval superiority on Lake George. And as to the French positions on Lake Champlain, a new plan was drawn up over the winter of 1758. Abercromby was replaced by Amherst, who was to personally lead a new effort against Fort Carillon once spring arrived.

THREE

The Destruction of the French Lake Champlain Fleet

ENERAL JEFFERY AMHERST CAST A SMALL FROWN TOWARD HIS optimistic young aide. The two men slowly walked along the shore of Crown Point, stopping occasionally to speak with groups of men who were struggling to right overturned vessels and haul ashore those half-filled with water. The devastation wrought by the midsummer tempest both surprised and depressed the forty-one-year-old British commander-in-chief in North America. Boats lay jumbled along the length of the shoreline, while others a few yards away bobbed partially submerged in the cool mountain waters. The general paused before the conspicuous wreckage of one of his gunboats, his eyes tracing the trail of destruction. A small fleet of these twenty-five-foot vessels had been specially built to carry a single twenty-four-pound cannon in their prow. The addition of a ton of iron had made them questionable sailers from the outset, but now as he surveyed the damage he reluctantly concluded that they were incapable of handling the inclement weather on Lake Champlain.[1]

Amherst removed his hat, idly examining the gold lace along its brim while he reflected on the moment. Until now things had gone remarkably well. The British campaign of 1759 in North America was a three-pronged attack on the borders of New France. To the west an Anglo-Colonial force under General John Prideaux supplemented by Sir William Johnson and his Mohawk warriors was to launch an assault against the French fortress of Niagara on Lake Ontario, while along the St. Lawrence General James Wolfe and Admiral Charles Saunders with nearly a quarter of the English fleet at their disposal were to lay siege to the city of Quebec. The third element of the plan, which Amherst was to personally lead, called for the capture of the French fortresses at Ticonderoga and Crown Point along the southern portion of Lake Champlain, followed by an advance down the lake with the ultimate aim of seizing Montreal. Although he had been slow in getting his campaign under way due to the late arrival of his colonial forces, the general had made short work of Fort Carillon, forcing the badly outnumbered French to blow up the fortress once he had erected his siege guns and retreat back to Fort St. Frédéric at Crown Point. The French commander, Brigadier General Charles Bourlamaque, had no intention of standing his ground at Fort St. Frédéric, an even older and less capable stronghold than Carillon. The fort was quickly stripped of anything useful and demolition charges set. By the time Amherst reached Crown Point in the opening days of August, all that remained of the once-feared post was a smoldering mass of timber and broken stone.[2]

Amherst had done well. In the course of two weeks he had reduced the French position at the southern end of Lake

A portion of a map detailing Amherst's position at Crown Point in 1759. The larger fortification is Fort Amherst, while the smaller structure to the east, on the water's edge, is Fort St. Frédéric.

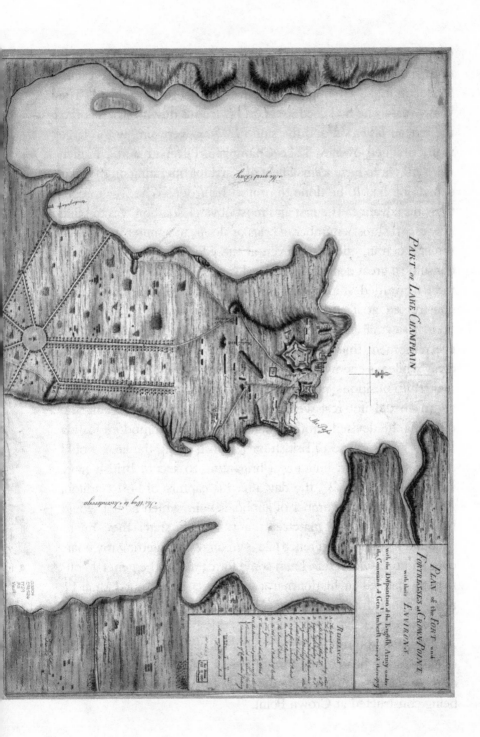

Champlain at the cost of some sixty-eight casualties, a distant cry from the failed attempts of the previous four years. Once established on Lake Champlain, however, he faced a problem. The heavy vessels he had used to escort his troops down Lake George, the radeau *Invincible* and the sloop *Halifax*, were simply too large to be dragged over to Lake Champlain. Given that the French were known to have a small fleet of warships operating on the lake, something had to be done to protect his troops if he was to continue his advance. The first and most obvious solution was to build new escort ships, a number of brigs or sloops to counter the French threat. Such an effort, however, at the edge of civilization would consume a great deal of time. Naval supplies and tools would have to be forwarded, shipwrights and carpenters assembled, dockyards constructed at Ticonderoga, and most important the shattered French sawmill at Ticonderoga would have to be repaired. And every moment that Amherst waited, his army's initiative slipped away while his enemy was afforded the opportunity to secure their makeshift positions at the northern end of the lake. Such an approach did not rest well with the general and, foreseeing the dilemma, he devised another plan. Although Commodore Joshua Loring, in command of British naval efforts along the lake, would still be tasked with building a brigantine to secure British navy superiority, on July 27, the day after his capture of Fort Carillon, Amherst ordered a number of gunboats built, which he felt would prove more than a match for any French ships they might encounter. "They [the French] depend on my not getting my boats over and being forced to build some for cannon," the general confidently penned in his journal a few nights later, "but I shall be ready sooner than they imagine."[3]

Now a week later, surrounded by his battered gunboat fleet, Amherst found himself having to alter his plans. The general could only shake his head at the turn of events, and after writing Loring of the urgency of his task, he turned his attention to the new fort being constructed at Crown Point.

The storm that derailed Amherst's plans was perhaps fortuitous. On August 16 a French deserter was brought into camp. The man, a marine aboard one of the French warships, stated that the French had fortified themselves at Ile aux Noix, a small island in the center of the Richelieu River which drained Lake Champlain into the St. Lawrence. The man then testified as to the number of cannon on the island and his previous duties. When asked about the French fleet, however, he startled the general and his officers with what he had to say. There were four French warships operating on the lake, the *Vigilante* (an older schooner armed with ten guns, six and four pounders), two sloops (the *Brochette* and *Esturgeon*, both armed with eight guns, six and four pounders), and a third sloop the *Musquelongy*, the fleet's flagship, armed with a respectable complement of two brass twelve pounders and six iron six pounders. All of these vessels carried detachments of French regulars aboard and were armed with various numbers of swivel guns. In addition, the Frenchman informed a now alarmed Amherst, a fifth vessel was undergoing repairs at St. Jean.[4]

The next day Amherst summoned Loring up from Ticonderoga and met with him and Major Thomas Ord of the Royal Artillery. The French fleet was clearly larger and better armed than first thought, Amherst informed the pair after they had a chance to review the deserter's testimony. Loring quickly agreed and informed the general that the brigantine he was working on was not sufficient to contend with such a force. As the smaller boats had proven incapable of carrying twenty-four pounders, Major Ord suggested that a radeau be built, similar to the *Invincible*. The three agreed that a radeau carrying six twenty-four pounders would be the quickest and best response to the threat, and Ord, who had built the *Invincible*, agreed to oversee the project, estimating that it would take him ten days to complete.

By the end of August Ord's radeau was nowhere near finished nor was Loring's brigantine. Part of the problem was difficulty keeping the Ticonderoga sawmill in working order. Another issue was that the demand for timber simply outstripped the mill's capabilities. Everyone wanted wood. Ord asked for planks for his radeau, the new fort at Crown Point made its demands, the repairs for Fort Ticonderoga and the dockyard facilities at the fort made theirs, rafts had to be constructed to ferry cannon to Crown Point, and Loring asked for wood for his brigantine. There simply was not enough production to go around. Interservice rivalries only compounded the problem. Lt. Colonel John Bradstreet in charge of transportation, Loring in charge of the navy, Ord in charge of the artillery, and Lt. Colonel William Eyre of the Royal Engineers vied with each other for supplies to carry out their assignments, and when these were not to be had, they accused one of the other department heads of usurping their shipments and undermining their efforts. Amherst attempted to keep all of them on friendly terms and focused on the common goal, but when the constant bickering finally tried his patience he penned a letter to each reminding them of their duty to the king.[5]

To monitor French efforts Amherst dispatched two scouts toward Fort St. Jean in late August. One of these, led by veteran Ranger sergeant-major Joseph Hopkins, managed to capture three French marines near Ile aux Noix via an impressive feat of deception before returning to Crown Point on September 1. Hopkins reported, and his prisoners confirmed, that a newly launched sloop pierced for sixteen guns was being fitted out near the island. Amherst frowned at the news. Clearly a naval arms race was taking place on the lake, one that was consuming the season, and with it, his opportunity to strike at the enemy. The general met with Loring the next day and ordered him, once the brigantine was completed, to undertake the building of a sixteen-gun sloop. Loring agreed that this could be done, and left Amherst with the good news that the brigantine, christened the *Duke of Cumberland*, was ready for launching. In the meantime Amherst attempted to even the odds by entrusting Hopkins with the task of burning the new enemy sloop. The commando squad of fifteen Rangers, provincials, and regulars arrived opposite Ile aux Noix around 10 P.M. on September 11. Here it was agreed that Hopkins and four others would swim out to the enemy vessel and under cover of darkness attach fire darts to its hull. The daring ploy came close to succeeding. Two of Hopkins's men had nearly secured their incendiary devices when a French sailor standing watch on the ship's deck spotted them and sounded the alarm. Within moments the waters about Hopkins and his men turned into a cauldron of geysers as the ship's watch fired into the darkness, followed a few moments later by the island's sentries standing guard along the shore. Hopkins and his men escaped, but by the skin of their teeth. As they assembled on the opposite shore and hastily pushed off for Crown Point they found that the only injury was to one Ranger who had been grazed by an ax that was thrown at him.[6]

General Sir Jeffery Amherst. Amherst quickly captured Forts Carillon and St. Frédéric, but was delayed by the need to build a fleet on Lake Champlain to challenge French naval forces on the waterway. Although he eventually succeeded in securing control of the lake, the advanced season and the retreat of the French army from Quebec to the vicinity of Montreal forced him to abandon his campaign.

The failure disappointed Amherst, but he viewed it as just one more crack in his slowly eroding patience. Ord's radeau, which was to have been constructed in ten days, was still not finished, and Loring's estimations were that it would be several more weeks before the agreed-upon sloop would be ready to sail, if of course the sawmill at Ticonderoga didn't break down again. Repairs were still ongoing at Fort Ticonderoga and the new fort at Crown Point was turning into a sprawling monstrosity. To complicate matters a distinct chill was now in the air. The season was slipping away.[7]

At the other end of the lake Amherst's adversary Brigadier General Charles Bourlamaque was nothing short of delighted by the British delay. The French commander had initially been against fortifying Ile aux Noix, at first preferring La Pointe à Margot, a hook-shaped peninsula a little over a mile south of the island where the river narrowed to a width of a few hundred yards. The initial objections were based for the most part on this island's size. With the resources at his disposal, some three thousand regulars, marines, and militia, the brigadier worried that the island was simply too large for his forces to effectively fortify such that they could bar the river's passage on both its eastern and western sides. But with no better location to be had, and a good deal of hard work and the time granted to his force by Amherst's delays, the French commander was eventually able to report that he was confident that the post could not be taken by storm.[8]

At the moment, however, Bourlamaque's true deterrent lay in his little fleet and the British need to build one of their own to match it. In this he was inadvertently aided by the deserter who spoke with Amherst, for the man had greatly overestimated the strength of the French fleet. Currently four vessels were operating on the lake. The oldest was a seventy-ton topsail schooner named *Vigilante*, commanded by veteran captain Joseph St. Onge. The last three vessels were all current additions started in the fall of 1758 and launched the following spring. Unlike the *Vigilante* they were sixty-five-ton xebecs, slim vessels used by the Mediterranean pirates of the age who favored speed over sturdiness. The vessels' trademark, however, the short-masted triangular lateen sails, were replaced in favor of a more conventional sloop-style rigging, a decision no doubt based on the availability of naval supplies. Levasseur's choice of xebecs was odd, and several French officers, Bourlamaque for one, questioned the vessels' usefulness, especially in the narrow Richelieu waterway, as they did not possess oars and were known to require a favorable wind to get under way – a true oddity for a ship rigged as a sloop. The first of these three vessels was the fleet's flagship, the sixty-foot-long *Musquelongy*. It was armed with two brass twelve-pound cannon and eight iron four-pounders, easily making it one of the deadliest fish on the lake. The remaining two xebecs, of the same size, were the *Brochette* and *Esturgeon*, each of which carried from six to eight four-pound cannon, as well as a handful of swivel guns mounted along their deck rails. Eighty-two sailors manned the four vessels, supported by ninety-six regulars and militiamen who acted as marines for the fleet.[9]

At the head of this squadron was Lieutenant Jean d'Olabaratz *dit* Laubaras. Although St. Onge was the most experienced sailor on the lake he was not a regular naval officer, and with a naval encounter likely it was felt that a commander with a military background was needed. Experienced naval officers however, were in short supply in New France, and as such, the choice of Laubaras seems to have been based more on his availability than any other factor. It was an unfortunate decision on the part of the colony. Although Laubaras was certainly an experienced sailor, his recent career had been mired in bad luck. Raised in a seafaring family, Laubaras joined the Navy in 1745, serving first in administrative positions at the port of Bayonne and then later on a number of warships during the War of Austrian Succession. In 1750 his father was appointed port captain at Louisbourg, which in turn led to the younger d'Olabaratz's appointment to the position of port ensign later that year. In 1755 Laubaras returned to France and a year later was given command of the frigate *Aigle* which he sailed to Louisbourg that fall. After having once again returned to France, Laubaras left for Quebec in early 1757 in the *Aigle*, this time accompanied by the frigate *Outarde*. He captured a number of British merchant ships before the two vessels became separated near Newfoundland. Proceeding on alone, Laubaras elected to make his way to Quebec through the dangerous Straits of Belle Isle and, as a result, ran aground. When informed of his plight, officials in Quebec dispatched two vessels to assist him; unfortunately, these ships collided and sank in a storm not long after reaching the stranded crew. Determined to reach Quebec, Laubaras requisitioned the old fishing schooner *Roi du Nord*, loaded it with what could be salvaged from the three wrecks, and set course for the colonial capital only to have the dilapidated vessel sink on him a hundred miles short of his destination. Once again Laubaras and his crew waded ashore, this time finally reaching their goal by foot. Thus, when the governor of New France, Pierre Vaudreuil, began looking for an officer in early 1758 to command the fleet being constructed on Lake Champlain he found the downcast lieutenant, whose father Vaudreuil knew well, without a ship, and appointed him to the position.[10]

Throughout the late summer and fall Laubaras's squadron, supported by a number of makeshift gunboats, operated on the lake looking to gather information on Amherst's impending advance, and interdict British scouting parties moving north. They achieved little in the way of accomplishing either goal. There was nothing to report on Amherst, and scouting parties, both large and small, routinely slipped past them unnoticed. Even so, their very existence was enough to buy Bourlamaque the time he desperately needed.

By mid-October matters were about to come to a head. On the morning of the tenth Loring sailed the newly built *Duke of Cumberland* to Crown Point and anchored it near Ord's radeau *Ligonier*. Around them the camp and nearby waters bustled with activity. With his navy ready Amherst had given the order that the army would depart the next day. While the army busied themselves with loading their boats and seeing to final details, Loring met with Ord and Amherst. The sloop *Boscawen*, Loring informed the general, would arrive from Ticonderoga the next morning.

Amherst nodded at the report, and informed the commodore that he now felt strong enough to advance against the French fleet, but Loring was hesitant, expressing concerns that the *Duke of Cumberland* and *Boscawen*, neither of which had undergone a shakedown cruise, were not equal to the combined strength of the French squadron. Having waited the better part of the summer and fall Amherst was not interested in the commodore's assessment and dismissed it with little in the way of discussion. He ordered Loring to take his two warships up the lake, with the aim of slipping past the French fleet to cut their communications with Ile aux Noix. The hope was to isolate the enemy warships, thereby delaying any warning the defenders of the island might have of the English advance. If this was not possible and he was discovered by the French squadron, Amherst ordered him to "do his utmost to come up with and attack them . . . without any regard to the army you leave behind." The army, he assured Loring, would be well enough protected by the *Ligonier* and the gunboats he had used earlier.[11]

Armed with his sailing orders, Loring set out late on the afternoon of October 11, quickly leaving Amherst's four long columns of bateaux and whaleboats in his wake. The commodore stationed himself aboard the *Duke of Cumberland* while command of the *Boscawen* was given to Lt. Alexander Grant of Montgomery's Highlanders, an officer with prior sailing experience. Although he did not know it at the time, Loring's concern as to his ships' ability to meet the French on equal terms was unfounded. At 115 tons, carrying four six-pound cannon, twelve four-pound cannon, and twenty-two swivels with a complement of 112 sailors, officers, and marines, his smaller ship, the *Boscawen*, was more than a match for any two ships in the French fleet. The *Duke of Cumberland* was even more powerful. Carrying twenty more men than the *Boscawen* and mounting two extra six-pounders, the 155-ton brig more than evened the odds against the combined French fleet.[12]

In keeping with his orders Loring moved up the lake and under the cover of darkness slipped past Laubaras's squadron. At first light the two English vessels found themselves nearing the passage between Grand Island and Cumberland Head, and as dawn took hold, a cry rang out from a lookout aboard the *Duke of Cumberland*. The French schooner *Vigilante* was dead ahead. Loring signaled the *Boscawen* to give chase, and cleared his ship for action.

Since late September Bourlamaque had stationed the *Vigilante* and a few bateaux to guard the entrance to East Bay and Missisquoi Bay in an attempt to prevent British Ranger forays behind his lines. It had proven dull work until the morning of October 12 when a lookout on the *Vigilante* spied the British warships at almost the same moment they spotted him. St. Onge was quick to react. He gave orders for the bateaux accompanying him to scatter and then raised every square inch of sail his vessel had. As the pursuit pressed north it became clear to the French captain that he had neither the speed to escape, nor the firepower to turn and face the British. He did, however, have one advantage. He knew the lake better than any man alive. As the British vessels edged closer he saw his opportunity. Ahead about three-quarters of a mile off the northwest coast of Grand Island lay two small islands known at the time as the Two Brothers. The waters around the twin rocks were laced with shoals and sandbars. If the consequences were not so dire the whole thing might have brought a smile to the mariner's face as the timing could not have been better. When the larger of the enemy vessels was almost upon him St. Onge ran the rudder hard over passing between the two islands. Thinking that the *Vigilante* was aiming for the passage into East Bay, Loring steered a course between the Two Brothers and Grand Island with the aim of cutting off the Frenchman's escape. A few moments later a scraping noise reverberated down the length of the *Duke of Cumberland*'s hull followed quickly by another, and then a jarring jolt as the vessel bottomed out. Lt. Grant, not far behind in the *Boscawen*, screamed at his crew to spill the air out of the sails and spun the wheel hard to port, but it was too late. The *Boscawen* touched bottom and then shuddered to a stop on another shoal. As the *Vigilante* disappeared behind Grand Island, a furious Loring shouting a dozen orders to his crew couldn't help but pause and give the departing vessel a reluctant nod. He had been outdone and knew it.[13]

Opposite: A map of the naval actions on Lake Champlain, October 11 and 12, 1759. which culminated in the scuttling of the French fleet.

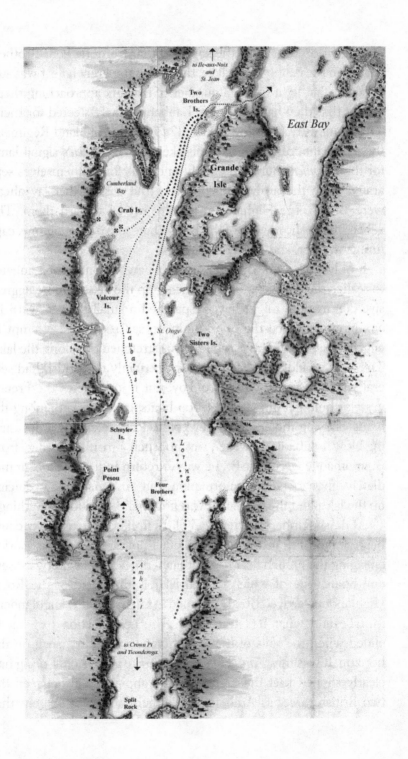

A few dozen miles to the south, not far from the Four Brothers Islands in the center of the lake, the rest of the French fleet was surprised at first light to see a number of bateaux approaching them. Seeing that they had no escort, Laubaras slowly steered for them. The boats were from the British 42nd Royal Highland Regiment, the occupants of which had mistaken the *Boscawen*'s signal lamp for the *Ligonier*'s during the night and thus found themselves separated from the army. Thinking that the vessels that lay ahead were British, the Highlanders calmly rowed toward them. The xebecs made short work of the British bateaux: damaging one, capturing another, and scattering the rest.

It only took a few minutes with his new prisoners for Laubaras to realize that Amherst was advancing up the lake. A more aggressive commander might have dispatched a small boat to warn Ile aux Noix and used the opportunity to sail south and attempt to engage the British flotilla while it was stretched out along the lake. The risks would have been high, for certainly the British had several warships escorting the convoy, but if just one of the French vessels could get among the troop boats, or better yet among the boats carrying the artillery, they could deal the enemy a devastating blow. Laubaras, however, was not such a man. His orders from Bourlamaque were specific, he was to return to Ile aux Noix immediately upon obtaining information that Amherst was advancing up the lake, and the lieutenant was not one to question such things.

At dawn Amherst at the head of his flotilla in the *Ligonier* could hear cannon fire in the distance, but thinking that it was Loring engaging the French fleet he continued on. Not long afterward several boats, one of which carried Major John Reid of the Royal Highlanders, arrived. Reid informed Amherst of the Highlanders' mistake and what had transpired. The conversation had barely ended when the sails of the French xebecs could be seen on the horizon. It was now Amherst's turn to make a decision. Loring had clearly slipped past the French fleet, trapping them between the two British forces as Amherst had hoped, but unfortunately, that now placed his troops in a precarious position. The *Ligonier*, although heavily armed and an excellent gun platform, was a poor sailer being nothing more than a barge with sails, and his little gunboats which could barely handle the rough waters of the lake were no match for several well-armed sloops. If the French acted aggressively he might well have a disaster on his hands. As a precaution he ordered the bateaux to form one column along the west shore of the lake while his gunboats and the *Ligonier* moved into position to cover the column's right flank. Several anxious moments passed before it became apparent that the move was unnecessary. The French vessels were headed north at full speed.[14]

Loring and Grant spent the better part of the day alternately cursing St. Onge and the shoals they were stuck on. The *Boscawen* was freed fairly easily, but the *Duke of Cumberland* proved to be stuck fast. After removing eight guns and sixty men, the vessel was finally refloated to the cheers of all, and the relief of Loring. Neither vessel was damaged and after transferring the guns and men back aboard, the two warships headed back out into the main channel. They had no sooner done so when a cry from a lookout drew everyone's attention. To the south three vessels could be seen tacking north. It seemed to all that the French fleet had found them and not the other way around, but with the wind in his favor Loring was not going to argue the point, and ran up the signal to close in on the enemy.

With the wind gauge against him and his route north blocked, Laubaras had little choice but to reverse course. It now became a matter of who was faster. If Laubaras could outdistance Loring before nightfall he might be able to turn back under the cover of darkness and make his way past the Englishman. Such was not the case, however. Loring pressed the French squadron, and with dusk falling Laubaras saw no option but to take shelter in the lower portion of Cumberland Bay near the southern end of the Isle of St. Michael (or Crab Island as it is known today). With the two British warships anchored not far away he called together Captain Rigal of the *Brochette* and the captain of the *Esturgeon* to discuss their options. Strangely, the decision was made to put the crews ashore and scuttle the fleet. It was an odd course of action, primarily because nothing had been attempted. Although Laubaras's fleet was south of the British warships, it was far from an iron trap. It was nightfall and the channel north between Cumberland Head and Grand Island was close to a mile and a half across, covered by only two warships whose crews were unfamiliar with the waters. At the very least one would have thought that an attempt could have been made to slip past the British. Given that there were three French ships and only two of the enemy, the odds were good that even if things went badly that at least one of the French vessels would have escaped. Nor was choosing to fight out of the question. The three xebecs, although outgunned and outmanned, were hardly facing overwhelming odds. The weather, however, which was beginning to deteriorate, may have had much to do with the decision. The xebecs were poor sailers under the best of circumstances, and without oars to counter the contrary winds Laubaras seems to have judged both flight and fight impossible.

The act of scuttling the fleet was accomplished almost as fast as the decision was arrived at, and with nearly the same thought process. The brass twelve-pounders from the *Musquelongy*, a few swivel guns, and a handful of muskets were thrown overboard, but in general the *Brochette* and *Esturgeon* were sunk intact in five fathoms of water, and the *Musquelongy*, with its masts cut, was simply run aground on the west shore of the lake opposite Crab Island. The work seemed to satisfy Laubaras, who along with the rest of the sailors and marines began the overland trek to Montreal. When dawn broke the next morning Loring was stunned to find the abandoned French fleet before him. When he, Lt. Grant, and a boarding party investigated the wrecks the shock turned to satisfaction. In both his and Grant's opinion all three of the vessels and most of the items thrown overboard could be salvaged. Leaving Grant and the *Boscawen* to handle this task Loring set sail north in hopes of catching the *Vigilante* before it returned to Ile aux Noix, but poor weather and contrary winds forced him to seek shelter before he got more than a few miles from Cumberland Head.[15]

The same storm that held up Loring had also forced Amherst's flotilla ashore. A letter from the commodore reached the general on October 14 with news of the French fleet's destruction, but there was little Amherst could do at the moment to take advantage of the situation. The winds were so bad that he could not even get a message back to Loring, and the lake was as choppy "as some seas in a gale." October 15 proved "impractical," the sixteenth no better, and the seventeenth just as bad, and on each of the evenings a hard freeze gripped the area making the troops' life ashore miserable. The weather lifted some on the eighteenth, but it no longer mattered. A courier reached the general from Crown Point that morning with news of Quebec's capture and General Wolfe's death. The fall of Quebec, while jubilant news for the British cause, spelt a death blow for Amherst's campaign. With the loss of Quebec the French army would be falling back on Montreal, which meant that if he proceeded he would now have to contend with a much larger force than Bourlamaque originally possessed. To add to the decision the air had taken on "an appearance of winter." The weather was not likely to improve, and by Amherst's estimation Ile aux Noix was a good ten days away at their current pace, plenty of time for the French to prepare a warm reception for his men. It all signaled the end of the campaign. "I shall decline my intended operations and get back to Crown Point where I hear the works go on but slowly," he wrote in his journal. The next morning he made his decision official. After detaching troops to assist Loring in his hunt for the *Vigilante* and to aid Grant in his salvage operations, Amherst ordered the army back to Crown Point.

For Bourlamaque the entire chain of events proved nothing less than irritating. From the beginning he had little faith in his navy's ability to halt the British advance, and although its loss was tempered by Amherst's decision to abandon his campaign, the French commander was mystified as to what had motivated d'Olabaratz's decision to scuttle his fleet. "[D'Olabaratz] has sunk his boats without trying to march, without firing his cannon, and without attempting to escape under the cover of darkness," he wrote to General Levis. Nor was an explanation forthcoming as Laubaras and his men elected not to return to Ile aux Noix, but instead marched straight for Montreal. Bourlamaque wrote Governor Vaudreuil demanding an explanation and the return of these men to bolster of the defenses of Ile aux Noix, but with the campaign season coming to a close, the whole matter soon faded into the background.[16]

For Amherst and his men the failure to reach Montreal was offset by the year's gains. Quebec, Fort Niagara, Fort Carillon, and Fort St. Frédéric were now in British hands, and in an impressive feat Lt. Grant had managed to salvage all three French xebecs and much of their armament. By November 16 these vessels, which more than doubled the British naval presence on Lake Champlain, were safely anchored alongside the *Duke of Cumberland* and the *Boscawen* at Ticonderoga.

The conquest of New France was still a year away, but for the moment at least, there were no questions—Champlain was a British lake.

With the turn of the year command of Ile aux Noix was handed over to Montcalm's old chief of staff, Colonel Louis-Antoine Bougainville. Having visited the island on several occasions, Bougainville was under no illusions of what his new assignment would bring. With a British attempt on the island all but certain he was forced to operate under a greater handicap than Bourlamaque had the year before. Until the end of June he had no more than five hundred men to work on the island's fortifications and man its defenses. Relief came not long after when Vaudreuil ordered the 2nd battalion of Berry and a detachment of militia to join him, but the lack of manpower crippled the young colonel's efforts to secure the post, and what he did possess after the reinforcements arrived was less than half of what Bourlamaque had found necessary to defend the post the year before. Even with these setbacks a great deal of progress was made. By August the island bristled with field fortifications. Most of the work was logically confined to the southern portion of the island where the initial attack was certain to fall. The northern part of the island, however, still lacked adequate defenses. Although the ground here was marshy there was still the possibility that the British might attempt to bring cannon over to this part of the island and attack the French fortifications via trench work in the fashion of a formal siege. Bougainville erected a few crude defensive works here, and stationed a number of troops to watch the area, the best that could be done given his limited resources.[17]

One of the most important elements of the island's defenses was the vessels assembled around the island. The loss of the three xebecs the previous fall had left the French scrambling for naval support. The *gabare* armed with four small cannon and the schooner *Vigilante* still remained, but little else. To fill the void left by the loss of Laubaras's squadron, two vessels known as *tartanes* were constructed at St. Jean during the fall of 1759 and the summer of 1760. The tartanes were in keeping with the Mediterranean theme set earlier by the construction of the xebecs. Essentially row galleys, these vessels employed a short lateen-rigged main mast, and a small sail on their bowsprit to go along with a lateen sail on a short mizzen mast. The larger of the two, christened *Grand Diable*, carried between forty and sixty oars and was originally to be armed with four twenty-four-pound cannon, but such guns were no longer to be found within the colony and three eighteen-pound cannon were substituted instead, two mounted in the prow and another firing astern. The smaller of the two, simply referred to as the "little one," carried twenty-four oars and was armed with a number of swivel guns and four pounders. Four small "Jacob" gunboats, armed with eight-pound guns in their prow, rounded out the naval forces at Bougainville's disposal.[18]

At Crown Point General William Haviland had spent a busy summer preparing for the upcoming campaign. Although he had previously commanded Fort Edward, the assignment was Haviland's first independent command of a corps, and he was eager to show that his recent promotion to brigadier general was well founded. Throughout May, June, July, and the first part of August his days were spent immersed in the details of forwarding troops and supplies to Crown Point, repairs on Fort Ticonderoga, work on Fort Amherst, and dispatching scouting parties north. To seize Ile aux Noix, the Richelieu Valley forts, and from there march on to Montreal, Amherst had given Haviland two regular British regiments, several provincial regiments from New Hampshire, Rhode Island, and Massachusetts, Rogers' Rangers, and a detachment of Royal Artillery. To protect his advance up the lake Haviland could look to the naval squadron under the command of the Highlander turned commodore, Lt. Alexander Grant. Although it was known that the French still had a few vessels at their command there was no question as to who controlled the lake. Grant had successfully raised and refitted the scuttled French fleet at Cumberland Bay, which meant that in addition to the *Duke of Cumberland* and the *Boscawen* he now had three more sloops at his disposal, and in addition to the *Ligonier* Lt. Colonel Ord had seen to the construction of three more radeaux to carry his artillery. Added to this were a number of gunboats, whaleboats, and smaller flat-bottomed vessels, all of which more than ensured British naval superiority.[19]

By August 11, 1760, all the details having been seen to, Haviland pushed out onto the lake. Rogers' men took the lead in whaleboats followed closely by the grenadiers and light infantry. Behind them in three columns were the provincial troops and the two regiments of British regulars. The *Ligonier* and three smaller radeaux carrying Ord's artillery and supplies along with the army's provision boats followed. As compared to previous years, the flotilla was small, but in all it consisted of some 3,400 troops in eighty whaleboats, 330 bateaux, and four radeaux–more than enough for the task at hand. Added to this was Grant's squadron which had been ordered to lie off Windmill Point in expectation of the fleet.[20]

By daybreak of the sixteenth Haviland's troops columns had joined with Grant's fleet forming two four-mile long columns on the lake, which when cast against the perfect weather "made a very beautiful appearance," according to one provincial soldier. Led by the *Ligonier*, the other artillery radeaux, and a few small gunboats the columns entered the confines of the Richelieu River where they encountered two small French boats that quickly beat a retreat at the sight of the armada. Around noon Haviland ordered the columns to halt just above La Pointe à Margot out of sight of Ile aux Noix. The radeaux and gunboats were sent ahead to "amuse the enemy" while the order was given for Lt. Colonel John Darby's advanced guard of Rangers, Grenadiers, and light infantry to land on the east bank of the river. After scouring the shore for an hour Darby gave the all-clear signal, and the rest of the army disembarked shortly thereafter with little incident. By nightfall over three thousand men were ashore in the woods south of the island, secure behind a mile-long wooden breastwork that Haviland ordered built.[21]

Louis-Antoine Bougainville, later Admiral and Count de Bougainville. This portrait shows Bougainville as he appeared during the American Revolution while in command of the French man-o-war *Auguste* at the siege of Yorktown. Bougainville's appointment to command the fortifications at Ile-aux-Noix left him under no illusions. At best he could only hope to delay the British advance. (*Library of Congress*)

Haviland spent the next few days shuffling his army forward along the east shore, throwing up new breastworks, and securing a point of land within musket shot of the fort. A wharf was constructed to land the artillery, and crews toiled away on the road to move the guns forward, while others saw to fashioning fascines and firing platforms to mount the cannon on the swampy ground. The French fired a handful of cannon at the advancing British, but it did little to distract them, and more often than not it brought forth a barrage from Colonel Ord's artillery radeaux which hovered about the southern end of the island.[22]

Bougainville was quickly finding himself in an impossible situation. A few militia had reached him on the opening days of the siege, but nowhere near what was needed or promised. His garrison of 1,453 men which included workers, sailors, and domestic servants was simply not enough to defend the extent of the island's works. As much as he would have liked to have opposed the British landing he simply couldn't spare the men to do so, and to make matters worse the Abenaki with him had deserted, depriving him of scouts and badly needed intelligence. Although Haviland had no intentions of doing so, Bougainville's first concern was to prevent an English landing on the island, especially on the northern part where the enemy might appear suddenly via the Rivière du Sud which entered the Richelieu a few hundred yards below the island. If they secured a foothold there they could entrench themselves and haul cannon forward against the weaker north wall of the fortifications. To prevent this, at the start of the siege he sent Captain Jean Valette with 230 men and four cannon to this part of the island with orders to man the blockhouse there in hopes of hindering any British landing. St. Onge in the *Vigilante*, Captain Lesage with the *Grand Diable*, the gabare, and four gunboats were posted at the mouth of the Rivière du Sud, not only to block any British descent down the river, but to keep the supply and communications lines to St. Jean open. It was hardly a formidable position, nor the ideal approach, Bougainville informed Levis, but "The isle is immense and I must avoid all arrangements which would put me in the position of being taken by a coup de main." Still, he assured

Levis, regardless of the defects in the position he and the garrison were up to the task of defending it.[23]

On the afternoon of August 23 Bougainville's statement was to be put to the test. Haviland's men had completed three batteries, the first consisting of six twenty-four pounders, the second comprised of three twelve-pound cannons, three "Royal" howitzers, and seven five-and-a-half-inch mortars, and the last, a heavy bomb battery of two thirteen-inch and two ten-inch mortars. At four o'clock a signal gun was fired, and in keeping with the formalities of the age, the sound of fife and drums carried from one end of the British line to the other. For ten minutes the martial music filled the air finally ending with the echoed command to fire. With a deafening crash the British batteries fired five quick salvos against the island, "beating down all before them," according to one observer. As the fire steadied to a more reasonable pace the *Duke of Cumberland*, with fascines fitted to its sides for added protection, approached the island and added its guns to the onslaught. Initially the French remained silent, but as the evening wore on a few guns came into action, firing the occasional mortar round or cannonball across the channel. Haviland used the barrage to send several parties out to cut the boom blocking the east channel, but with little success. Each found the structure much stronger than anticipated, and each was eventually chased off by a hail of grapeshot and small arms fire.

At dawn the British batteries fell silent as the crews were changed and munitions brought forward, but the reprieve was short lived. Within an hour the guns were once again pounding the island through a low-hanging mist that scattered showers across defender and foe throughout the day. As night descended Haviland ordered parties forward to construct a fourth battery of two guns near the east boom "within a musket shot of the island." Their activities brought an immediate response from the French, who quickly realized that this battery would not only enfilade their position but also cover any attempting to remove the boom as well. Volley after volley of grapeshot ripped through the woods in an attempt to dissuade the working parties. Although two provincials were killed in the attacks and a dozen wounded, it was the onset of heavy rains and not the French guns that eventually brought the work to a halt for the evening.[24]

In the early morning hours of August 25 Colonel Darby's detachment of Grenadiers, light infantry, and Rangers plowed through the mire along the east shore dragging two twelve-pound cannons and a pair of five-and-a-half-inch howitzers behind them. It was grueling work, manhandling several tons of iron through the muck and between the trees, but by mid-morning Darby's men had reached their destination and erected their little battery on a point of land just south of the confluence of the Rivière du Sud and the Richelieu. Across from them, anchored below the northern tip of the island, were three French vessels, the objective of their trek. Haviland had ordered Darby to destroy the French fleet in order to cut the island's communications with Fort St. Jean and open a passage for British vessels once the boom was cut. Around ten o'clock that morning Darby opened fire on his unsuspecting targets. Onboard the *Grand Diable* Captain Lesage responded instinctively to the attack by ordering the anchor cable cut so that the vessel could be rowed to safety. Darby's men, however, were quick to find the range and the next few shots crashed into the *Grand Diable*, killing Lesage. With the tartane under fire, and drifting slowly under a northwest wind toward the British battery, the crew thought better of the matter and either swam to safety or surrendered. With the *Grand Diable* aground on the east shore Darby turned his attention to the *Vigilante* moored a few hundred yards to the north. St. Onge had slipped his anchor at the start of the engagement in an attempt to run down the river, but quickly found himself sliding toward the east shore under the prevailing winds. Soon he too was aground on a peninsula north of the Rivière du Sud. The gabare which accompanied his flight met a similar fate running aground not far away. The gabare, stuck fast, was doomed,

The Destruction of the French fleet, August 25, 1760. With the loss of the remaining elements of the French fleet at Ile aux Noix the defense of the island, and the entire French position in the Richelieu Valley became untenable.

but with luck the *Vigilante* might still be able to free itself, if it had the time. Darby had no intention of allowing his quarry to escape. He ordered Rogers across the Rivière du Sud while he and his men, now in control of the *Grand Diable*, attempted to free it. Rogers and his men made their way across the river, and once opposite the two vessels, laid down a barrage of musketry. A few of the Rangers armed with tomahawks swam out to the gabare and boarded it with little in the way of opposition. The *Vigilante*'s crew put up slightly more resistance, banging away with its small cannons, but when the *Grand Diable*, now manned by red-coated sailors, came into view, St. Onge resigned himself to the futility of the situation and struck his colors.[25]

The engagement was an unheralded success for Haviland, and the end of the French Lake Champlain fleet. Twenty French sailors including St. Onge had been captured, the garrison's communications with Fort St. Jean had been cut, and the British now had three vessels under their control below the island. To make matters even better, the entire venture had been accomplished without the loss of a single British soldier. The general was quick to exploit the victory. He ordered Lt. Grant and seventy sailors down to Darby's position to man the prizes, and followed this with supplies and new cannons for the vessels. Ten whaleboats were also sent forward with orders for Darby to use them to ferry his men across the river to seize control of Prairie de Boileau on the west bank, further tightening the noose around Ile aux Noix.[26]

The loss of the three warships placed Bougainville in an intractable situation. His lifeline to St. Jean was cut, and what remained of his fleet, even if he had any faith in their abilities, could not contest the waters with the British. In addition, the enemy had made repeated efforts against the east boom and it seemed only a matter of time before they managed to cut it and open the channel to their vessels. The turn of events called into question his entire position. To a large extent the defense of Ile aux Noix hinged on naval control of the river below the island. Once this was lost, the island's fortifications could at best only serve to pin down a portion of the British army while the rest circumvented the island and carried their advance farther downriver. The conclusions were clear, and the next evening under the cover of darkness Bougainville abandoned the island.[27]

It then only became a matter of days for New France. Haviland cut the boom blocking the east channel and with the captured *Grand Diable* in the lead arrived at Fort St. Jean on the afternoon of August 30 to find it a smoldering ruin. Here lay the last two elements of the French Lake Champlain fleet, "one on ye stocks and one burned." The vessel on the stocks was the unfinished xebec *Waggon* that Bourlamaque had used as a floating battery. In November of the previous year he had ordered this vessel towed to St. Jean and pulled out of the water in preparation for winter. The problems encountered with the earlier xebecs, their lack of oars needed to navigate the Richelieu River, and the real possibility that such a vessel might be surprised and boarded in the narrow waterway, coupled with the shortage of resources and manpower, led to the decision not to finish her. The ship reported as burned was in all likelihood the *Saintonge*, the only major vessel not accounted for in the French Lake Champlain fleet.[28]

Fort Chambly fell quickly on September 4 after a few shots, the only artillery rounds ever fired at the structure in its ninety-five-year history. With the forts and towns of the Richelieu Valley secured, Haviland turned his army to the west to take part in the final moments of New France. At one o'clock on the afternoon of September 8 his troops arrived on the south bank of the St. Lawrence opposite Montreal. General Amherst was encamped on the island to the west of the city with his army, while General James Murray was on the eastern end of the island marching toward the last French stronghold. At almost the same moment as Haviland appeared, Governor Vaudreuil, realizing that further resistance was useless, gave the official order surrendering the colony.[29]

FOUR

Valcour Island

ROM THE QUARTERDECK OF THE *Maria* BRITISH GENERAL GUY Carleton gave an approving smile. Carleton was not prone to such displays, but given that he now found himself at the head of the most powerful fleet to ever ply the waters of Lake Champlain, the crack in his exterior was understandable. Directly behind his ship, the *Maria*, was the sixty-foot twelve-gun schooner *Carleton*, followed closely by the gondola *Loyal Convert*, aptly named given that it started its life as an American vessel. Behind it came one of the odder craft on the lake, the radeau *Thunderer*. At almost ninety-two feet in length and thirty-three feet in breadth, this flat-bottomed box was a modified version of the vessels built by Amherst and Ord a generation before. Fitted with oars and a pair of short masts and rigged as a ketch, the *Thunderer* was not the most elegant sailer to ever try the northern lake, but with its complement of six twenty-four-pound cannons, four twelve-pound cannons, and four howitzers it was certainly the most heavily armed. Next, ranged in columns across the narrow northern confines of the lake, came twenty gunboats. Basically longboats, these rowed craft were manned by twenty or so sailors and artillery men. Each carried a single cannon in their prow ranging in size from six to twenty-four pounds, and with the wind being fair, the lot moved forward under the power of the small sails employed on a single mast. Splayed out behind these warships were the army's longboats and bateaux carrying the artillery and provisions, and strung out for miles beyond this was Carleton's main force of some seven thousand red-coated British regulars and blue-coated German mercenaries. Three longboats, a gift from the Royal Navy warships anchored in the St. Lawrence River, slashed a path through the waters in front of the *Maria* forming the vanguard of the British fleet as it made its way south toward Point au Fer.[1]

It was a spectacular sight further magnified by the crimson and gold brushed foliage of early October. As pleased as Carleton was at the moment, he realized it had not been an easy journey. Just eleven months before he had found himself pinned behind the walls of Quebec as a pair of American armies under Generals Richard Montgomery and Benedict Arnold gathered in a swirling snowfall for an assault that would expel the British from Canada and perhaps change the course of the American rebellion against the crown. The Americans had seized most of Canada during the summer and fall of 1775, forcing the unprepared and severely out-numbered Carleton to consolidate his forces at Quebec while rein-forcements were mobilized in England. Overextended, lacking siege guns, and facing the Canadian winter as well as the British, the American dream of making Canada the fourteenth colony faulted before the walls of the city amidst a pair of ill-advised attacks that left Montgomery dead and Arnold severely wounded.

It then only became a matter of waiting for the Governor-General of Canada. In early May the first reinforcements reached the city, and with their arrival the American army, already decid-ed upon retreat, began to disintegrate. Carleton used the meager addition of manpower to march out of the city and scatter the besiegers. Too weak and too dispersed to support one another, the American army encircling the capital broke into a headlong flight toward Montreal. Most of the American shipping on the St. Lawrence was captured by the newly arrived British warships, as was the American artillery train. The Americans attempted to make a stand at Deschambault, forty-five miles west of Quebec, but then reconsidered and withdrew to Sorel at the mouth of the Richelieu River. A counter-attack on Three Rivers failed, and as spring changed to summer the American army of Canada, wracked by smallpox and desertion, abandoned their positions, falling back first on Fort Chambly, and then on Fort St. Johns. Carleton, now reinforced by a succession of British and German regiments under General John Burgoyne, followed close behind. On the evening of June 18, 1776, his vanguard reached Fort St. Johns to find it in flames, deserted by the Americans just a few hours before. The American army still clung to Ile aux Noix, but by the end of the month they had abandoned this post as well, withdrawing up the lake to the safety of Crown Point.[2]

In six months the Americans had been chased out of Canada and the situation was restored to what it had been the summer before; with the Americans entrenched at the southern end of the lake while the British held the northern end. But this time there was a difference: with a handful of warships in their arsenal the Americans controlled the lake.

Without supplies to pursue his fleeing enemy and more important, without warships of his own to counter the American vessels operating on the lake, Carleton halted the pursuit. For him and his men it now became a matter of logistics and preparation. Supplies and artillery would have to be forwarded to Fort St. Johns, a fleet of warships built to contend with their American counterparts, and boats constructed to ferry the troops south. The effort was aggravated by the destruction left behind by the retreating Americans. All the bridges between Chambly and St. Johns had been leveled, the docks at St. Johns had been demolished, and the barracks, the

General Richard Montgomery reviewing his troops at Crown Point before their advance north on Fort St. Johns. (*Library of Congress*)

nearby sawmill, and the fort itself put to the torch. Everything from cannonballs to the nails needed to construct a fleet had to be carried around the half dozen miles of rapids to the fort. In many respects Carleton's plight was reminiscent of Amherst's a generation before. He had dislodged his opponent from their strongholds with little effort and secured a base of operations at one end of the lake, and like Amherst, he was now in the position of having to build a fleet to continue the pursuit. There were, however, two major differences between the commanders. First, even though the Chambly and St. Therese rapids lay in the way, the supply route to St. Johns from the British logistic centers in Canada was far simpler than that faced by Amherst at Ticonderoga and Crown Point. And second, to construct his fleet Carleton could immediately draw upon a supply of skilled manpower and naval experts from the sizable elements of the Royal Navy operating in the St. Lawrence.[3]

The governor had in part already foreseen the problem at hand, if not exactly the circumstances of its execution. Shortly after the Americans had seized control of Lake Champlain in 1775 he wrote

Admiral Graves in Boston requesting the men and materials needed to build two warships at St. Johns, and a fleet of bateaux to carry
British troops south. At the time Graves was in no position to ful-
fill this request, and within a few months Carleton was more interested in holding onto Canada than in launching an attack on
Ticonderoga and Crown Point. The petition, however, did not go
unanswered. Graves forwarded Carleton's letter on to the admiralty, and when the Royal Navy relief squadrons arrived at Quebec
the following spring they carried with them ten disassembled gunboats along with a bounty of much-needed naval supplies.

The thirty-six-foot-long gunboats would prove easy enough to
transport to St. Johns, where they would be reassembled and supplemented by another dozen or so to be built at the fort. But it
would take more than just gunboats to seize the lake back from the
Americans, and therein lay Carleton's problem. Although he possessed the resources to do so, building several large warships at St.
Johns would take too long, and would allow the Americans time
to add to their fleet, creating something of a naval arms race that
would consume the campaign season. Instead, the decision was
made to transport several warships currently operating on the St.
Lawrence intact to St. Johns. The plan called for the first two, the
fourteen-gun 129-ton schooner *Maria* and the twelve-gun 96-ton
schooner *Carleton*, to be lightened and floated over the Chambly
rapids by the use of air bladders known as camels. The ambitious
approach was not all that different than what had been attempted
by the advancing Americans the previous fall. The difference, however, was that the Americans were able to take advantage of the
higher seasonal water levels, and even with this they wrecked one
of their vessels in the effort.[4]

It did not take long for Royal Navy captain Charles Douglas,
who Carleton had placed in charge of the effort, to realize that the
plan would never work. As work crews toiled to rebuild the dockyard and facilities around Fort St. Johns, Douglas turned to a second approach, that of transporting the heavy vessels around the

rapids via the Chambly–St. Johns road-
way. Heavy rollers fashioned from felled
trees and teams of horses were dispatched to the area as well as hundreds
of men to mend the war-torn road. The
Maria was winched out of the water at
Chambly and placed on a sled balanced
upon a set of wooden rollers. This effort
alone was impressive, but after a few
hundred yards of pulling the sled forward the engineers in charge gave up;
the road was simply in too bad a condition to support the vessel's weight.
Either the plan would have to be abandoned, or the ships dismantled and
transported in pieces. There was really
little choice, and the latter approach was
soon adopted. Both the *Maria* and the
Carleton were stripped down to within a
few boards of their keel and hauled to St.
Johns like a whaler's trophy. It was slow,
grueling work, especially at the numerous stream and river crossings where the
vessels often had to wait until the
bridges had been rebuilt. And even after
the structures were erected, navigating
the hulks down the riverbank, across the
narrow wooden stretches, and back up
the opposing riverbank proved a trying experience.[5]

Governor-General of
Canada Sir Guy Carleton.
A capable general and
administrator, Carleton
weathered the American
attack on Canada in 1775,
successfully directing the
defense of Quebec until
British reinforcements
arrived in the spring of
1776. Carleton's counter-
attack threw the American
army out of Canada, but
like Amherst, he was forced
to halt his advance in order
to build a fleet to gain control over Lake Champlain.
And like Amherst, although
he succeeded in securing
control over Lake
Champlain, the delay cost
him the campaign season.

By early August the *Maria* and the *Carleton* had reached Fort St.
Johns. The smaller gondola *Loyal Convert* followed in similar fashion a few weeks later. As crews tended to the rebuilding and re-

arming of these ships, another vessel began to take shape along the shore. The ungainly *Thunderer* caught the eye of many stationed at Fort St. Johns, but oddly, beyond its proportions and a few external changes, the floating box was nothing new to the region. Amherst and Ord had built several of these flat-bottomed vessels a generation before to act as gun platforms and haul their artillery across the lake. The largest of these, however, the *Ligonier*, was dwarfed by the new vessel's proportions and impressive armament, but the two shared a common trait; drawing only a few feet of water, they were difficult to manage, especially when the weather on Lake Champlain took a turn for the worse.

By now St. Johns had been transformed into a flurry of activity. Douglas had scoured the Royal Navy vessels on the St. Lawrence for volunteers, and after assembling some 450 of these, he turned his attention to the transports in the river. Another 250 sailors and carpenters were recruited from these ships, leaving some vessels to make their way back to England with near skeleton crews. Carleton also called out the Canadian militia, setting them to work repairing roads, building bridges, transporting supplies, and erecting fortifications and storehouses at St. Johns. A new sawmill was constructed as well, the whine of its blades frequently rising above the backdrop of hammer and saw that echoed across the valley from dawn till dusk.[6]

Although work proceeded rapidly on the four major vessels and a dozen new gunboats, the total was not considered sufficient to challenge the American fleet, which by current reports had grown to a dozen vessels. What was needed, in Captain Douglas's mind, was a vessel powerful enough to tip the scales and ensure British supremacy over the mountain waters regardless of what the Americans might build. To accomplish this, his focus landed upon a vessel currently under construction at Quebec. The 204-ton *Inflexible* had barely finished having its floorboards laid when Douglas ordered Lt. John Schank, commander of HMS *Canceaux*, to have the vessel disassembled and shipped to Chambly for transport to Fort St. Johns. Douglas gave the command of the *Inflexible* to Schank, and to equip and man the new warship he ordered Schank to strip the *Canceaux* of its crew and supplies.

The same carpenters who had just completed the *Inflexible* mumbled at the orders and then carefully disassembled the craft over the next few weeks, cataloging and marking each piece. A parade of thirty longboats hauled the pieces to Chambly, and from there they were loaded onto ox-drawn carts and transported to St. Johns. In a display of peerless skill and determination, two dozen shipwrights reassembled and completed the eighty-foot vessel in twenty-eight days under Schank's supervision. On September 29 it slid down its launch skid and splashed into the Richelieu River, rocking gently to the repeated "huzzahs" of Carleton's army. The next day it sailed for Ile aux Noix to take on guns, already drawing too much water to dare try this at Fort St. Johns.[7]

Even though the *Inflexible* was still occupied in taking on its guns, by October 5 Carleton felt secure enough to move forward. That morning the general and his army left the confines of the Richelieu and entered Lake Champlain. Not sure where the American fleet was currently operating, Carleton had the bulk of the army make camp at the La Colle River while he and the armed elements of the fleet, now under the overall command of Captain Thomas Pringle of the Royal Navy, dropped anchor at Point au Fer, some nine miles further south. Carleton spent the better part of the next week at Point au Fer waiting on the *Inflexible*, and news from his scouts who were busy scouring the lake for signs of the American fleet. His plan was simple. The army would wait at the La Colle and Point au Fer while he and the fleet sought out and destroyed their American counterparts. Once this was accomplished the entire invasion force could move forward at its leisure.

On October 9 the *Inflexible* joined Carleton. The ship-rigged three-masted frigate bristled with a new complement of eighteen twelve-pound cannons and ten swivel guns mounted along its deck rails. With its square sails billowing before the autumn breeze and flags snapping atop its masts, it was a creature more commonly encountered upon the open seas than the confines of a mountain lake. The sight of the warship sent a surge of confidence through the troops and made a lasting impression on one young British lieutenant encamped at Point au Fer. "It certainly was a noble sight to see such a vessel on a fresh water lake in the very heart of the Continent of America," he noted in his journal after watching the warship glide by.[8]

Carleton was pleased to see the vessel as well. Earlier that day the sound of cannon echoed from the south, which he took to be the Americans clearing their guns. The time had come. The rebel fleet was near, and with the *Inflexible* now joining him, he would set off in search of them the next day.[9]

The last American out of Fort St. Johns was Brigadier General Benedict Arnold. For Arnold the previous year had been an impressive cycle of highs and lows. In April 1775, as a colonel in charge of a Massachusetts contingent, he had been one of the first men to enter Fort Ticonderoga, seizing it and its stores in the name of the new republic. While others, satisfied with the effort, debated the next step, Arnold acted. To capture Fort Ticonderoga was one thing, but to hold it against a British counterattack required control of the lake, and to this end, he ordered Captains Eleazer Oswald and John Brown to retrieve the forty-ton schooner *Katherine* seized at Skenesborough (Whitehall) from retired British major Philip Skene. Renamed *Liberty*, the little schooner was fitted with four light cannons and half a dozen swivel guns at Ticonderoga on May 13, and the next day carried Arnold as he advanced down the lake toward Fort St. Johns. Arnold's intention was not to capture the fort, but the only other vessel of consequence on the lake, the British sloop *Betsy*. Just as with Ticonderoga, the British garrison at Fort St. Johns was taken by complete surprise. Without a shot being fired the Americans captured the fort, the garrison's bateaux, and more importantly, the fifty-ton *Betsy*. Arnold renamed the vessel *Enterprise*, gathered together what supplies he could carry, destroyed the garrison's bateaux, and sailed back to Ticonderoga with his prize. The attack had gone flawlessly, and upon his return he was able to boldly inform the Massachusetts Committee of Safety that "we are masters of the Lake."[10]

True to his word, Arnold spent the next month securing the lake while contemplating and pushing for an attack on the tenuous British position at the northern end of the waterway. In Arnold's mind the importance of Lake Champlain to the American cause was not only to protect the colonial backcountry from a British invasion, but also to serve as a conduit from which all of Canada could be seized. Along these lines he submitted a plan to the Continental Congress in early June 1775 which outlined the timing, and the benefits such an operation would bring. With the worsening conditions around Boston and elsewhere, the plan was promptly ignored. Worse yet, Arnold's political enemies maneuvered the Connecticut and Massachusetts Councils to place Arnold under the command of Colonel Benjamin Hinman of Connecticut. Given his service, ability, and active ego Arnold refused to accept the demotion, and instead resigned his commission in mid-June, deeply in debt as he had been forced to use his own funds to maintain his troops and vessels on Lake Champlain.

Not long after, Arnold visited General George Washington outside of Boston to offer his services. In conversations with Washington, Arnold went over his plan to invade Canada and remove it as a threat to the northern colonies. Washington was so impressed by the Connecticut merchant turned soldier that he authorized the invasion. He also agreed to Arnold's bold plan to appear before Quebec by marching 1200 men up the Kennebec and Chudière rivers. This force would rendezvous with the American army advancing from the west, and together they would launch a combined assault on the Canadian capital.

Arnold's trek across the frozen woodlands of northern Maine has become legendary. Overcoming a series of obstacles through tenacity and sheer will Arnold and 600 of his men appeared on the south bank of the St. Lawrence on the morning of November 9, 1775. The colonel crossed the St. Lawrence a few days later with his worn-out battalion planning to surprise the garrison of Quebec, but Carleton was alerted to Arnold's presence. Exhausted and ill equipped, Arnold decided to wait for General Montgomery, who arrived with nearly a thousand men on December 1. After consulting with Arnold, Montgomery agreed that a conventional siege was unlikely to succeed. The ground had frozen, making the digging of siege trenches nearly impossible, and the Americans simply did not have the artillery needed to reduce the fortress in any case. Instead, the two decided to take the Canadian capital by storm. The plan was doomed from the outset, and amidst a howling snowstorm on New Year's Eve it collapsed. Wounded, Arnold continued the ineffective siege of Quebec until he was relieved by Major General David Wooster in April 1776. Now promoted to the rank of brigadier general, Arnold took command of the American forces occupying Montreal until Carleton's counteroffensive in May forced him to abandon the city and fall back on St. Johns.[11]

At St. Johns Arnold showed himself worthy of his new rank. He voluntarily formed a rear guard with his men to cover the flotilla of overcrowded vessels moving south, and then turned his attention to stripping the fort of anything useful. When this was accomplished, he ordered the rest set ablaze. After sending off his men, and making one last sweep of the area on the night of June 18, the brigadier rode down to the waterfront, shot his horse, and boarded the last American boat moving south as the outlines of British grenadiers formed amidst the flames.[12]

The reversals suffered by the invasion of Canada had now placed the American position along the Champlain corridor into question. What was left of the Army of Canada, perhaps some 3,500 men, congregated among the ruins of Fort Amherst at Crown Point. Most of the artillery and supplies gathered for the expedition had been lost, and sickness ran rampant, threatening to consume what was left of the army. General Horatio Gates, who

had traveled to Crown Point to attend
an emergency council of war, was
appalled to find "not an army but a mob,
the shattered remains of twelve or fifteen
very fine battalions, ruined by sickness,
fatigue and desertion." Gates's superior,
General Phillip Schuyler, commander of
the Northern district, was equally
shocked, informing Washington in a letter a few days later that, "the most
descriptive pen cannot describe the condition of our Army: sickness, disorder,
and discord, reign triumphant."[13]

Brigadier General Benedict
Arnold. Arnold rightly surmised early on that naval
control of Lake Champlain
would be crucial to the
American cause. In large
part, Arnold's efforts along
this front bought the poorly
equipped and ill-trained
Americans a year in which
they grew strong enough to
defeat a British army under
General John Burgoyne at
Saratoga, New York, in
1777.

As the senior officers of the Northern
Army met at Crown Point on July 7,
1776, to discuss their options, Arnold
presented a plan. First, the army had to
withdraw to Ticonderoga. Fort Amherst
was untenable before a British attack.
Most of the fort had been destroyed in a
fire in 1774, and what was left was simply not worth repairing. With some
effort Ticonderoga, and fortifications on
Mount Independence across the lake from it, would serve as an
excellent defensive position. Second, the troops infected with
smallpox must be transported to Fort George. If this was not done
soon, there would be no army. Third, and most importantly, the
army needed time; time to repair and improve the works at
Ticonderoga and Mount Independence, time to resupply and
recruit, and time for America's ally France, to send money and
arms. Carleton's advance had to be delayed, hopefully long enough
that the onset of winter would dissuade the British commander
from carrying through with any attack. In Arnold's estimation
there was only one way to accomplish this goal; by securing naval

superiority over the lake. After all, the only reason they even had the luxury to discuss the matter, he pointed out to the stern faces of the council, was because of the handful of American warships currently operating on the waterway. If those had not been in place, and the British so wary of their presence, right now they would be discussing either how to lift the siege of Ticonderoga or how to stop the British from advancing into the upper Hudson Valley. For every vessel the Americans put onto the lake the British would be forced to build one of their own in order to secure their vulnerable convoys, and every day that Carleton spent at St. Johns seeing to this effort, the young brigadier emphasized, was one day less he had before the walls of Ticonderoga, and one day less until the rains of autumn either ruled out an advance down the lake or forced him to lift his siege. At the moment the army could not survive a direct confrontation with the British, but if the matter could be turned into a naval arms race there was at least a chance of success.[14]

General Schuyler nodded at the plan. He had already come to the same conclusion and had set the groundwork into motion a month earlier. In late May Schuyler responded to a plea for more gondolas (squat sixty-foot long shallow draft vessels that could be rowed or sailed) by visiting the town of Skenesborough at the southern end of Lake Champlain. The location of Skenesborough at the junction of South Bay and Wood Creek was an excellent choice based on the fact that south of Ticonderoga the lake narrowed to an easily defensible corridor known as the "drowned lands," which ended at Skenesborough some 120 miles from the British position at St. Johns. But this aside, the choice was really driven by the fact that Skenesborough already had docks, warehouses, and critically, a pair of sawmills and an iron foundry. All the elements needed to build ships. Schuyler brought with him thirty carpenters and set them to the task at hand. The initial steps were slow, but with the American army on the verge of being expelled from the Richelieu Valley, the work at Skenesborough took on even greater importance. The British, Schuyler was informed, had transported a number of gunboat frames over from England with the intent of quickly putting these together at St. Johns and continuing their advance up the lake. It was now imperative that the Americans build a number of vessels "with all possible dispatch" to counter their adversary's efforts. Schuyler asked Washington for shipwrights, tools, and an individual knowledgeable in the construction of gondolas to accelerate this plan.

Some of the requested manpower arrived, and on June 24 the general reported to Washington that "One gondola is finished at Skenesborough and another is planking," and that it was his plan to "build one every six days." With the expulsion of the American army from St. Johns a week earlier, the matter crystalized. The next day Schuyler sent an urgent appeal to Massachusetts and Connecticut for ship's carpenters and naval supplies. A naval arms race was starting, and to the winner would go control of the lake. Given the Americans' head start, however, Schuyler was convinced that "we can out build them."[15]

With an aristocratic wave of the hand Schuyler motioned for Arnold to continue. Currently, Arnold began, there were three schooners and a sloop operating on the lake. One of the schooners, *Liberty*, was in the process of being refitted at Skenesborough, while another, the *Revenge*, was still being armed at Ticonderoga. Added to this was a pair of gondolas, the *New Haven* and *Providence*, recently finished at Skenesborough and currently waiting to be rigged and armed at Ticonderoga. Although a start, what was needed in the brigadier's estimation was a sizable fleet of some twenty vessels; half gondolas, half row galleys, stiffened by a large schooner or frigate which would lead them. To construct this fleet would require a thousand men along with another five hundred shipwrights and carpenters. There was also the matter of crews for the vessels. Some nine hundred or so seamen, gunners, and marines would be needed to man the fleet. Arnold wiped at his brow and shrugged. Unfortunately, the naval stores which could have been used to partially equip this fleet had been lost at Chambly when the fort was abandoned. They would have to be replaced. Most of the cannon needed to arm the fleet could be taken from the captured stores at Ticonderoga or Crown Point, but naval supplies such as anchors, rigging, and rope, along with most of the tools needed to build the fleet would have to be rushed to the area.[16]

Schuyler thanked Arnold, and after discussing a few administrative matters adjourned the meeting to consider his reply. It was not necessary. The commander of the Northern Army Department was won over by the plan, and he had no doubts that Arnold was the right man to lead the effort. Arnold had been a ship's master before the war, involved in the lucrative Caribbean trade. He understood ships and, given his actions along the lake from the onset of the conflict, there was little question as to his knowledge of the waterway. The general approved of Arnold's plan the next morning with one caveat; Arnold could construct his row galleys and gondolas, but there would be neither the time nor the resources to construct a frigate. The brigadier accepted the modification without a second thought, and for the next few weeks busied himself in overseeing the details at Ticonderoga. He personally led crews out into the woods about Crown Point to select trees from which the fleet's oars (sweeps) would be fashioned, and marshaled the army's blacksmiths together under Captain Edward Williams who, along with half the army's carpenters, were dispatched to Skenesborough. Since it was agreed that the ships would be rigged and armed at Ticonderoga, the armorers under Lt. Solomon Bowman would stay. Half the army's carpenters, some thirty-four in number, along with a number of wheelwrights, were set to work making gun carriages, and a dozen ship's carpenters were assembled to rig the vessels once they arrived at Ticonderoga.[17]

By the end of the month Arnold was at Skenesborough. Here he found a finished gondola and five others in various states. The mood of the frontier town alarmed the brigadier almost immediately, and after a conversation with Brigadier General David Waterbury, in command of the Connecticut militia stationed there, he understood why: one Colonel Jacobus Wynkoop. Gates already had reservations in regards to Wynkoop's focus after a few encounters, and the matter would eventually come to a head after Arnold's appointment as commander of the American fleet, ending in Wynkoop's arrest and dismissal from the service.

With his characteristic fervor Arnold was able to instill some camp discipline and impose organization on the project. He was greatly helped by the arrival a few days later of the shipwrights and carpenters from Connecticut, Massachusetts, and Philadelphia, the latter of whom were led by Thomas Casdrop whose firm had recently built row galleys for the Pennsylvania state navy. With their arrival Arnold passed orders that no more gondolas were to be built, even though he had originally intended to construct ten not eight of these craft. It was a question of resources and priorities, and both were better spent on constructing galleys, which being larger and better armed would prove a major deterrent on the lake.[18]

The influx of shipwrights allowed work to begin on three galleys, which immediately launched a cloud of procurement officers across New York and New England for the rigging and the naval supplies needed to fashion this effort into a fleet of warships. When they were finished in late September the seventy-two-foot *Trumbull, Congress, Washington,* and *Gates* each displaced a little over 120 tons, carried a crew of eighty sailors and marines, and were armed with eight to ten guns, the largest being eighteen pounders and the smallest six pounders. Arnold had wanted heavier guns, twenty-four pounders, for the vessels' main armament, but they were simply not to be had.

The brigadier turned commodore, however, did not have the luxury to wait on the galleys. By late August he had a fleet of six gondolas, the schooners *Royal Savage, Liberty,* and *Revenge,* and the sloop *Enterprise* anchored at Crown Point. Shortages of naval supplies abounded, as did a shortage of experienced sailors, gunners, and marines. Arnold complained to Gates, but to little avail. Experienced sailors abounded along the New England seaboard, but if their livelihood didn't keep them busy, the lure of big paydays privateering did. In either case the money being offered by the Continental army was not enough to make them venture west, leaving Arnold to complain that, "without a larger number of seamen than can be found in the Northern Army our navigation will be useless." Such matters, particularly in terms of manpower, would haunt Arnold, causing him to write at one point that "Saving and negligence, I am afraid, will ruin us at last."[19]

These issues were not enough to prevent Arnold from taking his fleet down the lake on August 24. It initially proved a trying experience when a storm blew in and tested the new gondolas' seaworthiness. The *Connecticut* lost its mast and had to be taken in tow, and although the fleet managed to find shelter in Buttonmold Bay, the gondola *Spitfire* was unable to make way against the storm and was forced to ride the tempest out on the lake. By September 2 Arnold was anchored off of Isle La Motte. Here he spent the next week putting his vessels in order. On September 5 he sent crews ashore to gather timber to make fascines which would be fastened to the sides of the gondolas to help ward off shot and small arms fire. One of these wood-cutting crews from the *Boston* was set upon by a British and Indian war party soon after landing. The fleet responded with swivel guns and small arms fire which allowed the landing party to extricate themselves, but not before they had suffered several killed and half a dozen wounded. The next day brought better news as the cutter *Lee*, which had been fashioned from a ship frame captured at the siege of St. Johns, and the gondola *New Jersey* joined the fleet. News also arrived from the captain of the gondola *New York*, who joined the fleet a few days later, that the galleys being built at Skenesborough were nearly finished.

Two weeks later at St. Amand Bay Arnold was writing Gates with his regular request for more seamen and gunners. He also pressed the general for news on his new warships, saying, "I am greatly at loss what could have retarded the galleys so long." Confined to the northern part of the lake Arnold had no idea how badly smallpox and malaria had hindered the American ship-building efforts. General Waterbury had informed Gates that illness had struck down most of his carpenters, making constructing more than four of the eight galleys Arnold had requested out of the question. For that matter, even getting these four finished was proving to be a trying experience.

It was not good timing as Arnold was anxious to strengthen his forces after disturbing news reached him about the British fleet at St. Johns. One report from a British deserter put the enemy forces at a pair of schooners carrying six-pound guns, and two or three more sloops or schooners as well as some gondolas and a few floating batteries. Another more questionable report came from a local Frenchman whom Arnold had sent to St. Johns as a spy. The man returned to inform the brigadier that there were a pair of schooners there, one mounting twelve guns and the other fourteen, a captured American gondola, a two-masted floating battery carrying twenty-four heavy guns, and a large number of smaller vessels afloat and on the stocks. He estimated that the entire force would be completed in a fortnight. Based on his scouts' reports and those of prisoners he had recently taken, Arnold concluded that the Frenchman was an English plant, and dismissed his report, which ironically, was fairly accurate.[20]

The news coupled with his tardy galleys was enough for Arnold to sail up the lake on September 24 and anchor his fleet in the channel west of Valcour Island. From here he could monitor any English movement up the lake, and either engage the enemy, if the odds were in his favor, or retreat if they were not. For the next week Arnold lay at this location drilling his crews, and even with the shortage of powder and shot, allowing the fleet to occasionally practice with their guns. On September 30 the first galley, the *Trumbull*, arrived at Valcour Bay. The brigadier's initial delight soured some when he looked over the ship. Its guns were too small, and it was only partially rigged. In addition, the promised reinforcements of one hundred sailors were not on board, nor were any of the supplies he had requested such as the winter clothing for his wet and wind-chilled crews. Although Gates had written him that everything humanly possible was being done to forward his troops, supplies, and ships, Arnold could not help but lash out in his typical style. "I hope to be excused (after the requisitions so often made) if with five hundred men, half naked, I should not be able to beat the enemy with seven thousand men, well clothed, and a naval force, by the best accounts, near equal to ours."[21] At least there was some good news; General Waterbury, Arnold's second in command, was a few days behind the *Trumbull* with the *Washington* and the *Congress*. The last galley however, christened the *Gates*, was still waiting at Ticonderoga for cordage to finish its rigging.

When the *Washington* and *Congress* joined the fleet a few days later on October 6, even with Arnold's logistics issues and man-power shortages he still had managed to assemble a powerful fleet. It now numbered sixteen vessels, carrying eighty-nine cannons of various caliber, and crewed by over 650 men. The addition of the three galleys alone had increased his striking power by a third.[22]

The fleet hung on their cables at Valcour Bay for the better part of a week. The weather had turned cold and blustery leading Arnold to conclude that if Carleton didn't move by the middle of the month, he would not attempt it this year. Reconnaissance boats were sent out each morning, and each evening they returned without incident. A member of the gondola *Providence*'s crew, Bayze Wells, noted as one of the few highlights during the inactivity, that the ship purchased "Eight Gallons of West india Rum, and two Gallons of Sider brande." Further south the silence was simple. "No news is good news," Gates wrote Schuyler.[23]

Carleton, however, was about to change this. Now reinforced by the *Inflexible*, on the afternoon of October 10 Captain Pringle,

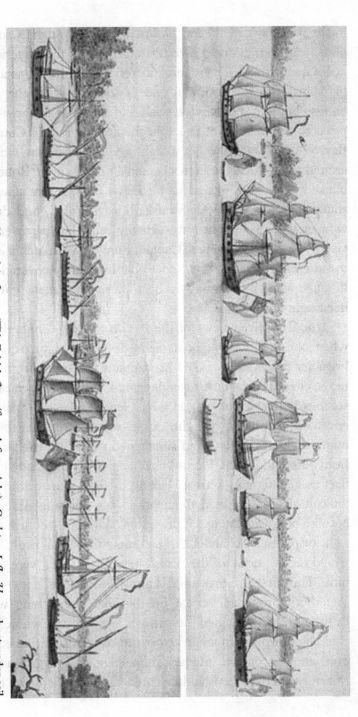

The British (top) and American Lake Champlain fleets, 1776. British fleet (from left to right): *Carleton, Inflexible,* gunboat under sail, *Maria, Loyal Convert,* and *Thunderer.* In the background can been seen more gunboats under sail. American fleet: (center) *Royal Savage,* (left to right) *Revenge, Washington, Philadelphia, Congress, New Jersey, Lee, Boston, Spitfire, New Haven, Providence, Connecticut, New York, Enterprise,* and *Trumbull.*

in the *Maria* with Carleton on board, led his warships south in a line ahead formation to investigate reports of the American fleet near Grand Island. The reports proved false, and Pringle anchored his ships near the southern end of the island for the evening. Sunrise brought a northwest wind and the sight of snow-covered peaks to the west. With first light the fleet set sail for Cumberland Bay to investigate the latest sighting. The bay was empty, but around ten o'clock Carleton's personal physician Dr. Robert Knox blinked at what appeared to be sails half a dozen miles to the south. The image quickly vanished, leaving the good doctor to wonder what he might have actually seen, but persistent in his claims, he at last convinced Captain Pringle to dispatch a longboat toward Valcour Island. The scout boat had barely covered half the distance when its cannon was heard, a signal that the enemy had been sighted.[24]

Arnold received news of the British fleet in Cumberland Bay when one of his scout boats arrived around eight o'clock. The brigadier immediately called his captains together. Given the size of the enemy fleet, some seven large sail, and two dozen or so vessels nearly the size of his gondolas, General Waterbury, an experienced sailor in his own right, expressed concerns that the British might divide their fleet and simultaneously attack the Americans from both ends of the Valcour channel. He recommended that the fleet make a fighting retreat back up the lake. For Arnold it was a difficult decision. He had anchored his ships in Valcour Bay because of the advantages it presented. With his fleet tucked out of sight of the main channel, Arnold knew that in all probability he would receive news of the British before the latter were aware of him. This in turn presented him with options. He could, as Waterbury proposed, retreat up the lake, skirmishing with the British until they reached the narrows at Split Rock where his fleet could be drawn up in a line across the lake. At the moment, however, another option intrigued him—standing his ground. If the British sailed past the island he could either then emerge from his shelter behind them with the weather gauge in his favor, or entice them toward his battle line running from Valcour Island to the west shore of the lake. In either case he would hold the weather gauge during the encounter. There was a problem with the plan, however. If he waited, and the British appeared at both the north and south entrances to the Valcour channel, he'd be trapped. What he really needed was news that the British had passed the northern part of the island. To answer this question he ordered his third in command Colonel Edward Wigglesworth, the captain of the *Trumbull*, to take a long boat to the north end of the island and investigate.[25]

The problem was that Wigglesworth would not be back for forty-five minutes or so, more than enough time for the British to close their trap. Weighing the risks Arnold agreed with Waterbury, and ordered the fleet to get under sail. The anchors were hauled up and the sails unfurled as the crews scrambled to make way. The galleys and schooners, better sailers on the open lake, would go first to act as a screen for the slower, less maneuverable gondolas. The effort was proceeding when Wigglesworth returned with news that the enemy was in the main channel passing to the east of Valcour Island. With the news Arnold recalled the galleys and schooners, and ordered the fleet to into a battle line across Valcour Bay.

Whether he realized it or not Arnold's initial response had inadvertently lured the British past Valcour Island. The vessel Dr. Knox had spied and that Pringle's scout boat sighted was the *Royal Savage*, which had already made its way into the main channel in keeping with the brigadier's original orders. With the alarm sounded Pringle hoisted his flags, ordering the fleet south in pursuit. It proved to be an unorganized effort. The *Carleton, Maria*, and *Inflexible*, being the best sailers, leapt into the lead with the rest of the fleet following behind as best they could. In allowing the fervor of the moment to dictate the action, Pringle lost a golden opportunity to send part of his fleet into the northern portion of Valcour Bay, where reports had surfaced that the enemy had anchored its fleet. Instead the fleet of over thirty sail slipped past the eastern shore of Valcour Island behind which a rebel schooner had just disappeared.[26]

Captain Joseph Hawley of the *Royal Savage* already had cleared the southern point of Valcour Island and entered the main channel of the lake when he received the order to return. With British sails sighted to the north Hawley attempted to comply, but the northwest wind was making any headway back into Valcour Bay extremely difficult. At length Hawley managed to clear the southern portion of the island and enter the channel, but in doing so he had taken the schooner dangerously close to the west shore of Valcour Island. Around eleven o'clock as the crew of the *Royal Savage* clawed their way north, the *Inflexible* rounded the southern end of Valcour Island and punctuated its presence with the sound of a broadside which raked the schooner. As the three-masted warship came into view, the more seasoned sailors among Arnold's fleet winced. To these men of the New England and New York coast, the sight of a full ship-rigged vessel boded poorly for their chances in the upcoming duel. With eighteen twelve-pound cannons, alone it outgunned nearly half the American fleet. Another broadside from the *Inflexible* lashed out at the *Royal Savage* sending forth a shower of wooden projectiles when the balls found their mark and the echo of splintering wood across the bay. As the *Inflexible* slipped further west the six- and four-pound guns on the *Royal Savage* barked at it. The British warship responded with another volley of twelve-pound shot, which damaged one of the schooner's masts and tore away chunks of its rigging.[27]

A cannon went off from Arnold's line. The brigadier looked down the line at the culprit, cursed, and put a quick end to such actions with a flurry of signals from his flagship the *Congress*. The range was still over a thousand yards. Hawley's vessel was already wrecked in the unequal contest when a British schooner was spotted to the southeast. As the crew struggled with what sail and lines remained, Captain Hawley made the decision to run the *Royal*

Savage aground on Valcour Island. As another round of shot sprayed the waters about him and ricocheted along the rocky shore a shimmer moved down the length of the ship as it touched bottom. Hoarse shouts followed, but were quickly drowned out by a groaning shudder as the schooner ran aground on the southwestern tip of the island. Defiant, the guns on the *Royal Savage* fired again, but any thought Hawley had of maintaining his ship vanished when the *Carleton* was spotted holding tight to the southern shoreline and bearing down on them.

By now the other British warships were rounding the southern end of Valcour Island. The *Maria*, the *Thunderer*, and the *Loyal Convert* came into view one by one, each further and further south of the *Inflexible*. The Americans eyed the vessels and the British crews pointed to the line of rebel warships strung across the channel. Soon a cluster of gunboats came into view, and then another, and another, as their numbers formed a white cloud upon the dark waters. The *Inflexible* launched another long-range volley at the American line, which fell in skipping splashes or whistled over their heads.

Although the Americans were clearly outnumbered and outgunned they held a major advantage, the weather gauge. The *Inflexible* was unable to overcome the wind, and already at long range was slipping slowly south. The *Maria*, *Loyal Convert*, and the *Thunderer* were also unable to make any headway and, already too far south to engage the American fleet, they were relegated to observer status in the upcoming engagement. The twenty-two gunboats, however, did not suffer under the same handicaps as their larger brethren. Their crews lowered their sails and took to their oars, advancing toward Arnold's position in a broken line. At three hundred yards Arnold gave the command and the American line loosed a ragged volley on the advancing formation.[28]

As the two sides fired away at each other the British schooner *Carleton* could be seen crawling its way north hugging the west side of Valcour Island. In a nice piece of sailing Captain Richard

Dacres had managed to clear the southwestern point of the island and make his way north, toward the eastern portion of the American line. As the ship passed the *Royal Savage* Dacres's crew greeted the former British vessel with a pointblank broadside of six-pounders and the bark of half a dozen swivel guns, all of which more than convinced Hawley to abandon the vessel. Before long Dacres had moved the *Carleton* to within musket shot of Arnold's left wing. Here he tossed out his anchor and quickly added the schooner's guns to the din.[29]

As the battle intensified into an exchange of grapeshot, chain, and ball, Arnold's deficiencies became clear. The end-on profiles presented by the low-lying British gunboats were not easy targets for experienced gun crews, and Arnold had few of these, which meant that most of the American shots were too high. To compound the matter the British had landed a large party on the western shore of the lake who sniped away at the fleet from behind the tree line. At least some results were being seen when it came to the *Carleton*, the general noted after stopping to aim one of the guns on the *Congress*. A closer and easier target, it had already been hulled several times.

Pringle's gunboats had no such problems with their crews. Manned by detachments of British and Hessian artillery troops, these vessels began to repeatedly score hits on Arnold's vessels; nor were Dacres's guns less well served, although the focus of the American effort was starting to show on the schooner. The initial emotion soon wore off and both sides reduced their rate of fire to a more manageable pace. Around one o'clock Arnold's men scored one of their few successes. A well-placed round struck the powder box aboard one of the British gunboats, setting off an explosion that lifted the vessels gun and several of its crew into the air. The occurrence caught both sides' attention, and for a moment the firing slackened, its noise replaced by colonial cheers, but it did not take long for the guns in both camps to return to their former pace.[30]

Arnold's fleet was taking a slow pounding from the *Carleton* and the gunboats' Hessian and British gunners. The *Congress* had been hit several times, the *Washington*'s rigging had been shot away, and several of its senior officers had been killed or wounded. The *New York* had been badly hit, and the *Philadelphia* repeatedly hulled. Clouds of grapeshot left their pattern on the waters short of their mark, but occasionally the aim was true and an express of angry buzzes and dull thumps swept the decks of one of Arnold's ships. The American vessels shifted their positions slightly to throw off their opponents' aim, and the gondolas even turned end on to use their heavier bow guns, taking the risk of being raked stem to stern by a well-aimed British cannonball. There was, however, little room for Arnold's vessels to maneuver. The same could not be said for the gunboats which frustrated the Yankee gunners with their movement, darting to and fro before falling back slightly to avoid the clusters of grapeshot.

The *Carleton*, which had not moved an inch for several hours, sustained a concentrated fire from a good part of Arnold's line. By half past four the schooner was nearing the edge. The captain had been badly wounded early in the engagement, was taken for dead, and was about to be thrown over the side when his second in command, midshipman Edward Pellew, who would one day become Admiral Viscount Exmouth, intervened. With Pellew in charge the *Carleton* fired defiantly into the center of the rebel line toward the *Congress* and *Washington*. Its guns were well served even though the casualties to their crews began to mount. There was nothing left of the vessel's rigging, and it had been struck several times at the waterline, resulting in two feet of water in the hold.[31]

Pringle had seen enough. The battle was entering its sixth hour when he signaled the recall to the *Carleton* and his gunboats. Pellew cut the *Carleton*'s anchor cable to allow the wind to push the schooner south, but to little avail. Seeing the schooner's plight Pringle sent a pair of artillery boats to tow the vessel away. They had no sooner gotten under way with the crippled warship when

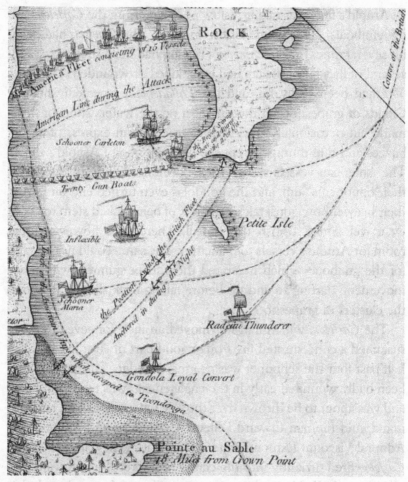

A plan of the Battle of Valcour Island, October 11, 1776, showing the movements of the participants during the battle, the deployment of the British fleet after the battle, and the escape route of the American fleet.

a well-aimed shot struck the prow of the *Carleton* and cut the tow-line. With the deck being splattered by grapeshot Pellew dashed forward and resecured the line allowing the vessel to be towed out of the fight. The gunboats answered the recall as well, and after covering the *Carlton*'s retreat, dropped back to seven hundred yards from the American line. As the sun dipped toward the white-laced Adirondacks a pair of boats from the *Inflexible* and the *Loyal Convert* landed on Valcour Island and took control of the *Royal Savage*, but proving an easy target for the rebel gunners, they withdrew after putting the vessel to the torch. Sometime after five as the shadows grew longer the flames reached its magazine and it exploded in a fireball that lit up the western cliffs of the island.[32]

By six it was over. Pringle had withdrawn his ships further south to form a line across the southern portion of Valcour Bay. He had lost two gunboats, and the *Carleton*, with nearly half its crew killed or wounded, was in dire need of repair. In all there were some thirty casualties in the fleet, half of which were onboard the schooner. As for the rest of the fleet, beyond the *Carleton* the larger elements had barely been involved in the engagement. The day belonged to the gunboats and their British and Hessian artillery crews. They had borne the brunt of the fighting, often closing to within a few hundred yards to inflict a toll upon their opponents.[33]

Arnold was not so fortunate. As the *Royal Savage* burned to the southeast with all his papers on board, he met with his senior staff. The reports soon started filtering in; the *Washington* was hulled half a dozen times, and one of its main masts was shot through; the *New York* had lost all of its officers save the captain; the *Trumbull* had been hulled and had a main mast damaged, the *Philadelphia* had been abandoned and was sinking; the *New Jersey* was taking on water, as was the *Spitfire*; Arnold's flagship the *Congress* had been struck twenty times and both of its masts were damaged. Almost every ship in the American fleet had been hit. All told, there were some sixty casualties that the hospital ship *Enterprise* struggled to cope with.[34]

There was only one path forward, in the brigadier's opinion: retreat to Crown Point. His fleet was badly shot up, but just as important, they had expended three-quarters of their ammunition, making another engagement out of the question. If they stayed it would only be a matter of time before the wind shifted and the British were able to bring their entire force against them, perhaps this time from both ends of the channel. No, they had to leave, and the sooner the better. "But how?" was the question asked by a senior officer. The British had no doubt erected a line to the south to bar the American retreat, and with the wind still from the northwest, going around Valcour Island was out of the question. Arnold tapped the map on the table before them. "We'll sail right through them," he responded. There were slow nods of agreement given that there were no other alternatives.

The Americans were helped by two things. First, although the sky was clear there was a new moon. The cloak of dark that descended over the lake was further accentuated by the contrast struck between it and the glow of the *Royal Savage*, which must have fixated the gaze of more than one British crewman. Second they were aided by their enemy. Although Captain Pringle would later blame being "frustrated by the extreme obscurity of the night," the escape of the American fleet was as much due to the captain's deployment as anything else. As Arnold surmised, Pringle had thrown up a screen of vessels across the southern portion of Valcour Bay, but it was haphazard at best. Most of the gunboats were busy taking on ammunition, and there was a wide gap between the major British surface vessels, leaving nearly a mile uncovered between the western shore of the lake and the left-most vessel in the British line.[35]

Around seven o'clock Arnold gave the signal for the fleet to move south, keeping close toward the western shore. Wigglesworth in the *Trumbull* was ordered to take the lead, showing a lamp pointed astern. Each vessel would then follow the lamp of the other in a long line feeling its way along the shoreline. To everyone's delight, "they did not give us one gun nor we did not fire one at them," recorded a crewman onboard the *Enterprise*. Once through the British position Arnold ordered all ships to make their best speed. Every hour under the cover of darkness put them a mile further from their enemy, and one mile closer to Crown Point.[36]

By noon the next day most of the American fleet was anchored off Schuyler's Island. There was little choice; most of the vessels' rigging was so damaged, or the ships leaked so badly that they had to stop. The gondolas *New Jersey* and *Spitfire* were taking on so much water that the decision was made to scuttle both of them, and the cutter *Lee* was nowhere to be found. Waterbury's *Washington* was a wreck. "The wind being against us," Waterbury testified of the incident, "and my vessel so torn to pieces that it was almost impossible to keep her above water; my sails . . . so shot, that carrying sail split them from foot to head." With British sails in sight, at two o'clock Arnold's fleet pushed south again. The contrary wind impeded their progress and, forced to row, Arnold's galleys and gondolas did not make much headway, while the nimbler sloop and schooner fared little better. The fleet pushed on through the night, a true testimony to their crews, who had already rowed through part of the previous night and fought a battle the day before.[37]

At first light on October 12 the British reconnaissance boats went forward, but their report was not needed. The calls soon rang out from the lookouts. The rebel fleet was half a dozen miles to the south pressing on toward Crown Point. Pringle was shocked, but immediately ordered the fleet to raise sail and set off in pursuit. After beating to windward all day with little to show for it, he gave the command to come to anchor before evening. After sunset the winds abated, which put the British force into motion once again. As the sun splayed over the Champlain Valley on the morning of the thirteenth the *Maria*, the hastily repaired *Carleton*, and the *Inflexible* found themselves just north of Schuyler's Island with eleven enemy sails in sight about eight miles to the south. The rest of the fleet had fallen behind, but the good news was that a fresh breeze had sprung up from the northeast. The sails of the three warships crackled as they billowed out, filled for the first time in days. With Carleton pacing the quarterdeck of the *Maria* it now became a race between the tattered rebel fleet and the three best sailers in the British fleet.[38]

Arnold eyed the British sails to the north and passed an apprehensive glance toward the wind that now filled the *Congress's* torn sails. Around Ligonier's Point he met Wigglesworth in the *Trumbull*, who outpacing the rest of the fleet had come to anchor here on the previous day to repair a shattered main mast and wait for the rest of the fleet. Near Split Rock Arnold signaled the *Trumbull*, *Enterprise*, *Revenge*, and the gondola *New York*, which were farther south, to make their best speed to Ticonderoga. Leaving the remaining four gondolas in front of him he slowed the *Congress* down to help cover the stricken *Washington*. With his vessel a wreck, and unable to keep up, Waterbury sent a boat to ask permission to run the galley ashore and burn it. "No," Arnold replied. The galleys and the gondolas would form a line across the narrows at Split Rock. They would make a stand there.

But time was up for the *Washington*. The *Maria* had outsailed its companions and now was bearing down on the stricken galley. Waterbury's shattered vessel was in no condition to fight a fourteen-gun schooner. The *Maria* launched a pair of broadsides at the *Washington*, and with the *Inflexible* now bearing down on him Waterbury struck the ship's colors. The *Maria*, *Inflexible*, and the *Carleton* a little further astern slipped past the *Washington* one by one, aiming their sights on the next American vessel, the *Congress*.[39]

Around ten o'clock the *Maria* pulled aside the *Congress* and unleashed a broadside of seven six-pounders. Although he was outgunned, Arnold was fortunate in one respect. Clearing Split Rock he had entered one of the narrower parts of the lake. The half-a-dozen miles from Split Rock to North West Bay narrowed at one point to some 1,300 yards from shore to shore. It was tricky enough sailing, especially for a crew who had never seen the strait, such that the *Inflexible* and the *Carleton* stayed astern choosing to join the fray with their bow chasers.

"They kept up an incessant fire on us for about five glasses," Arnold wrote, "with round and grape shot which we returned as briskly." For two and a half hours, the *Congress* traded fire with the

Maria some three hundred yards away. Both sides struck their opponents. On board the *Maria*, General Carleton had a splinter glance off his forehead after the *Congress* scored one hit, but in general, it was Arnold's ship that took the worst of it. His second in command had been killed, and "the sails, rigging, and hull" were "torn to pieces."[40]

When the lake widened at North West Bay, room presented itself for the other British warships to bring their guns to bear. It now only became a matter of time for the *Congress* and the four gondolas just ahead of it. With his galley in shambles and a score of casualties on board, Arnold signaled for the gondolas to follow him into what was at the time Ferris Bay, a small alcove on the east shore, south of Buttonmold Bay. Here Arnold scrambled to remove the wounded and small arms from his ships while the British warships fired at him from offshore. With his flags still flying, the brigadier, who had just lost his country's first naval battle, put all five vessels to the torch, and when he was satisfied that they were consumed, set out with his crews toward Crown Point.[41]

With this act Pringle called off the chase. He was later criticized for not pursuing the rest of Arnold's fleet—a galley, a gondola, a sloop, and a schooner—but in fairness to Pringle his task was complete. The rebel fleet had been soundly beaten and the lake was safe for the army to move forward. Not far ahead lay Crown Point, which had been secured by the Americans at least well enough that three warships were not going to dislodge them. Nor were the vessels that escaped much of a threat to landing operations at Crown Point with his fleet nearby.

Pringle's task was thorough indeed. He had lost two gunboats and had suffered fewer than forty casualties in clearing the lake. He had sunk, or the enemy sunk for him, seven gondolas, a schooner, and a galley. He had captured another galley, and along with Arnold's second in command, had collected over 120 prisoners over the course of the campaign. One of the gondolas sunk near Schuyler's Island, the *New Jersey*, could be salvaged, he was informed, and a few days later the rebel cutter *Lee* was found beached on the western side of the lake, and was refloated as another prize. The victory was overwhelming. "The Rebel fleet upon Lake Champlain has been entirely defeated," Carleton informed the minister of war.[42]

There was little question as to the status of the American Lake Champlain fleet. The *Enterprise*, the damaged *Trumbull*, the *Revenge*, and the damaged gondola *New York* reached the safety of Ticonderoga where they joined the newly outfitted galley *Gates* and the schooner *Liberty*. Arnold had lost eleven ships, two-thirds of his fleet, and what was left was not strong enough to ever venture out again against the British. Some two hundred men were either casualties or prisoners, although Carleton, in a gesture of good will, would release the American prisoners he held in the next few days. Yet, were it not for their miraculous escape on the night of October 11 it is likely that none would have survived.

With the rebel fleet dealt with, it only was a matter of days before thousands of British troops were encamped about Crown Point. Scout boats probed south, drawing fire from the American guns about Ticonderoga, and parties of Canadians and Indians moved forward to assess the American positions about the fort. The moment Carleton had fought so hard to see was upon him, but so was the season. He had little doubt of the outcome should he besiege Ticonderoga. Although the Americans outnumbered him he had with him professional British and German soldiers, and an impressive train of artillery manned by seasoned specialists. Ticonderoga would undoubtedly fall, but how long would it take? It was now mid-October and a cold rain was pelting the general's tent. How long did he have? Two weeks of good weather, perhaps. And after that? Even if he did push the Americans out of Ticonderoga, if they destroyed the fort there, which they were certain to do, he would not be able to leave a garrison. (Not to mention find a way to supply them through the winter even if he could have maintained the garrison.) Carleton muttered to himself about the situation, and after a few weeks of inactivity gave the order for the army to withdraw to St. Johns. The decision, and the general's pointed reply to its official criticism, would cost him command of the next year's expedition, which was perhaps fortunate for him, but more likely, fortunate for the American cause.[43]

For men like nineteen-year-old private Charles Vanderford of Poor's New Hampshire regiment, Carleton's withdrawal was a fitting culmination to a dizzying campaign spent between Canada, Ticonderoga, service on the *Boston*, and now, cattle guard duty at wet and dreary Skenesborough. Still, he realized as the rain swept over him, that it was sweet news. Almost every other American soldier agreed. "Their retreat will have very near the same effect as a defeat," one Pennsylvania trooper wrote home, "their great preparations for this Campaign in Canada, has ended in nothing more than destroying a number of our vessels." Arnold could not have agreed more. The man who would one day betray his country had spent a summer building a fleet only to lose it in three days, but in doing so he had bought his fledgling republic a precious year; a year in which the Northern Army grew stronger, strong enough, to finally face an English army at Saratoga. Almost a year after his defeat at Valcour Island, Arnold, wounded once again, would force the surrender of a British army, a feat that would forever alter the fate of his country.[44]

FIVE

The Masters of the Lake

I N JUNE 1777, EIGHT MONTHS AFTER THE BRITISH WITHDRAWAL down the lake, General John Burgoyne, who had served as second in command for Carleton, was at the head of another British army moving south. This time, however, there would be no naval engagement. Carleton's previous campaign had settled this matter. But just to be certain, Burgoyne's troops were led by a sizable array of British warships. First among these was the newly built *Royal George*. Laid down at St. Johns the previous winter, the 384-ton three-masted vessel was the largest ship launched on the lake to date. It carried twenty twelve-pounders on an enclosed gun deck, and another six six-pounders on the main deck. To support this warship, which could have single-handedly defeated the remaining elements of the American fleet, were the veterans of Carleton's 1776 campaign; twenty-eight gunboats, the ship *Inflexible*, the schooners *Carleton* and *Maria*, the gondola *Loyal Convert*, and the radeau *Thunderer*, which proudly flew the royal standard of England, typically reserved for the presence of a member of the royal family. The banner had been unfurled on this occasion as a mark of loyalty to the king of England, and as a rallying sign for any loyalists in the area.[1]

As if this level of force was not enough, several additions accompanied the fleet. The captured cutter *Lee* and the captured gondola *Jersey* now flew the Union flag on their masts, as did the galley *Washington*, which had been repaired and refitted as a sixteen-gun brig. When the naval forces gathered near Ile aux Noix, it became clear to Royal Navy captain Skeffington Lutwidge, who had been placed in command of the squadron, that the captured vessels' firepower would not be needed, and as such, he ordered them to be stripped of their guns and outfitted to carry the army's supplies.

On June 19, 1777, Lutwidge's fleet, trailed by Burgoyne's army of some 6,900 British regulars, Canadian auxiliaries, and German mercenaries in bateaux, headed up the lake to a fair breeze. "This day was very fine and the passage pleasant," one participant recorded, "the Lake affording many beautiful prospects." Another, a German mercenary in the main body of the army, agreed. "No finer and more beautiful sight can be imagined than a fleet of about 800 boats propelled on smooth water by hundreds of oars." The lead elements of the fleet dropped anchor at Split Rock, and the next morning General Burgoyne arrived in the *Maria*. By the end of the week Burgoyne's army was encamped at Crown Point, which the general had decided to use as a staging point for his operations against Fort Ticonderoga.[2]

With the details seen to, on June 30 Burgoyne gave the order to advance. The army led by a flotilla of gunboats began landing below Ticonderoga at Three Mile Point to the sound of fife and drum. With the *Royal George* and the *Inflexible* guarding the channel leading south there was little chance of an American naval foray against the position, but just to be sure a boom was thrown out in front of the warships to halt any fireship that the rebels might consider sending their way.

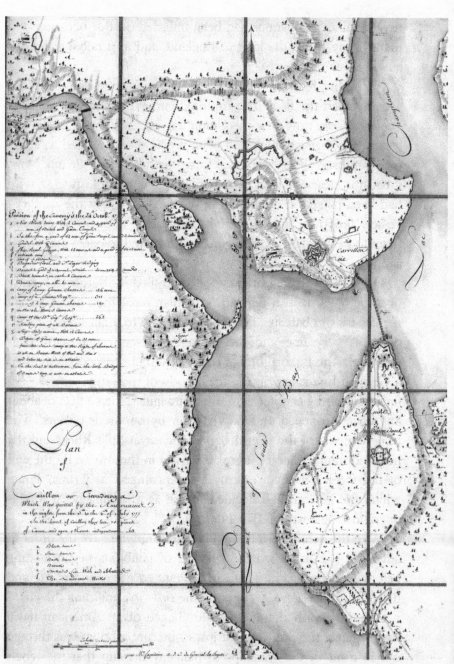

A 1777 map of the British positions at Carillon (Ticonderoga) and Mount Independence. The floating bridge built by the Americans can be seen extending from the east shore of the lake to the Ticonderoga Peninsula.

The British army moved methodically over the next few days, probing the American works on the heights before Ticonderoga and hauling their guns forward. Along the lake several gunboats moved forward to inspect the boom and bridge thrown up by the Americans between Ticonderoga and Mount Independence, only to withdraw under an increasing number of shots from the American batteries. Along the heights to the northwest of the fort the Americans had repaired the old French lines and added works of their own. The batteries along these lines fired on the advanced elements of Burgoyne's army, while at night, patrols of Canadians and Indians tested the rebel sentries and sought out prisoners.[3]

A formal siege seemed to be the course of the day. Burgoyne would cut off the Ticonderoga Peninsula, haul up his heavy cannons from the landing site, and destroy the rebel outworks. Once the defenders were pushed out of these fieldworks, Burgoyne's army would start digging trenches for their artillery to engage the fort. The trenches would then be advanced closer to the American stronghold until a parallel trench was dug for a new battery of guns. The principle, in general agreement between belligerents of the day, was that once one of a fort's walls was breached, or even in the imminent position of being breached, the fort's commander was faced with a decision. He could surrender and his garrison be taken prisoner perhaps with honors of war, or he could fight on, but doing so came at a risk. The unwritten code was that a garrison which resisted after their walls were clearly breached could be put to the sword should the besiegers be forced to storm the structure through the breach. It was a rule seldom if ever employed, but the Americans were rebels in the eyes of the British, and as such, the rules might not apply to them. Last, if the fort's commander was lucky, he had one other option; he could abandon the structure and retreat.

This methodical approach had taken Fort Ticonderoga before in 1759 under General Jeffery Amherst and, given the state of the American army, would certainly do so again. But it might prove a lengthy proposition. Pushing the Americans off the heights above the fort would take some time, as would the formal approach toward the fort. Several weeks perhaps, more than enough time for the American garrison to destroy the fort at an opportune moment and conduct a retreat. For Burgoyne it would all amount to time. Time for the siege and time to repair the fort and its facilities, which the general desperately needed as a supply depot when his army moved farther south.

Fortunately for Burgoyne, Royal Engineer lt. William Twiss had other ideas. Twiss, who would one day become a general, had helped oversee Carleton's preparations at St. Johns the previous year. Carleton was so impressed with Twiss, and the efforts of several senior naval officers in the building of his fleet, that in the official record of the expedition he noted that "Captain Pringle, Captain Dacres, and Captains Schanks and Starke of the Navy, and Lieut. Twiss of the Corps of Engineers deserve particular distinction in this acknowledgment, it being to the indefatigable attention of these gentlemen that the surprisingly expeditious advancement of the important works carried on is owing."[4]

Twiss's eye was quickly drawn to the summit of Mount Defiance, which overlooked the Ticonderoga Peninsula, and Mount Independence, a little farther away across the lake. On July 4 with the British army encircling the peninsula work crews focused on repairing the bridge at the sawmills on the La Chute River. This was no sooner accomplished, when a pair of light twelve-pound cannons crossed the structure destined for Mount Defiance. Twiss had found a path to the summit. As he gazed down at the American positions some 1,500 yards away, he quickly realized that the spot "completely commanded the works and buildings both at Ticonderoga and Fort Independence." The ground at the summit of Mount Defiance, Twiss informed his superior, Major General William Phillips, could be cleared to take a battery of guns, and while it would prove difficult, he could build a crude road to the summit in twenty-four hours. Phillips was delighted with the news, and settled the matter in terms of difficulty by informing Twiss that, "Where a goat can go a man can go, and where a man can go he can drag a gun."[5]

The next morning General Arthur St. Clair, commanding some five thousand American troops at Fort Ticonderoga and Fort Independence, clasped on his sword belt as a sentry anxiously pointed to the summit of Mount Defiance to the southwest. St. Clair and his aides turned their spyglasses to the dominant peak about three-quarters of a mile from the fort. One by one the officers confirmed the sighting with a dismayed comment. The British had indeed dragged cannons up the steep face of the mountain, something considered impossible until now. It would only be a day, maybe two at the most, before they had leveled the ground and constructed firing platforms.

The matter seemed settled at this point, but St. Clair summoned a council of war to clarify the situation. The council unanimously recommended an immediate withdrawal from Fort Ticonderoga and Fort Independence. The sick and wounded, along with whatever supplies and arms could be saved, were loaded into two hundred bateaux under the command of Colonel Pierce Long of New Hampshire. Long was to proceed to Skenesborough under the escort of the remaining elements of the American fleet, the schooners *Liberty* and *Revenge*, the sloop *Enterprise*, the gondola *New York*, and the galleys *Trumbull* and *Gates*. In the meantime the main body of St. Clair's army would leave Fort Independence along the road to Castleton before swinging southwest at this village to rendezvous with Long's detachment at Skenesborough. Like Bougainville at Ile aux Noix a generation before, St. Clair was faced with the tricky prospect of withdrawing his army when opposed by a superior foe. If the British should get wind of the retreat and attack while the withdrawal was in progress, they might overrun his jittery army. Stealth and secrecy were the order of the day, meaning that there would be no opportunity to destroy the fortifications at Ticonderoga or Mount Independence.[6]

On the night of July 5 Long's boats were loaded in secrecy above the boom. His convoy of two hundred bateaux pushed off after midnight, screened by the remaining elements of Arnold's fleet. The calm moonlit night transformed into morning dews when dawn broke. The sullen procession entered the narrows of the drowned lands near the headwaters of Lake Champlain and marveled at the sight. "The shore on each side exhibited a variegated view of huge rocks, caverns and clefts, and the whole was bounded by a thick impenetrable wilderness," one witness wrote. "My pen would fail in the attempt to describe a scene so enchantingly sublime." In an attempt to cheer his troops up Long ordered the fife and drum to be played, but this was not as effective as the bottles of wine and liquor scattered throughout the fleet.[7]

Around 3 o'clock in the afternoon of July 6 Long's flotilla arrived at what they believed was the safety of Skenesborough. They certainly had a head start on the British, but more important, months of labor had gone into the construction of a four-hundred-yard-long boom blocking the lake above Ticonderoga. Twenty-two piers had been sunk across the channel as anchor points, and a floating bridge built to link Fort Ticonderoga and Fort Independence. Beside this, "a boom, composed of large pieces of timber, well secured together by riveted bolts, is placed on the north side of the bridge, and by the side of this is placed a double iron chain, the links of which are one and a half inch square." All were convinced that it would take the British a week to remove these obstacles.[8]

Two hours later the Americans realized how wrong they had been. Once Burgoyne's troops occupied the American fortifications and detachments were dispatched to harry the retreating rebels, the general turned his attention toward advancing on Skenesborough. The boom, so long in the making, was attacked by Burgoyne's engineers and sappers. The timber was cut, and the matter only became a question of the chain the Americans had strung across the channel. Strong as the chain might be, no one

had considered that it would have to
survive the impact of a well-aimed
twelve-pound cannonball. The reality of
it was that it took Burgoyne much
longer to marshal his forces back into
their boats than it did to undo the barri-
cade.

At Skenesborough around 5 o'clock
everyone's attention was drawn north as
the guns on the American galleys and
schooners came to life. Because of the
crowded harbor the warships were
anchored farther down the channel.
There was quiet for a moment and then
a ragged response as the sound of a
dozen cannons filled the air. Near panic
took hold along the waterfront where
the Americans had yet to finish unload-
ing the stores and arms they had sal-

General John Burgoyne.
Although Burgoyne quickly
seized Fort Ticonderoga
and destroyed the remains
of the American fleet at
Skenesborough, a tenuous
and difficult to defend supply line down the length of
the Champlain Valley ultimately contributed to his
undoing.

vaged from Fort Ticonderoga. Men raced to their baggage to
obtain their possessions, while others set items to the torch before
disappearing into the surrounding forest.⁹

Royal Artillery captain John Carter's two dozen gunboats
exchanged fire with the Americans for about half an hour, slowly
creeping forward as they did so. For the undermanned American
vessels, the end was approaching. They were clearly outgunned,
and when large masts could be seen approaching it was enough to
settle the matter. The crews of the *Revenge, Enterprise*, the gondola *New York*, and the galley *Gates* set their vessels ablaze, and darted into the treeline, while the schooner *Liberty* and the *Trumbull*
lowered their colors before the inevitable.

Carter pushed on to the Skenesborough dockyards, his vessels
firing their cannons into the lines of densely packed bateaux along
the way, setting dozens ablaze, which culminated in a series of

explosions as the flames reached cargoes of powder and munitions. Amidst the chaos of explosions, burning buildings, and swirling smoke Carter landed marines to secure the town, but he need not have. Most of the Americans had fled south in a panic. Artillery, powder, provisions the Royal Artillery officer found for the taking, and conveniently still onboard boats ready for transport. Burgoyne and the army arrived not long after. The American rout was so complete that only thirty prisoners were taken.[10]

St. Clair's main force departed Fort Independence a few hours after Long, and probably would have gone unnoticed until daylight were it not for a dwelling being set ablaze by mistake during the retreat. A pair of British detachments crossed the damaged floating bridge the next morning and set off in pursuit of the American army. On the morning of July 7 the lead British detachment under Brigadier General Simon Fraser made contact with the American rear guard at Hubbardton, Vermont. Fraser attacked, and the outcome of the affair was in doubt for much of the action. The Americans threatened to turn Fraser's flank when a detachment of German troops came on the scene and broke the American lines. The British called off the pursuit and fell back to lick their wounds, while the American rear guard made a scattered retreat through the woods toward Castletown.[11]

With Skenesborough secure and no threats to his movements on Lake Champlain, Burgoyne ordered his larger warships back to St. Johns. The *Carleton* and *Maria* were sufficient to protect the lake and would stay near Ticonderoga, while the rest of the heavy vessels were to be stripped of their guns and turned into transports, as he had already done with the *Thunderer* a few days before. Supplies for an army moving south were now the general's primary concern.

While Burgoyne's army marched from Skenesborough for Fort Edward, a British force crossed from Ticonderoga over to the outlet of Lake George. Although Burgoyne had not chosen this traditional route for his army, the waterway was important to him nonetheless. The road from Skenesborough to Fort Edward was too vulnerable to attack, and in too poor a condition to transport the army's heavy artillery and supplies which were still at Ticonderoga.

Burgoyne's intelligence had informed him that the Americans had built several vessels at Fort George that spring, and that they planned to contest the lake. In this he was correct. In March 1777 Colonel Jeduthan Baldwin, the chief engineer of the Northern Army, was dispatched to the outlet of Lake George to determine if caissons could be sunk across the channel to block entrance to the lake from Ticonderoga. Although the matter did not prove practical, a sizable naval reinforcement was required for the lake to convoy supplies and guard its waters. Currently a number of bateaux were at Fort George, as well as a schooner in need of repairs. To increase the American naval presence

General Arthur St. Clair. St. Clair was later court-martialed for his decision to abandon the American posts at Fort Ticonderoga and Mount Independence, being accused of neglect, treachery, incapacity, and cowardice. There was little foundation to the case and St. Clair was exonerated. He later became a trusted aide-de-camp to General Washington and was with Washington at the surrender of Yorktown.

on the lake, a week later General Schuyler dispatched the recently reinstated Jacobus Wynkoop and a company of ship's carpenters to the head of Lake George with orders to build "two strong schooners of sixty feet keel and twenty feet beam." Three row galleys were to be constructed as well, each to carry a twelve-pound cannon in their bow, and as many additional small guns as possible. Orders also went out the same day to Captain Isaac Seaman authorizing him to raise a company of sailors, and gunners to man the new fleet.[12]

An existing schooner was repaired and along with a number of bateaux shuttled supplies down the lake to Fort Ticonderoga throughout the early summer of 1777, but work on the new vessels had barely started when Burgoyne seized Ticonderoga and Skenesborough. With British troops busy dragging their bateaux and gunboats over to the outlet of Lake George to the north, and Burgoyne's main force advancing toward the Hudson River to the south, Commodore Wynkoop had little choice and abandoned the American position on the lake on July 18. Wynkoop sent off whatever he could in wagons, set his row galleys and old schooner ablaze, and then turned his torches on the buildings along the shore. A pair of partially completed schooners on the stocks suffered a similar fate, before the order was given to set off the magazine in Fort George, which blew out one of the structure's stone walls.[13]

In all, it made the task before the transport wing of Burgoyne's army easier. Even so they were prepared. Captain Carter's gunboats returned to Ticonderoga a few days after their action at Skenesborough. A new task lay before them; the conquest of Lake George. One at a time the gunboats navigated the La Chute River up to the bridge near the sawmill. Here their supplies and guns were removed, and the vessels hauled out of the water by the Canadian auxiliaries and teams of horses. Lt. Twiss and Lt. Schank, who had overseen the effort the year before at St. Johns, directed the loading of large flatbed wagons carrying the procession of gunboats and bateaux along the portage road to the shores of Lake George. A handful of the gunboats were rearmed, and a small tender rigged as a sloop was dragged over and launched in the mountain waters. The rest of the vessels were stripped of their armament to carry the army's heavy artillery and supplies south.

By the end of the month Burgoyne's forces were transporting the artillery and supplies to the ruins of Fort George. To help cover the landing at Fort George, two companies of the 47th regiment, a detachment of royal artillery, and a pair of gunboats occupied Diamond Island about a half-dozen miles from the head of the lake. Throughout August Lake George was busy with small boat traffic as the sick and wounded moved north along the lake while supplies brought to Ticonderoga from Lutwidge's disarmed fleet were shuttled south.[14]

Burgoyne's long, thinly guarded supply line made for a tempting target, particularly when news came that the British general had crossed over to the west bank of the Hudson and was moving south. Although Burgoyne had already cut his supply lines to Lake George, General Benjamin Lincoln, in command of the militia gathering near Pawlet, Vermont, did not know this, and had already decided upon a sudden descent on Fort Ticonderoga in hopes of disrupting the enemy's supply lines, or at least, to place Burgoyne's line of retreat into question. The plan, hatched in mid-September, called for a three-pronged attack. Five hundred men under Colonel John Brown would strike at the Lake George portage and nearby Mount Defiance, while Colonel Benjamin Woodbridge would advance on Skenesborough with another five hundred men to secure Brown's retreat. To support Brown's efforts five hundred men under Colonel Samuel Johnson would launch a diversionary attack on Mount Independence from the Vermont side.

On September 12 and 13 the three detachments moved forward. Colonel Woodbridge's detachment arrived at Skenesborough a few days later, finding it abandoned by the British. The fresh reminders of Captain Carter's attack on the portage a few months earlier struck one witness. "Arived their att 4 o'clock & had a View of the Destruction of our Guard Boats Vessells Batteaus," he recorded in his journal. "The Destruction began att the Mouth of South Bay about 3 miles from Skeen & Continued to Skeen boath Sides of the Lake being Covered with Wreck of the Above Vessells, &^{C}." To the north Colonel Johnson's detachment made contact with the German troops holding Mount Independence on the seventeenth. Johnson's men spent the next several days marching and skirmishing with the Brunswickers of the Prince Frederick Regiment.[15]

Brown's detachment, which was the main striking component of the plan, had been picked among the best of Lincoln's contingents. The attack, reminiscent of one of Robert Rogers's raids during the French and Indian War, called for speed and self-sufficiency, and as such the more experienced among Lincoln's men such as Herrick and Whitcomb's Rangers and Colonel Seth Warner's Continentals were chosen for the task. The detachment crossed the southern portion of Lake Champlain at "the narrows" and proceeded at a steady pace through the red and yellow speckled forest for the outlet of Lake George. With no trail to speak off, it proved a tedious task, but by the evening of September 17 the column was a few miles from their target. Scouts went forward, and upon their return a plan of attack was devised. Captain Ebenezer Allen would lead a detachment up the face of Mount Defiance and attack the artillery battery at the summit at first light. Colonel Brown and Colonel Herrick's men would first seize the Lake George portage, before turning their attention toward the sawmills and the bridge across the La Chute River.

Brown's men crept forward toward their position once the sun set. The tangled woods and darkness scattered the detachments as they pressed forward. Fortunately a rallying signal had been agreed upon, as one participant recalled. "Our rallying signal was a hoot, like that of an owl, which caused a pretty frequent apparent hooting of the owls that night, while we were scrambling over logs and other impediments, and were frequently saluted with the jingling of rattle snakes, which was more terrific to many of us than the thoughts of the enemy."[16]

At dawn Brown struck, taking the British position at the Lake George portage by complete surprise. Brief bursts of gunfire were exchanged, but Brown's men quickly surrounded the enemy, forcing their surrender. As Brown organized guards for the nearly three hundred prisoners, Colonel Herrick ordered a detachment to advance on the sawmills. As this party advanced, firing could be heard coming from the top of Mount Defiance as Captain Allen launched his attack.

Allen and his men had spent most of the evening scaling the rocky sides of Mount Defiance. Not long after the sound of gunfire erupted from the portage Allen let loose an Indian war whoop and dashed for the British four-gun battery, his men following him "like a stream of hornets to the charge." A British gunner managed to fire a small field piece, but otherwise the surprise was near total. What enemy that did manage to escape were captured by Herrick's men near the sawmill bridge. A detachment of men under Captain Warner pressed over the bridge, intent on seizing a blockhouse on the dominating heights of the north shore. The men holding the structure's garrison proved too stubborn to be taken by simple musketry, but quickly changed their minds when a captured field gun was positioned before them. As Warner's men scrambled forward toward the old French outworks, everyone's attention was drawn to a distant thump and puff of smoke coming from the top of Mount Defiance. A few seconds later a fountain of water appeared near the *Carleton* and *Maria* anchored above Fort Ticonderoga. Another shot followed a few minutes later, and although it was no closer than the first shot it was enough for the two schooners to shift positions.

While Warner's men dragged their single field gun to the old French lines, and began exchanging cannon fire with Fort Ticonderoga, Brown penned a quick letter to General Lincoln. He had carried the Lake George portage, the sawmills, and Mount Defiance at the cost of less than dozen casualties, he informed his commander. In the process he had taken 293 prisoners, and freed more than one hundred American prisoners of war. Better yet he had taken an armed sloop, seventeen gunboats, and two hundred bateaux on Lake George and the lower part of the La Chute River, as well as a number of cannons, "which may be of great service to us," he noted. Currently his forces occupied the old French lines, and he had sent a summons to the commander of Fort Ticonderoga demanding his surrender.[17]

Brown was hardly surprised when Brigadier General Henry Powall in charge of Fort Ticonderoga scoffed at the surrender demand. Nor was there much he could do about it. Traveling light, the expedition had not brought any cannons, and those captured were far too small to threaten the fort. The Americans made demonstrations against the British positions for several days, but there was never a serious threat to Ticonderoga or Mount Independence.

With nothing more to be accomplished around Ticonderoga, on the evening of September 22 Brown marshaled together a small fleet at the Lake George portage. He had loaded most of his command, some 420 men, onto the three-gun sloop, a pair of armed gunboats, and seventeen other vessels. The rest of the vessels he destroyed, along with the docks, storehouses, and anything else of value. Given that Fort George was known to be lightly defended, Brown looked to secure the lake for the American cause by seizing Diamond Island, the last British post of consequence on the lake. His flotilla spent a stormy night at Sabbath Day Point, and the next morning a debate broke out regarding the escape of a small British ship that had been taken along with Brown's forces. Even though the enemy would be warned of their approach, the agreement among Brown's officers was to press on. The weather prevented the little American fleet from reaching Diamond Island until the morning of September 24. When they arrived Brown announced his simple plan. The three armed vessels would engage the British shore batteries, while the rest of the vessels searched for a landing spot on another part of the island.[18]

Two companies of the British 47th regiment, a detachment of artillery, and a pair of gunboats had been stationed at this oblong island about five miles from Fort George, and a little after 9 A.M. they started that last naval battle on Lake George when they fired at Brown's advancing sloop. One by one plumes of water emerged near Brown's vessel. The colonel ordered his men to return fire, and he maneuvered the sloop closer. As the British guns zeroed in on Brown and his warships it became clear to the American commander that the enemy was much stronger than he had imagined. Much of this, however, was due to the German gunners who

A view of Fort St. Johns near the end of the American Revolution. Several members of the British Lake Champlain fleet are shown, the most prominent being the three-masted vessels *Inflexible* and *Royal George.*

manned the island's guns, being much better at their craft than Brown's militiamen. The little sloop was struck several times, sending men and splinters flying across the deck and shredding its rigging. One of the American gunboats fared no better, moving off after being struck several times by the British gunners. The British gunboats added their heavy cannon to the fire and discouraged Brown's landing force from approaching too close.

A shot that struck Brown's sloop at the waterline brought the Battle of Diamond Island to an end around 10:30. Brown had the crippled vessel taken under tow, and with the rest of the fleet turned toward the east shore of the lake. The American flotilla, slowly pursued by the two British gunboats, took shelter in Dunham Bay. Although Brown claimed that he burned all the vessels, he did a poor job of it. The British recovered the sloop and one of the gunboats as well as the vessels' cannons, two of which had burst during the action.[19]

Brown and the rest of Lincoln's command retired unmolested on Pawlet a few days later. The British scrambled to reinforce Ticonderoga and their positions on Lake George. News of Burgoyne's surrender at Saratoga hastened their work as fears of an

American attack on Ticonderoga circulated. By November any threat of an American expedition had passed. For Carleton, however, it had now become a question of what to do with the posts along the lakes. The answer was obvious. It would take a large garrison to defend them through the winter, and a nearly indefensible supply line over the frozen skin of Lake Champlain to support them.

On the afternoon of November 1 Captain Lutwidge departed Ticonderoga with the *Inflexible, Thunderer, Maria, Carleton*, and the munitions ship *Camel.* The vessels were bound for Fort St. Johns with the garrison's stores and sick. Smoke from the Lake George portage could be seen by the departing vessels as General Powall's men destroyed everything of worth. Fort George and the breastworks on Diamond Island had been demolished earlier, and these troops withdrawn to Ticonderoga. The *Lee* and several of the fleet's larger vessels departed in the following days as the British army occupied itself in destroying the fortifications and outworks at Ticonderoga and Mount Independence. Finally, "On November 8th before daybreak," one German officer wrote in his journal,

> the signal was given to start the fires and to leave by blasting the last cannon. All at once we saw all the log houses, the store houses, the hospital, all the huts and cottages, everything which could be ruined by fire, in flames. The soldiers were very busy, thinking this to be the end of their trials. The floating bridge was also cut down and burned. We embarked and departed. Immediately after, the explosion at Fort Ticonderoga took place; it had been filled with powder to which fire was set at the last moment.

The sound of Ticonderoga's fate echoed through the valley and to all within earshot watching the long columns of smoke emanating from the area the meaning was clear; the British were withdrawing from Lake Champlain.[20]

The war along Lake Champlain still had many more years to go, but neither side showed interest in upsetting the status quo.

The British had clear control of the lake with their navy, and on numerous occasions paraded about with these vessels to remind the Americans of the fact. There were raids upon the New York and Vermont frontier as well, to support this display of force. Major Christopher Carleton led a series of raids along the shores of the lake, which beyond the minor military gains that were achieved, served to keep the Americans from moving against Ile aux Noix and St. Johns. The success of this approach meant that there was no reason for many of the vessels at St. Johns and Ile aux Noix, and hence an opportunity to reduce the cost and manpower demands required to operate these vessels. Several of the principal warships remained active, particularly the *Maria*, *Carleton*, and *Lee*, but the bulk of the fleet languished. With news of the Treaty of Paris in the summer of 1783 there was even less reason for the British Lake Champlain fleet. To reduce costs the Governor-General of Canada, Sir Frederic Haldimand, ordered that the Lake Champlain fleet be reduced to three officers and thirty men. Two or three of the light warships would be kept in service, while the rest were to be dismantled at St. Johns.[21]

Although an occasional warship, including the twelve-gun HMS *Royal Edward* built in 1794 to secure the waterway in the event of a conflict, could be seen upon the waters of Lake Champlain, it was the new ferries running from Grand Island to Cumberland Head and from Burlington to the growing town of Plattsburgh, and the raft fleets of timber moving north to markets in Canada, that would dominate the lake scenery over the next generation. Soon schooners and sloops built along the shores of Burlington, Essex, N.Y., and Whitehall (Skenesborough) took to the northern waters traveling the length of the waterway from Whitehall to St. Johns in search of commerce.[22]

For the moment the lake belonged to merchantmen.

SIX

The Battle of Cumberland Bay

CLEAR OF THE WHITE MOUNTAINS, COMMANDANT THOMAS Macdonough finished the second half of his trek to Burlington, Vermont, by crossing the northern portion of that state during the most spectacular time of the year. Two days later, on October 8, 1812, he finished his journey, and after taking some time to refresh himself, he officially took command of all naval operations on Lake Champlain.

At twenty-nine Macdonough was already a twelve-year veteran of the navy. He had seen service in the West Indies during the undeclared war with France, and as a member of the *Enterprise* he had participated in the attack on Tripoli during the campaign against the Barbary pirates. An additional item from his past was to be of help to the recently promoted lieutenant. For a short time he had been assigned to Captain Isaac Hull in Middletown, Connecticut, where Hull was busy overseeing the construction of a number of gunboats. No doubt the saltwater veteran found the small vessels interesting, particularly given his time in Ancona, Italy, spent supervising the outfitting of four gunboats destined for service against the Barbary pirates. After a brief absence Macdonough was to return to Middletown and take command of gunboat detachments there, another at Norwich, Connecticut, and a number posted on Long Island. It was Macdonough's first true command, and for an officer of his experience, an undesirable posting. Although he spent only seven months there, no doubt the experience with handling several vessels, the navigation of the channels and inland waterways, and mastering their tactics made its mark on him.

Bored with a posting that the secretary of the navy would later characterize as "a service in which those who are to form the officers of the ships of war ought not to be engaged," Macdonough obtained a furlough to the merchant service to make a cruise to the East Indies as captain of the brig *Gulliver*. Leaving from New York, Macdonough sailed to Liverpool and then Calcutta, and on his way back stopped at St. Helena, the future prison of Napoleon Bonaparte. Upon his return in August 1811, Macdonough asked for another fourteen-month furlough to make a second voyage to India. The request was denied, but Macdonough, pleading a case of having already contracted his services to the vessel's owners (of which it turns out he was one), submitted his resignation to the secretary of the navy. The resignation was accepted, and had it continued being processed via its normal path, the future victor of Lake Champlain's most contested naval battle might well have been in India, but for some reason, no doubt a comment made by a colleague as to Macdonough's excellent service, Navy Secretary Paul Hamilton later crossed out the comment "to be accepted" on Macdonough's resignation, and wrote him a letter granting him this one-time "indulgence."

Macdonough returned to his naval duties in June 1812 when war was declared on Great Britain. He was posted as first lieutenant on the frigate *Constellation*, but as this vessel was being over-hauled and would not be in service for another six months, the impatient Macdonough applied for, and was granted, command of a division of six small gunboats stationed at Portland, Maine. Macdonough would spend less than a month in his new assignment. On September 28, 1812, a letter arrived from the navy secretary ordering him to take command of the American naval forces on Lake Champlain. "You will therefore," Hamilton wrote, "immediately, upon receipt of this letter, proceed to Lake Champlain, & make every arrangement necessary. Six vessels, have been purchased, by the War Department and there are two gunboats, built by the Navy Department, on the Lake, the whole of which is to be under Your direction & command."[1]

The waterway that Macdonough had taken command of had changed significantly since Arnold's and Pringle's fleets clashed. Vermont, now a state in the union, had become settled farther north, along the shores of the 120-mile-long lake. Burlington, a town of some 1,500 souls nestled along the eastern bluffs near the exit of the Winooski River, had taken form in the 1790s, as had smaller towns like St. Albans and Swanton to the north and Vergennes to the south. The mills at Winooski Falls and lake commerce, primarily the selling of timber and potash to Canada, had flourished, leading to the construction of some twenty-two merchant vessels ranging in size from thirty to fifty tons. Of greater importance, the influx of settlers after the American Revolution had also brought infrastructure; roads linked Vermont and the western New York shore of the lake to points south, and to points north. Armies could now march north or south along the banks of Lake Champlain, the Richelieu River, and the Hudson. The flotillas of bateaux built by Amherst and Carleton, along with all the labor and manufacturing that they entailed, were no longer required. This, in turn, changed the strategic importance of Lake Champlain. Whereas in the past the lake waters had been the primary mode of transportation for advancing armies, they were now viewed as a supply line or as a potential threat to an advancing army's flank. In either case American control of the waterway was paramount, and this translated into building a fleet.[2]

Fortunately for Macdonough, he was told that work had already begun on this task, but when he surveyed his gunboats at Basin Harbor he was not so sure. One of the vessels had sunk, a victim of neglect, and the other was on the verge of doing so. Macdonough ordered the vessels repaired and directed that each be re-armed with a single twelve-pound bow gun. This matter attended to, he traveled to Whitehall, as Skenesborough was now called, where he found five of the six vessels purchased by the War Department. After a cursory inspection he declared three of the vessels too old to carry guns, and left them to continue with their duties supplying the troops stationed at Plattsburgh under General Henry Dearborn. The two remaining sloops he renamed the *Growler* and *Eagle*. Within a few weeks both had been refitted with six six-pound cannon and were patrolling the lake. The third vessel, the seventy-five-ton sloop *President*, "being the largest and best vessell on the lake," became ensnared in an argument with General Dearborn, who refused to release it to Macdonough despite the commandant's orders from the secretary of the navy. The matter was soon resolved, and in mid-November Macdonough supported Dearborn's push north with his "poor forlorn squadron." After a skirmish with a British detachment near the LaColle River, Dearborn retraced his steps to Plattsburgh, and a few days later suspended operations for the season. Macdonough followed suit shortly thereafter and laid up his fleet at Shelburne Harbor, where he spent part of the winter repairing his gunboats and modifying the *Growler*'s and *Eagle*'s quarterdecks to allow them to carry four more guns apiece, including his recently arrived eighteen-pound carronades.[3]

Spring brought new challenges to the commander of the U.S. Lake Champlain fleet. Just as with the lake, several things had changed in naval warfare during the intervening years, and most important among these were cannons. Simply put, cannons were better made and lighter than their forefathers. Techniques at foundries and iron works, pushed by the expanding field of metallurgy, had improved. So too had gun tactics. The advent of the short-barreled carronade near the end of the American Revolution had divided naval guns into two categories; long and short. The long guns, which because of their barrel lengths allowed for higher projectile velocities, were those designed to hurl solid shot in a standoff engagement and are perhaps the standing notion of cannon from these times.[4] They employed shot ranging from two pounds to thirty-two pounds, the latter typically being reserved for the lower decks on a British ship-of-the-line. The carronade, on the other hand, invented in Scotland in 1779, was a short-barreled version of the traditional cannon. The benefits of barrel length were traded for increased shot size and a significant reduction in gun weight. A thirty-two-pound carronade, for example, weighed several hundred pounds less than a light eighteen-pound long gun, the latter of which came in at a little over a ton. Yet the thirty-two-pound ball was capable of causing almost as much damage to a vessel's hull and framework, not to mention the destructive power such a weapon possessed when it came to firing grapeshot or canister. The reduced design had another benefit as well; smaller gun crews, which when coupled with its reduced weight and size, meant that ships could carry more guns and hence greater firepower than a vessel of the same size carrying just long guns. But the sacrifice of barrel length did have one detriment, reduced range. A twenty-four-pound carronade, for example, had a point-blank range of 300 yards, while a long twenty-four pounder had a point blank range of 1,750 yards. The basic difference in the use of the two gun types boiled down to tactics. A ship armed only with carronades would be at the mercy of one carrying long guns if the latter was a better sailor and kept its distance, but the moment the two closed to within a few hundred yards, the tables would quickly be turned.[5]

In general the gun of choice along Lake Champlain was the carronade. Much of this stemmed from tight maneuvering and tricky winds on the lake, which made long-range engagements less likely. More important, the vessels on the lake, both British and American, were limited in size, making gun weight an important consideration, as was the reduced manpower associated with carronades given the shortage of sailors available for lake service. Macdonough asked for carronades for his vessels, summarizing his reasons in a letter to the secretary of the navy: "18 pr Carronades I think the best kind for these vessels, as they are light and carry a greater quantity of grape shot than long guns of about the same weight and it is likely they will be used principally against small vessels with many men exposed in them, or against sloops."[6]

Master Commandant Thomas Macdonough. Macdonough would oversee the trials and tribulations of the American Lake Champlain fleet throughout the War of 1812, ultimately culminating in his decisive victory at Cumberland Bay on September 11, 1814.

There was another advance in naval gunnery as well. The Americans had developed a pivot mount that allowed a gun to be traversed through 180 degrees. Macdonough had one of these mounts, carrying a long eighteen-pounder, placed amidships on both the *Growler* and the *Eagle*. Such an arrangement allowed these vessels to use their eighteen-pounder on either broadside or in limited off-angle shooting situations. "The armed schooners of the United States often appear with their guns fitted in a manner, that, one would think, requires only to be known, to be generally adopted," one contemporary British writer penned in regard to the ingenious mount that would prove to be the great-grandfather of the modern gun turret.[7]

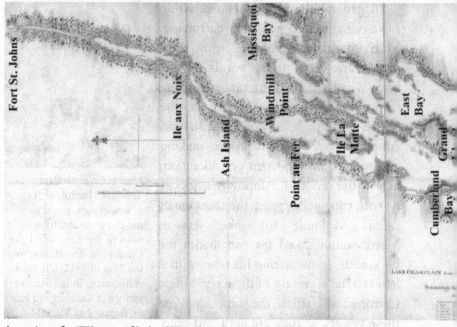

A portion of a 1779 map of Lake Champlain showing the Richelieu River from Ile aux Noix to Windmill Point. To help safeguard the naval post at Ile aux Noix and bar American passage down the river the British would later fortify Ash Island.

With the *Eagle* and the *Growler* refitted with more guns the shortage of sailors, seemingly a tradition in the lake service, meant that Macdonough had to lay up his gunboats until more men arrived. Still, with the opening of the lake he took his fleet of three vessels north to blockade the outlet of the lake. Unfortunately Macdonough's flagship, the *President*, struck bottom during one of these patrols and had to be laid up for repairs at Plattsburgh in late May. Not long after this, reports arrived that British gunboats had come out onto the lake. In response, Macdonough dispatched Lt. Sidney Smith north with the *Growler* and the *Eagle* to investigate.

Late on the morning of July 2 Smith proceeded with his orders. The *Growler* and the *Eagle* both ran down the lake under a light southerly breeze toward the entrance of the Richelieu River. The

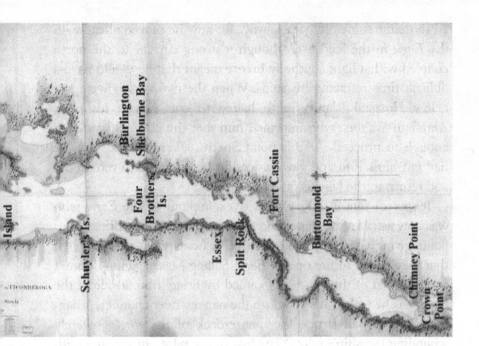

pair anchored near Rouses Point for the evening and sent their long boats ahead to gather intelligence. Thirty reinforcements, infantry under Captain Oliver Herrick, arrived that evening. Smith divided them between the two ships and waited for his boats to return. In the early morning hours the long boats reappeared with news that the enemy had retreated down the river toward Ile aux Noix.

For reasons that are not clear, Smith used this information to enter the confines of the Richelieu River the next morning. It was a dangerous proposition, given that the waterway could be covered by a musket shot. Strangely, the night before Smith had ordered the *Eagle* to shift its position throughout the night fearing that an enemy boarding party might try to take it from the wooded shoreline some fifty yards away. Yet now he moved ahead with the *Eagle* in the lead even though a strong current to the north coupled with a light southerly breeze meant that he would have a difficult time retracing his steps. When the two vessels were just below Hospital Island, Smith halted to confer with his pilot, Abraham Walters, who informed him that the channel was deep enough to proceed. At this point Smith realized the position he had put himself in and gave orders for both vessels to turn about and return to the lake as quickly as possible.[8]

It was too late. A little after 6 A.M. a lookout on the *Eagle*, who was now astern of the retreating *Growler*, spotted three British gunboats giving chase. By 6:30 the British boats were close enough that they began to fire on the *Eagle*. Sailing Master Jairus Loomis, in command of the *Eagle*, responded by firing a broadside at the enemy as he tacked his vessel up the narrow river channel. A half-hour later a ball struck the quarterdeck of the *Eagle*, severely wounding the ship's pilot. "The loss of the pilot put me in a critical situation," Loomis later wrote Macdonough of the incident. "Not a person onboard that was even in this part of the lake before. I was obliged to follow the motions of the *Growler* as much as possible."[9]

As the American vessels zigzagged south toward Ash Island, small arms fire began to splatter against their hulls. British detachments sent out from Ile aux Noix fired from both sides of the river. Their fire slackened after a few rounds of grapeshot were loosed from the American warships, which temporarily allowed the *Eagle* to return its attention to the three gunboats gaining ground on it. The resistance did not last long. By nine o'clock all of the *Eagle*'s guns but one were out of action, not from the application of British gunnery but because the ring bolts that confined the recoil of the gun carriages had all torn away from their mounts, making it impossible to use the weapons. The *Growler* was having similar problems, so around nine o'clock the pair of vessels hauled into the wind, and within a half an hour the problems had been rectified.

Soon both vessels were back on course, and busy engaging the British once again. The current, headwind, and narrow channel to tack in meant that neither American warship was making much headway, and the *Eagle* in particular was paying the price for it. Its top lines had been cut, and the mast damaged eighteen feet above the deck by a well-aimed cannonball. What was worse was that the British gunboats were maneuvering to keep their range such that they could use their long twenty-four pounders while the American vessels were at the maximum range for their carronades.

Gauging that he could not outrun the British warships, and slowly being whittled away by their fire, Smith sent the signal to close on and board the enemy. Neither vessel had executed a turning maneuver when the plan was undone. Around eleven o'clock a twenty-four-pound ball smashed through the *Eagle*'s hull on the port side while it was on a starboard tack and exited the other side leaving a gaping hole a few inches above the waterline. Given its route, the vessel was doomed. The next time it tacked over to port the wound was submerged. The ship quickly filled, and within minutes sank in shallow water. The *Growler* continued on, but about fifteen minutes later a cannonball cut the gaff on its main sail, leaving it a folded flapping mess. As the *Growler* was now unmanageable, its ammunition nearly expended, and facing the entire British force alone, Smith hauled down his colors.[10]

Smith's decision to enter the Richelieu River and the loss of his vessels was to unhinge the naval campaign on Lake Champlain. On the eve of the War of 1812 the British defense of the Richelieu River–Lake Champlain frontier was in shambles. Control of Lake Champlain, which the British had established twice in the past, had been lost through years of neglect that left Fort St. Johns and its naval facilities in ruins. Not that it mattered, as there were no longer any ships to guard the approaches along this front, the last one of any size, the twelve-gun schooner *Royal Edward* had been launched in 1794, and was unserviceable long before the start of the war. The matter was further complicated by the road networks that linked Canada, Vermont, and New York. These routes effectively bypassed Fort St. Johns and the old works at Ile aux Noix, making naval considerations along this front a secondary consideration for Canada's governor general George Prevost. That is, until an American naval presence was established on Lake Champlain in the fall of 1812. Realizing that the superior American fleet could use this waterway as an avenue of invasion, or at the very least as a supply line for an army striking north along one of the coastal lake roads, Prevost changed his strategy in the region.

In September 1812 the governor decided to establish a naval facility at Ile aux Noix and restore the old defensive works there, even though the year before Royal Engineer Ralph Bruyeres had reported that the works were not worth repairing. Prevost dispatched several flank companies from different regiments along with militia troops, a detachment of Royal artillery, and some engineers to secure the location. To establish an immediate naval presence on the Richelieu he ordered three gunboats currently on station in the St. Lawrence to be carried around the St. Jean rapids and transferred to the island. New gunboats would be built as well, and to see to this new naval presence a detachment of Royal Marines would be forwarded to the island. The reliance on a fleet of small rowed gunboats and galleys, coupled with improving the defenses of the island, which by nature split the waterway into two channels, both a point blank cannon shot away, meshed nicely with the governor's limited resources. It was a simple approach wholly defensive in scope with the added benefit that the troops stationed at the island could quickly be deployed to help cover part of the road network leading north.[11]

The first three gunboats to reach the island—the *Beresford*, *Popham*, and *Brock*—were quite like those employed by Carleton some thirty-six years before. They were similar in size, carried a long twenty-four pounder in their prow, and could be rowed or sailed with a simple rig just like their predecessors. To shelter this fleet whose dockyards rested on the east side of the island, the old fort and redoubts were revived, and heavy cannons were hauled into place to contest the river with any American vessel. Two new additions to the small fleet also appeared in the spring. The first was another galley of the same general design as those already on station, while the second was a small schooner that carried four six-pound guns. In all, nearly a thousand men would be stationed at the island by the summer of 1813, making it one of the most defended positions in Canada.[12]

Still, Prevost had no plan to switch to the offensive. That is until the *Growler* and *Eagle* fell into his hands. Major George Taylor of the 100th Regiment was quick to secure his new prizes. The ninety-ton *Growler*, which he characterized as "a fine vessel," was temporarily renamed the *Shannon*, and given that it was not badly damaged was put in service almost immediately. The *Eagle*, however, resting on the bottom in six feet of water, was more problematic. Its guns and stores, along with the ninety-nine captured Americans, were transferred to Ile aux Noix, while crews busied themselves with patching the hull and refloating their prize.

The turn of fortune presented Governor Prevost with an opportunity. The American fleet, as confirmed by the captured crews, now only consisted of a pair of old gunboats and the sloop *President*, which was being repaired at Plattsburgh. The enemy had inadvertently given him naval superiority on the lake, and as a gracious recipient, Prevost was happy to accept. More importantly, he was anxious to create a diversion that would shift American focus away from the Great Lakes. A raid in force up Lake Champlain was agreed upon, and to advance this effort the senior naval officers at Quebec were ordered to supply crews for the newly acquired sloops. After gathering together some eighty sailors, the force, which consisted of detachments of royal artillery, Royal Marines, and British regulars, amounted to almost six hundred men.

The raid, known as Murray's Raid, after Lt. Col. John Murray who was in command of the army contingent, was under the direction of navy commander Thomas Everand of HMS *Wasp*. It involved the *Shannon*, the *Broke* (as the *Eagle* was now called), three gunboats, and some three dozen bateaux. The task force met no opposition in burning government storehouses and buildings near Plattsburgh, the naval storehouses at Swanton and Rouses Point, or burning the fifty-ton merchantman *Essex* when they found it hiding in Shelburne Bay. On the afternoon of August 2 Everand stood outside of Burlington harbor, where Macdonough was busy reconstructing his fleet, and attempted to draw the American commander out to "afford him the opportunity of deciding the naval superiority on the Lake." Macdonough, however, was not interested, and after some long-range exchanges between the British vessels and the shore batteries at Burlington, Everand leisurely returned to Ile aux Noix content with his success and his clear command of the lake.[13]

The raid accomplished little materially, but it did shake the Americans, which escalated British talk about keeping naval control over the lake. Clearly, with the Americans outfitting another fleet in Burlington, now was the time to act. A master carpenter, William Simmons, sent to examine the *Growler* and *Eagle* after their capture, informed Major General Roger Sheaffe in Montreal that with the timber and supplies available that he could launch a sixteen-gun brig in six weeks to augment the fleet. A few days after the raid, departing Commander Everand and the newly appointed naval commander at Ile aux Noix Captain Daniel Pring both recommended that "a Brig to carry sixteen guns, and two Gun boats with two heavy guns each be built immediately, to enable us to contend for superiority on the lake." Although the idea was shelved for the moment, it would soon resurface.[14]

Macdonough grimaced at the sight of Everand's warships drifting slowly on the wind outside of Burlington, but beyond directing some of his vessel's guns at the intruders, there was little he could do. The foolhardy loss of the *Growler* and the *Eagle* had left him scrambling to reassemble a new fleet. The day after the two sloops were lost Macdonough wrote the secretary of the navy. Although he could not give any details as to the loss of the ships, he laid out the steps necessary to reassert control over the lake. It called for the immediate purchase of two commercial sloops which would be used to replace the lost vessels. Some 112 officers, gunners, and sailors would also be needed to man these vessels. And most important, he needed guns. "My guns are gone sir," he informed the secretary, "and there is not a spare one on the Lake."[15]

The response was swift and decisive. Every one of Macdonough's requests was approved. "You are to understand," Navy Secretary William Jones informed Macdonough, "that upon no account are you to suffer the enemy to gain the ascendency on Lake Champlain." He was given permission to purchase his sloops, and twenty eighteen-pound carronades would be forwarded from Massachusetts. To drive the urgency of the matter home the secretary gave him permission to use his letter as authority to obtain any items required from the naval agents in New York or Boston, and to make it perfectly clear, he spelled out to Macdonough that he now had "unlimited authority to procure the necessary resources of men, material and munitions."[16]

Governor-General George Prevost. Prevost's insistence that Captain Downing bring his hastily prepared fleet into action coupled with his failure to support Downing's fleet during the Battle of Cumberland Bay was a running source of controversy. The governor's decision not to advance on Plattsburgh once the British fleet was defeated, however, was sound. It was clear that with the Americans in control of Lake Champlain that his army could not advance past Plattsburgh for fear of their flank and supply lines. As such, Prevost deemed the cost of seizing Plattsburgh too high for what was to be gained in its capture and ordered a retreat back to the border.

With his plan of action approved, Macdonough immediately purchased the fifty-ton sloop *Rising Sun*, which he renamed the

Commodore Preble. A month later, the newly promoted Macdonough purchased a larger sloop, which he christened the *Montgomery* and fitted out to carry eleven guns. There were two more additions to the fleet as well, both seizures that the commander thought necessary after hearing news of more British vessels arriving at Ile aux Noix. The first was the fifty-ton *Francis* which was converted to a five-gun tender, while the second was the small sloop *Wasp*, a dismal sailor who could barely take three twelve-pounders on its deck.[17]

Macdonough put his patched-together fleet out onto the lake as the leaves began to turn, and although it was hardly a formidable force, it proved strong enough to dissuade the British from conducting anything beyond a few insignificant raids with their galleys. By late December as the fleet prepared to enter winter quarters Macdonough began looking past his stopgap measures. With rumors circulating about British naval plans he debated two issues before him. Clearly the winter would be occupied in shipbuilding, but where? And what to build?

The where proved to be Vergennes, a small lake-faring town a few miles upstream from the outlet of Otter Creek. The location was well suited to both shipbuilding and defense. Located at the base of a thirty-seven-foot waterfall, the young town of Vergennes thrived on this natural power source. There was a blast furnace and eight forges here, and iron to be had from the nearby town of Monkton whose work had already been put to the test, having produced nearly a thousand thirty-two-pound cannonballs for Macdonough's fleet. The water also powered an iron-rolling mill and a fulling mill. Numerous sawmills dotted the landscape, all more than capable of turning the abundant supply of local timber into ships. Added to this was a shipyard facility and reports that the newly formed Steamboat Company of Lake Champlain planned to build steamboats there starting in the spring. Just as important in the selection was the location's ability to be defended. In Vergennes this required little thought. Although Otter Creek was deep enough to handle heavy vessels it was narrow, often twisting and turning the length of its seven-mile trip to Lake Champlain. These features made it easily defended against a naval attack and, coupled with the Vermont militias and American troops stationed at Burlington, relatively secure against a British landing. To be sure, on this last point Macdonough would set up a battery at the mouth of Otter Creek and station some of his gunboats in Field's Bay at the outlet of Otter Creek.[18]

For a number of reasons, the question of what to build was more difficult to answer. Foremost was intelligence on the British shipbuilding efforts at Ile aux Noix. Macdonough had heard reports of work on a twenty-four-gun brig, which if true, would outgun anything in his fleet. What worried him just as much was his enemy's ability to move small gunboats around the St. Jean rapids. His estimates were that the British now had from nine to twelve of these vessels at Ile aux Noix, but next year they might suddenly augment these numbers by shuttling gunboats currently operating on the St. Lawrence or built at Sorel around the rapids to the island. Two approaches were in order to counter these efforts. First, Macdonough could build a fleet of twenty to twenty-five of his own gunboats, or second he could concentrate on building a large warship to counter the enemy's brig. What he could not do with his limited resources was both. Each had their advantages, gunboats could operate in shallow waters, could be rowed, and if need be, because of their shallow draft, could retreat up creeks and rivers if facing a superior enemy. But such vessels, equipped with forty oars, required large crews to only bring a pair of guns into action. A large sloop or brig would require significantly fewer sailors and could bring more guns into action than half of the proposed gunboat fleet.

Writing Macdonough in late January 1814, Secretary of the Navy Jones argued the pros and cons of each approach, but ultimately left the choice of what to build up to Macdonough. "You are authorized to build either a vessel of such force as shall certainly exceed that of the enemy or the Galleys as you shall judge best adapted to the service," he wrote the master commandant. "Or you may build a ship and three or four of the Galleys. The object is to leave no doubt of your commanding the Lake and the waters connected, and that in <u>due time</u>." Guns and naval equipment would be forwarded to Albany and Macdonough was authorized to give a bounty of twenty dollars to any potential recruit for the fleet.[19]

As it turned out Secretary Jones was not completely prepared to accept Macdonough's decision. Although the commandant had made up his mind to build gunboats, in mid-February Jones, worried by the reports on the British brig, signed a contract with master shipbuilder Noah Brown to launch a twenty-four-gun warship at Vergennes in sixty days. To augment this vessel Jones informed Macdonough that he was also authorized to purchase the 125-foot steamboat *Providence*, under construction at Vergennes by the Steamboat Company of Lake Champlain.

The winter was mild by Vermont standards which allowed the crews to take to their work. While several gunboats began to take shape along the waterfront Noah Brown surveyed a patch of wood on the outskirts of the town, and by March 7 he had fashioned these trees into the 180-foot keel of the twenty-six-gun sloop *Saratoga*. True to his word Brown slid the *Saratoga* into the water on April 11, some forty days after the start of the project. He then turned his attention to the steamboat *Providence*. There was some debate on whether or not to keep its steam engine and the benefits that such an arrangement would provide, but in the end the first steam warship in the American navy would have to wait. Questions concerning the reliability of the new propulsion system were the overriding factor, and the decision was made to build it up as the twenty-gun schooner *Ticonderoga*.[20]

By the second week of April the finishing touches were being put on six new galleys and the *Saratoga*, but the vessels' guns had yet to arrive and the crews were not complete. Work on the *Ticonderoga* was moving forward, and the older vessels had all been

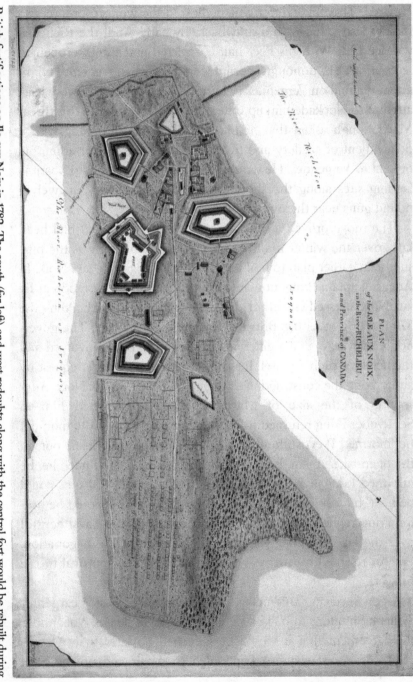

British fortifications on Ile aux Noix in 1782. The south (far left) and west redoubts along with the central fort would be rebuilt during the War of 1812. The north redoubt (on the right) was leveled to make room for a new dockyard and naval facility.

repaired. The mild winter which allowed the work to progress so rapidly also came with a drawback. By early April the Richelieu was ice free. With his fleet half completed and the lake open to navigation Macdonough became concerned the enemy might attempt a raid on Vergennes to burn his vessels, or at the very least attempt to blockade him up Otter Creek. In response to this threat Macdonough asked that militia be called out, and along with a detachment of artillery and five hundred troops from Burlington, be sent to Vergennes. He would use these troops to guard possible landing sites along the shore and establish a battery of twelve-pound guns near the outlet of Otter Creek.[21]

The move proved a wise precaution, for the British had been busy over the winter months. Their foremost action was the pursuit of an earlier plan to build a sixteen-gun brig at Ile aux Noix. In August Captain Pring, now in command of the naval station at Ile aux Noix, pressed Governor Prevost once again about building the 370-ton brig to assure British dominance on the lake. The governor, however, was of a different mind about the cost involved and the need for such a vessel. Instead he replied to Pring's request by authorizing the construction of two gunboats at Ile aux Noix. After reports of the size of Macdonough's fleet reached him in September Pring returned to the need for the brig. At the moment he informed Prevost, he did not dare face the Americans out on the open lake. Again, Prevost waivered on the idea. If need be, he informed Pring, a smaller vessel of not more than 120 tons could be built, but nothing more. Although such a vessel would be useful, Pring replied, it would not be enough to assure naval control over the lake. Seemingly having had enough of the negotiation, Prevost relented in early November and gave his approval to the project.

Upon receiving this news, Pring contracted master carpenter William Simmons to build a sixteen-gun brig at Ile aux Noix under the agreement that it would be launched no later than May 1, 1814. Simmons was also contracted to repair and upgrade the existing vessels at the island, as well as construct several more galleys. Not long after, Pring also received permission to purchase one of the prize vessels from Murray's Raid earlier that summer. The small forty-four-foot sloop renamed the *Canada* was assigned guard duty at the head of Ash Island with the primary purpose of alerting the garrison at Ile aux Noix of any American venture onto the river.

Taking form in the dockyards on the eastern end of the island alongside a pair of gunboats, the brig *Linnet*, as it would eventually be called, ended up being smaller than originally conceived. Even so, it displaced some 250 tons, carried a battery of sixteen long twenty-four pounders, and employed a crew of 120 sailors and marines. "First class" is how Macdonough would characterize the warship after seeing it for the first time, "A remarkably fine looking vessel." Simons also turned his efforts toward the gunboats. The existing vessels were repaired, and five more were built over the winter and spring ranging in size from fifty to sixty feet long, each armed with a long eighteen- or twenty-four pounder in their prow and a carronade in their stern.[22]

With the launching of the *Linnet* and his new gunboats in mid-April Pring was ready to take advantage of the early opening of the lake. On May 8 the *Linnet*, *Chub* (formerly *Shannon*), *Finch* (formerly *Broke*), the gunboats and galleys, a small tender, and a pair of captured merchant vessels set out from Ile aux Noix. Acting on orders received the month before, Pring headed for Vergennes to either burn the American ships being built there or sink his merchant ships in the mouth of Otter Creek. Contrary winds destroyed any element of surprise that Pring had hoped to achieve. His flotilla was spotted on the tenth and by the time he had reached Otter Creek on the morning of the fourteenth the alarm had been sounded across the length of the lake.

When dawn broke on the 14th Pring realized the strength of the American position. Otter Creek emptied into Field's Bay which was sheltered to the north by a thin peninsula of land that extended into the lake between it and the southern boundary of Porter Bay. At the head of this peninsula, where the lake narrowed to a mile and a half wide, the Americans had erected a redoubt and a battery of seven long twelve-pound guns. To support this battery ten of Macdonough's gunboats rode quietly in Field's Bay waiting for the signal to advance.

The battery at what would become known as Fort Cassin Point was not unexpected and a plan had been arranged to take the position by storm. After a preliminary bombardment one hundred Royal Marines manning the galleys would land in bateaux being towed behind these vessels. This force would be supported by another hundred marines packed aboard the *Linnet*. Together the two groups would storm the American stronghold.[23]

The British gunboats, several armed with mortars, began bombarding the American battery at Cassin Point as soon as their target was visible. The *Linnet* moved into range a half an hour later to cover the prearranged landing, but as Pring surveyed the situation he changed his mind and ordered the fleet to break off. The wooded banks on either side of the creek's entrance teemed with enemy infantry. The British commander had little doubt that his troops could seize the American battery, but there were simply not enough of them to hold it. Given the number of enemy gunboats still to be dealt with, and without the battery at Cassin Point disabled he would never get his merchant vessels close enough to sink them in the mouth of the creek. The Americans were too well prepared. Having missed his opportunity Pring cursed the winds before swinging back north.

The ninety-minute engagement produced little in the way of casualties on either side. Within a week it no longer mattered, Macdonough had brought his vessels out onto the lake. With the *Saratoga* and *Ticonderoga* added to the American arsenal the scales tipped once again, and on May 29 Macdonough was writing the secretary of the navy from Cumberland Bay that "there is now a free communication between all parts of this Lake, and at present there are no doubts of this communication being interrupted by the enemy."[24]

By June Macdonough had moved forward to blockade the entrance to the Richelieu River. An attack on Ile aux Noix was out of the question, particularly given news that the British had fortified Ash Island, but what concerned Macdonough more were reports coming out of Ile aux Noix. Spies had recently spotted the keel of a vessel laid at the shipyards there that rivaled, if not exceeded, the *Saratoga*. To go with this the enemy had done what Macdonough had feared. They had built a large number of galleys in the St. Lawrence and were now busy transporting them around the Chambly rapids on sleds. Three had reached the island by mid-June and reports were that eight more were soon expected. If true, when combined with the present building efforts, it would put the British gunboat flotilla at some twenty-two in number. There was also alarming news of four brig-sized frames having arrived from England, two of which it was said, were destined for Lake Champlain.

Macdonough expressed his concerns to Navy Secretary Jones, and in the process correctly sized up the emerging naval arms race between the two powers. "I am sure he [Pring] intends on risquing nothing, but will endeavor to out build us, and there is no knowing where this building may stop, for, as I before said, his acquaintance with our force will enable him to know exactly what force to bring against us, so there is a probability of his not meeting us unless he is pretty confidant of being successful."[25]

It simply became a question of what to build in response. Macdonough wanted galleys, but the available manpower was better suited to a large brig carrying twenty eighteen-pound cannon. The matter was accelerated when news reached Macdonough a month later that the British vessel under construction at Ile aux Noix was to take on the armament of a frigate, some thirty-two to forty-four heavy cannon. Although Secretary Jones saw no end to "the war of Broad Axes," in response to Macdonough's concerns he contracted Adam Brown, Noah Brown's brother and business partner, to proceed to Vergennes and construct an eighteen-gun brig to augment the American fleet. The twenty-gun brig *Eagle* was built in nineteen days by Brown and his company. It slid into the water on August 11, but lack of guns and, more importantly, lack of a crew kept it at Vergennes for two more weeks.[26]

British shipbuilding efforts were being accelerated as well. In late August the large keel Macdonough had received reports about had been transformed into a fifth-rate frigate named the *Confiance*. It was the largest and most powerful warship ever built for the lake. At almost 150 feet in length and thirty-seven feet in beam, the 1,200-ton warship carried twenty-seven long twenty-four pounders, ten carronades, and was manned by a crew of 270 sailors and marines. Like the *Inflexible* two generations before, it was yet another impressive feat of British naval skill and ability. But as impressive as the *Confiance* was, it was also a rushed ship; perhaps too rushed.[27]

While Macdonough and Pring pursued their "war of broad axes," the fortunes of America and Canada took a dramatic shift during the summer of 1814. Napoleon had abdicated, releasing a succession of seasoned British regiments for service in Canada. Some 14,000 redcoats arrived in Montreal over the summer, and almost all were slated for an invasion of upper New York along Lake Champlain. The signs of the buildup rattled the old invasion fears along these waterways. Talk of a British effort aimed at seizing the Hudson Valley, and cutting New England off from the rest of the country were revived, although Prevost had no such plans. His operation was similar to others conducted by the British over the next several months. The aim was to seize Crown Point and Ticonderoga, thereby blocking the Champlain Valley and threatening Albany and western New England. If successful, such a move would encourage the Americans to hurry the peace talks, as well as enhance Britain's position at those talks.

With an army of 11,000 men in Lower Canada Prevost was anxious to move forward before the season escaped him, but it was mid-August and he was stalled. Not due to troops, or cannon, or supplies, but because the Americans had asserted naval supremacy over Lake Champlain. Prevost could not move forward with his left flank exposed, to do so would be to invite disaster; the Americans could decimate his lengthening supply line or even shuttle an army across the lake behind him. With time running short the Governor ordered work on the *Confiance* to take priority, and when it slid into the water on August 25 he ordered its 270 man crew to be filled out by drafts among the vessels in the St. Lawrence. A week later he turned command of the frigate and the Lake Champlain fleet over to recently arrived Captain George Downie.[28]

The moment Downie assumed command Prevost began pressuring him to move against his American counterparts. He had yet to see the lake, oversee his charges, or meet the officers and crew under his command before Prevost, who was advancing on Plattsburgh with three brigades of regulars, was urging him forward. Throughout the first week of September Downie repeatedly responded to the governor's pleas by informing him that he was not ready. The last elements of the *Confiance*'s crew were arriving, its guns were still being mounted, and a host of other problems from its unfinished magazines to its incomplete rigging needed to be resolved.

Finally on September 10 Downie wrote Prevost that although his fleet was short on men, he was ready to move against the Americans the next morning. The overall plan agreed upon by the two commanders called for Prevost to attack Plattsburgh at the same time Downie engaged Macdonough's fleet, which reports indicated was anchored in Cumberland Bay. By seizing Plattsburgh and the American shore batteries the governor would be able to support Downie's attack, perhaps even catching the American's between two fires, or at the very least forcing them to withdraw to avoid such a situation. It was a simple plan, short on details, that was to prove a miserable failure.[29]

For Macdonough it was clear that a battle was approaching. He had withdrawn from his position blocking the Richelieu back to Cumberland Bay on September 1st when Prevost's army began marching towards Plattsburgh. From here he could cooperate with Brigadier General Alexander Macomb, who was busy preparing the outnumbered defenders. By fixing himself on Macomb's right wing, Macdonough all but guaranteed that the upcoming naval engagement would be decided at anchor. The American commander sent away the support vessels, and arranged his fleet in a north-south line, the upper part of which was partially covered by Cumberland Head a mile to the east. At the northern point of this line, some 800 yards from the shore, Macdonough stationed the newly built *Eagle* with its starboard guns bearing east. Stretched out behind the brig at roughly one hundred yard intervals were the *Saratoga*, the *Ticonderoga*, and the *Preble*. The ten gunboats were stationed about forty yards to the west of the main line just within range of the Plattsburgh shore batteries. Three of these sat to the port bow of the *Eagle*, another three occupied the interval between the *Eagle* and the *Saratoga*, and the remaining four filled the gap between the *Saratoga* and the *Ticonderoga*.

Each of the major ships had thrown out their bow anchor to which a pair of springs was attached, one running down the port side of the vessel and the other down the starboard side. By winching on one spring or the other the ship's bow could be shifted, which in turn would allow the vessel to bring its broadsides to bear on an enemy. In addition, kedge anchors attached to springs were thrown out on either bow quarter. If need be a ship could be winched against one of these anchors which would shift the direction of its bow allowing a vessel facing windward to fill its sails and turn to align herself with the wind. It would prove to be a crucial precaution.[30]

In positioning his ships Macdonough had considered two scenarios. There was a chance that Downie would try to tack his way up the lake against a southerly wind, and then turn on the

American line with the wind in his favor. Such an approach would unhinge Macdonough's current deployment, but the mitigating factor was that the American commander would have plenty of time to redeploy while the British crawled south past Cumberland Head in order to execute the maneuver. A more likely scenario in his mind was that Downie would bring his fleet up the lake under a northerly breeze. Working under this premise Macdonough had placed himself such that the British would have to haul into the wind after rounding Cumberland Head in order to come up with him, which in turn would subject the British squadron to fire from Macdonough's long range guns while they crawled forward against the wind. The real question that the American leader could not answer was whether Downie would stand off and turn the battle into a long range duel or close with the American fleet and turn it into a short range melee. Although Macdonough was prepared for the first scenario the second gave him a decided advantage given his superiority in carronades. There was one more advantage Macdonough possessed. His main vessels lay right at the extreme effective range of the Plattsburgh shore batteries. If anything went wrong, or if some of his vessels needed to retreat, they could do so under this protective umbrella.

Downie, who was gliding south from Isle La Motte on the morning of September 11 under a northeasterly breeze, scaled his guns as the agreed-upon signal to the land forces that he was making his approach. The fleet came to anchor around seven o'clock when the American mastheads were seen standing over the low lying Cumberland Peninsula. Captain Downie set out in his gig and a half an hour later returned with news that the American fleet had not shifted position.[31]

Downie assembled his captains and laid out the plan of attack. The fleet would round Cumberland Head and break into two parts. The southern portion consisting of twelve gunboats would advance on the *Ticonderoga*, fire once, and then attempt to board her. The *Finch* would accompany this gunboat flotilla and support their efforts before turning its attention to the sloop *Preble* stationed at the southern end of the American line. The *Linnet, Chub,* and *Confiance* would make up the northern element of the plan and would target the *Eagle* and *Saratoga*. All three vessels would haul around Cumberland Head, and in line ahead formation would tack their way north towards the head of the American line. The *Linnet* and the *Chub* would maneuver to anchor themselves off the *Eagle*'s bow, while the *Confiance* at the last moment would swing south firing its starboard broadsides into the *Eagle* before coming to rest between the *Eagle* and the *Saratoga* with a broadside bearing down on each. If successful the plan would leave the *Eagle* surrounded, the *Saratoga* raked stem to stern by heavy fire, the *Ticonderoga* captured, and the *Preble* destroyed. The American gunboats were not considered worth planning for; they would quickly scatter once their larger brethren fell.[32]

It was a bold plan and thoroughly impractical in terms of execution. Having never seen Cumberland Bay Downie probably didn't understand the fickle air currents that swirled across the bay when the wind came from the north, although it seems almost certain that one of his officers familiar with the bay must have pointed this out. The news did not deter Downie, even though the agreed upon maneuvers would pose a challenge, especially for the newly rigged *Confiance* whose crew had been together for less than a week. The approach north would also expose the *Linnet, Chub,* and *Confiance* to raking fire while they crawled their way up the bay, but this was put aside as well.

Of more importance was the question of why close with the American fleet at all? As pointed out by Macdonough, little could be kept a secret when it came to shipbuilding on the lake, meaning that Downie was well aware of his enemy's superiority in carronades. Yet, Downie proposed closing with the Americans when he possessed at least a marginal advantage in long range guns. It was true that if his maneuvers went flawlessly that he would be in a position to nullify the Americans carronade advantage, but

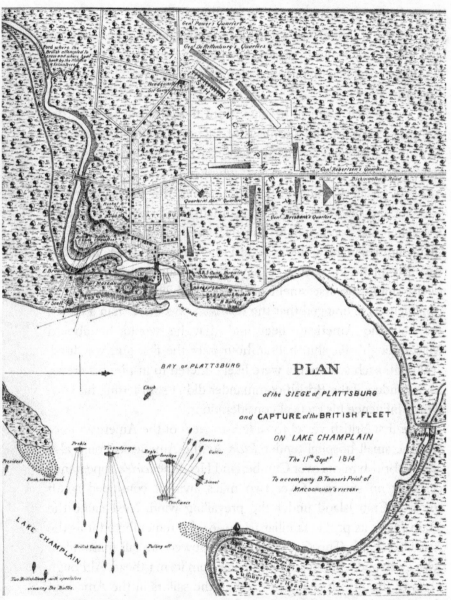

Map of the Battle of Cumberland Bay showing the positions of the British and American fleets approximately one hour into the engagement. The two British vessels in the lower left-hand corner are the hospital tender *Icicle* and the supply tender *Canada*. Oddly the *President* is shown positioned near Crab Island, which is incorrect as she was in Burlington at the time of the battle.

Downie was not a neophyte when it came to naval warfare. He had served in numerous actions throughout the Napoleonic Wars and had seen far more conservative plans go awry; and thus, with so much at stake, why pursue a plan that smacked of ill-timed desperation?

It seems that political pressure from the governor to push the campaign forward and promises of support by the army slanted Downie's risk analysis. It's unclear exactly what promises were made in terms of army support; whether it was to come in the form of artillery batteries erected along the north shore of Cumberland Bay once the action started, or a belief that Prevost's overwhelming force would quickly seize the shore batteries at Plattsburgh and turn them against the American fleet. In either case the plan also seems to have been influenced by Downie's overly optimistic assessment of his fleet's abilities and that of his opponents. He bragged that the *Confiance* was more than a match for half the American fleet and that he would be aboard Macdonough's flagship half-an-hour after the first gun was fired. Although such statements were likely uttered to inspire his crews, one wonders if the British commander didn't start letting his own words influence his tactical considerations.[33]

The first British vessel to slide into view of the American lines was the small hospital tender *Icicle*. As the Americans could also see the British masts over Cumberland Head the *Icicle*'s appearance came as no surprise. Over two miles away it continued south towards Crab Island under the prevailing wind. Next came the sloop *Finch*, its profile familiar to those who remembered it as the first USS *Eagle*. The *Confiance* soon followed, its tall masts filled with cloth and a broad pennant flying from its masthead. Although news of the British ship had reached the sailors in the American fleet it did not wholly prepare them for the sight. To many it appeared too big on the horizon. To others the frigate was the biggest warship they had ever seen, and to the slightly more seasoned among them, most had not seen larger. Another familiar profile, the *Chub*, came next, followed by the brig *Linnet*, and then a parade of gunboats.

When the *Linnet* cleared the shoals extending south from Cumberland Head it heaved west toward the American lines. The *Chub* and *Confiance* followed suit and soon the three vessels were moving toward Macdonough in a line-abreast formation. The *Finch* and the gunboats continued half a mile south before executing a similar maneuver toward the *Ticonderoga*.

For the moment, however, there was little to do on the American side but recite a short prayer and wait. Captain Robert Henley on board the *Eagle* loosed his starboard eighteen-pounders at the *Confiance*, but these rounds fell well short of their mark. As the range closed it became clear that the three British vessels' tracks were beginning to diverge. The *Linnet* and the *Chub* were aiming toward the head of the American line, while the British frigate appeared to be sighted on a point closer to the *Eagle*'s position. Macdonough personally tracked the *Confiance* with one of the *Saratoga*'s long twenty-four pounders. When the vessel came within range the commodore stepped back and gave the order to fire. The frigate presented nearly an end-on profile and the shot crashed into its port bow and carried down the length of the deck, scattering all about it before coming to rest. Macdonough ordered the "Close Action" signal raised as the remaining long guns on the *Saratoga* went off one by one. Soon the *Eagle*'s starboard battery echoed across the lake followed by the *Ticonderoga*'s guns not long after.[34]

For Downie and his three northern vessels, there was nothing to do but run the American gauntlet in order to reach their positions. The American gunboats soon joined the action with their long guns. The *Confiance* was clearly the target of choice and its two port anchors were soon shot away by well-aimed fire. As the American shot sheared through the frigate's rigging or splashed into the waters about them, Downie anxiously paced about the poop deck, looking to the shore, occasionally commenting to the vessel's sailing master, Robert Brydon, that he didn't understand why the army wasn't moving forward.

As they closed on the American line all three British warships were having trouble with the wind, which had not only shifted to the northwest when they rounded Cumberland Head, but now began to die off. As the hits on his frigate began to mount it became clear to Downie that he had misjudged the weather in the bay. Seeing that his planned maneuver to strike the *Eagle* and then turn and lay anchor between it and the *Saratoga* was impossible, the British commander hauled the *Confiance* into the wind about 350 yards from the *Saratoga* and dropped anchor. To the north the American focus on the *Confiance* did have one positive effect; it was allowing the *Linnet* and the *Chub* to proceed relatively unmolested.[35]

The *Eagle* and the *Saratoga* both poured a broadside into the British frigate before the latter finally secured its position and returned fire. When it did, its broadside of four thirty-two pound carronades and sixteen long twenty-four pound cannon, the latter loaded with double shot, were leveled at the *Saratoga*. The impact of nearly a ton of iron balls shook the hull of the American vessel sending a shower of wooden and iron debris whipping across its deck that disabled nearly a quarter of its crew.

As the *Eagle*, *Saratoga*, and *Confiance* exchanged fire, the *Linnet* dropped anchor about 300 yards off the *Eagle*'s starboard quarter. Captain Pring, who was familiar with the tricky winds in the bay, had done a masterful job of positioning the British brig. Lt. McGhie of the *Chub* was having a more difficult time, and was still maneuvering against the wind a few hundred yards astern of Pring. His crew had fired several broadsides at the *Eagle* and in doing so had finally caught the American warship's attention. The *Eagle*'s thirty-two-pound carronades shifted and then lashed out at the former merchantman, shattering its rigging and tearing into its hull. The head of the bowsprit was demolished and the jib boom carried away, leaving the foresail flapping chaotically in the wind when another broadside arrived from the American brig. The heavy balls splintered everything in their path, sweeping the deck with deadly wooden shards, one of which struck Lt. McGhie in the thigh, forcing him to be taken below. The *Chub* responded as best it could, but by now over half its crew lay dead or wounded. The next volley damaged the main boom and carried away the halyards that supported the gaff. The forestays were cut by more shot, and soon the unsupported foresail lay draped over its bow.

On fire, with its sails useless, its crew decimated, and the remaining crewmen rapidly deserting their stations, the *Chub* began drifting south out of control. Midshipman John Bodell, who took command from McGhie, ordered the crew to break out the sweeps in an attempt to stabilize the sloop, but these were quickly destroyed by enemy shot. With the ship now drifting toward the *Confiance* and *Saratoga*, McGhie summoned Bodell and ordered him to lower the colors. For the next few minutes the tempo of the battle subsided as the American vessels and the British frigate checked their fire while the surrendered vessel drifted between them; Bodell was the only figure to be seen upon its tattered deck.[36]

As the *Chub* drifted past the fight toward the Plattsburgh shore the *Linnet* unleashed its port broadsides against the *Eagle*. At point-blank range the twelve-pound shot tore down the length of the vessel, raking it stem to stern. It was nearly the ideal firing position for Pring, who began "a most destructive fire" upon the American brig, which was answered only by a pair of eighteen-pound bow guns; Henley focused the rest of his starboard guns on the greater threat, the nearby *Confiance*. The half a dozen American gunboats soon entered the fray with their guns, and by ten o'clock the northern part of the battle line was cloaked in rolling billows of blue-white smoke backlit by a series of staggered flashes as the belligerents unleashed grapeshot and ball at each other from point-blank range.[37]

Half a mile to the south Lt. William Hicks of the *Finch* turned into the wind and angled his sloop toward the *Ticonderoga*. Several hundred yards behind him gathered in a jumble were the fleet's three divisions of gunboats led by Lt. Raynham in the sixty-foot *Yeo*. Keeping to a southwesterly track Hicks edged closer to the *Ticonderoga* and around nine o'clock began to draw fire from the American schooner and the sloop *Preble* anchored a few hundred yards astern. Hicks's plan was to fire his starboard broadside as he passed by the *Ticonderoga*. The gunboat flotilla would follow up this attack by boarding the schooner while he continued on to engage the *Preble*. The balls from the Ticonderoga's eighteen- and twelve-pound long guns punched through the *Finch*'s hull and made tearing noises as they shredded their way through the sloop's sails. Hicks steadied his crew and when the sloop came within two hundred yards he loosed a broadside at the converted steamboat. For the next forty-five minutes the *Finch* divided its fire between the *Ticonderoga* and the *Preble*, all the while sliding further southwest toward the latter.

Among the gunboats there was confusion. Raynham finally managed to form his flotilla up some six hundred yards from the *Ticonderoga* and hoisted the signal to board. With calls to their crews, the officers in charge of the vessels ordered their men to pull on their oars, and the line started for the *Ticonderoga*. It soon became apparent, however, that not all of the crews were in favor of facing several broadsides of canister as they dashed forward to overwhelm the American schooner. Although together the flotilla outgunned the *Ticonderoga*, individually the little open boats seemed frighteningly vulnerable, particularly to their Canadian militia crews. These vessels chose not to row as hard toward their target, and as a result gaps opened in the line as two groups began to form. In the van the *Murray, Popham, Beresford*, and one other gunboat began closing on the *Ticonderoga* and at around three hundred yards began responding to the schooner's fire with their bow guns. Falling several hundred yards behind them were the remaining gunboats, and drifting behind these was Lt. Raynham's *Yeo*, the commander's signal flags now down.[38]

The Battle of Cumberland Bay showing the participants in the latter stages of the engagement from the northern shore of the bay. 1. HMS *Confiance* 2. USS *Saratoga* 3. HMS *Linnet* 4. HMS *Chub* (disabled) 5. USS *Eagle* 6. USS *Ticonderoga* 7. USS *Preble* 8. American gunboats 9. HMS *Finch* (aground) 10. British gunboats 11. HMS *Canada* and HMS *Icicle*.

The four lead boats bore down on the *Ticonderoga* as round shot and grape splashed around them, occasionally finding its mark. At a musket shot several of the gunboats brought their carronades into play, but none advanced any further. Without the support of more boats the venture would be suicide. On board the *Ticonderoga* Lt. Cassin calmly walked the gundeck encouraging his men, as fire from the British gunboats and the receding *Finch* struck the vessel. Cassin was particularly impressed with a young midshipman named Harim Paulding, who by necessity was forced to fire his section's cannons with the flash of a pistol throughout most of the engagement. Any initial fears Cassin possessed about being over-whelmed disappeared when he saw the bulk of the British gun-boats drifting south some five hundred yards away. When the schooner's thirty-two-pound carronades added their part to the swirling smoke, it was clear to the British gunboat crews that the warship was more than capable of repelling any boarders, and they withdrew to continue a long-range cannonade.

Slightly to the south the *Finch* had managed to bring its star-board guns to bear on the *Preble*, but not before the American sloop's captain, Lt. Charles Budd, let go of his anchor and, maneu-vering the vessel by sweeps, raked the British sloop with a broad-side of four nine-pounders. Within one hundred yards of one another, the *Finch* traded broadsides with the *Preble* and then turned to port heading out of the bay. The *Finch* had suffered the worst in its engagement with the *Ticonderoga* and *Preble*. Its main boom and bowsprit had been nearly cleaved, and the hull had been shot through and through five times, four of these at the waterline. Taking on water fast, it was just northwest of Crab Island being pushed by the shifting winds toward the island. Hicks needed to tack north, but with three feet of water in its hold and its sails a wreck, the *Finch* refused to respond. Not long after there was a scraping sound, then another, followed by a long vibration that tested the crew's balance, and the *Finch* came to a stop—stuck fast on a shoal that extended from the north point of the island.

A portion of a larger 1837 print showing the naval engagement at the Battle of Plattsburgh. In the foreground from left to right are the *Eagle, Saratoga, Ticonderoga,* and the *Preble.* These vessels are shown supported by a number of gunboats located closer to the shore. The British line in the background is (from left to right) the *Linnet, Chub, Confiance,* and the British gunboat flotilla. In the larger image the *Finch* is shown aground on the north point of Crab Island.

The *Preble* now faced a new danger. Several of the gunboats led by the *Blucher* and the *Prevost* were moving in its direction. Fearing being boarded, Lt. Budd let loose his jib and wheeled the vessel into the wind. The maneuver brought the *Preble*'s port broadside to bear on the advancing gunboats and in quick succession each of the fresh nine-pounders loosed a barrage of canister and ball at the advancing British vessels. With the wind now in his favor, Budd deployed the main sails and slipped away toward the shore.[39]

To the north one of the first casualties was Captain Downie. About ten minutes after his ship anchored, an American cannon-ball struck the muzzle of a twenty-four-pound gun Downie was standing behind. The impact of the round tore the two-ton cannon off its mount and propelled it into Downie, who survived barely long enough to be taken below. Lt. James Robertson assumed command and continued the cannonade. By the top of the hour the scene on board the *Confiance* was quickly deteriorating. The deck was strewn with casualties and the rigging was draped in places like a shroud over the vessel. "Never was a shower of hail so thick as the shot whistling about our ears," midshipman Robert Lea later confided in a letter to his brother. "There is one of our marines who was in the Trafalgar action with Lord Nelson, who says it was a mere fleabite in comparison."[40]

It was little better aboard the *Saratoga* and the *Eagle*. The latter was being particularly battered as most of the *Linnet*'s shots ripped down the length of the vessel's deck. An hour into the engagement Henley, with his anchor springs shot away, a third of his crew killed or wounded, and almost every starboard gun out of action, cut the *Eagle*'s anchor cable. Throwing out his jib sail Henley wheeled the vessel to port in a textbook maneuver, and under his topsails glided south past the *Saratoga* before throwing out his anchor a short distance astern and west of the flagship. Henley punctuated his new position by immediately firing his unused port guns into the *Confiance*.

Although Henley had removed the threat to the *Eagle*, in doing so he exposed the *Saratoga* to the combined fire of the *Linnet* and *Confiance*. On board the American flagship the repercussions were almost immediate. The fire coming from the British frigate had been slackening as the American warships slowly pounded away, but the *Linnet* had hardly been touched. For the moment it was quiet as the gunnery officers moved through the cannons in their sections aiming each at the new target four hundred yards away. When each station had reported ready, the command to fire was given and one by one the eight long twelve-pound guns flashed down the length of the vessel.[41]

The raking fire crashed into the *Saratoga*, which was already heavily damaged. Its masts had been splintered and the vessel hulled a dozen times over. First Lt. Peter Gamble was killed when a ball struck the gun he was sighting, and Macdonough himself had been knocked down on a pair of occasions, once when a round shot cut the spanker boom in two and a portion fell on him, knocking him senseless for several moments. But the *Saratoga* was fortunate. The inexperienced and hastily assembled gun crews on the *Confiance* failed to properly reset their pieces after firing. The progressive recoil on the weapons slowly raised their aiming point such that much of the shot tore through the *Saratoga*'s rigging and not into its hull.

At this point the outcome of the battle hung on the *Confiance*, which was taking the combined fire of the *Saratoga*, the *Eagle*, and a portion of the *Ticonderoga*, and the *Saratoga*, which was the focus of every gun the *Confiance* and *Linnet* could bring to bear. Almost every vessel involved had shredded rigging and sails. Simple maneuvering might still be possible, but no one was going to escape. The battle had devolved to a winner-take-all scenario. If the *Saratoga* surrendered, the *Linnet* and *Confiance* could make short work of the already damaged *Eagle*. The gunboats need only occupy the *Ticonderoga*, which was sure to run into Plattsburgh once the *Saratoga* and *Eagle* struck. But if the *Confiance* struck first, the three American warships could quickly turn on the *Linnet*, forcing its surrender.[42]

At this moment Macdonough had a choice thrust upon him. His last starboard gun, a carronade, flew off its mount after firing and fell down the main hatch. The American commander now did not have a single gun to oppose the *Confiance*. There was only one thing to do. Macdonough ordered the vessel's stern and bow cables cut, and using the kedge anchors he had thrown out prior to the battle he winded the ship, bringing it about in a classic maneuver that left its unused port guns bearing down on the *Confiance*.

The prospects of facing what was essentially a new ship with the four remaining guns on the port side left Lt. Robertson with no choice but to wind the *Confiance*. The matter was complicated by the damaged and missing bow anchors. With some effort a spring was bent onto the remaining bow cable. Led by the vessel's sailing master Robert Brydon, the crew hauled on the cable spring, and had managed to veer the bow through ninety degrees when a raking shot from the *Eagle* plowed down the length of the ship, killing or wounding several of the cable party. Exposed and exhausted from two hours of nonstop cannonading, the crew broke and deserted their posts. Robertson and his officers attempted to rally them, but to no avail. It didn't matter: the vessel was in shambles. "Our spring and rudder being shot away, all our masts, yards and sails so shattered the one looked like so many bunches of matches, and the other like a bundle of old rags." The hull had been struck over one hundred times, and the water in the hold was rising such that the wounded had to be moved for fear of their drowning. And now with the warship hung up in the wind end on to the *Saratoga*, not a single gun could be brought to bear against the enemy. There was simply no more sense in continuing, Robertson concluded, and with that he ordered the *Confiance*'s colors to be struck.[43]

If he could have, Captain Pring would have cut his cable and retreated at this moment, but the American gunboats and the *Eagle*'s forward guns had succeeded in cutting up the *Linnet*'s rigging. In hopes that the British gunboats clustered to the south would perceive the *Linnet*'s plight and come to its aid, Pring continued an unequal contest with the *Saratoga*, *Eagle*, and *Ticonderoga*. It only took a few minutes, however, before it was clear that the cause was lost, and to prevent further bloodshed Pring lowered the *Linnet*'s colors.[44]

To the south the last act of the battle played out. Not long after the *Finch* had run aground north of Crab Island, a pair of six-pound guns manned by the walking wounded from the hospital established on the island opened fire on the sloop. Hicks returned the fire and chased the gun crews away, but it was only a temporary reprieve. Two gunboats came to his aid, but were of little help. A kedge anchor was carried out in the ship's boat, but the vessel could not be winched off the shoal. To lighten the vessel Hicks ordered four carronades and some ballast over the side, but to little avail. The master carpenter informed him that a five-foot bilge plank had been ruptured below the water line. There was three and a half feet of water in the hold and rising. "I am confident that had I been so fortunate to get her afloat and in deep water," the ship's commander later testified, "she must have sunk." With the other British vessels either surrendered or retreating down the lake, Hicks apologized to his crew, and then lowered his flag, bringing an end to the battle.

With the major British vessels surrendered, Macdonough signaled the American gunboats to pursue the retreating British boats down the lake. A few minutes later, however, he rescinded the order, realizing that he needed the gunboats to help tend to the shattered fleet. There was still the matter of the battle ashore that would determine whether or not Cumberland Bay would prove a safe harbor, and given the state of his vessels Macdonough could not chance that the batteries at Plattsburgh might change hands. With the gunboats' help, the American fleet was moved south below the Plattsburgh batteries until news arrived that the British army was retreating north.[45]

Governor Prevost had held to part of his bargain with Downie, although many later questioned his actions both privately and officially. When Downie's fleet rounded Cumberland Head Prevost ordered his field batteries to open fire on the works at Plattsburgh. He then sent a brigade forward to carry three different crossings over the Saranac River. His troops were initially repulsed, but in the governor's mind the outcome of the naval battle sealed any prospects of continuing. Without control of the lake, seizing Plattsburgh was not worth the price it would take to storm its works. The invasion of upper New York was suspended, and Prevost moved the army back toward the border.[46]

As Macdonough and his staff surveyed their vessels and their new prizes over the next few days, the ferocity of the battle became more apparent. The *Saratoga* had suffered fifty-seven casualties, its rigging was mangled, and it had been hulled by fifty-five shots. Macdonough claimed that it had been set afire twice by heated shot, but the Royal Navy systematically refuted this claim, saying that they had not used this type of shot in the engagement. The *Eagle* suffered similar damage with thirty-nine shots counted in its hull, most twenty-four pounders from the *Confiance*. The *Ticonderoga* and *Preble* both sustained more moderate damage. In all some fifty-two seamen had been killed, and some fifty-eight wounded enough to be listed as such.

The American commander's prizes were in far worse shape. All the *Confiance*'s masts and yards had been fractured, and the hull was riddled with 105 shots, one of which ruptured a seven-foot plank at the waterline and nearly sent the frigate to the bottom. The *Linnet* was in better condition, although it too would require extensive repairs. The *Chub*, which had been towed out of the battle early on by an American galley, had been so badly damaged that it was hardly worth repairing the old warship, and the *Finch* was only spared from the bottom by virtue of resting on a sandbar. His adversaries had sustained nearly 200 casualties in the fight, 123 on the *Confiance* alone, and some 367 officers and men now sat as American prisoners. Nor had British naval losses concluded. In retreating from their advanced naval post at Isle La Motte the captured sloop *Burlington Packet* was overloaded in haste and sank in shallow water near the island.[47]

It was nothing short of a crushing victory. Macdonough had blunted a powerful British thrust toward New York and New England, securing the Lake Champlain corridor for America in the process. In the end the fleets were fairly well matched in terms of men and material. Downie's ambitious plan coupled with Prevost's failure to seize the Plattsburgh batteries certainly played a part in the British fleet's destruction, but the turning factor seems to have been the ships' crews themselves. The American sailors had simply performed better. One witness watching from a landward vantage point claimed that the American gunners fired two shots for every one of their opponents. When taken along with the extensive damage to the *Saratoga*'s rigging, the result of too high of an aiming point, this seems to lend credence to the poor performance of the British gun crews. More important, the lack of *esprit de corps* demonstrated by the British crews led to them abandoning their posts on the *Chub*, and ultimately on the *Confiance*.

Nowhere however, was this lack of effort more obvious than in the British gunboat flotilla. When the signal was given, only four of the twelve gunboats advanced on the *Ticonderoga*, too few to damage it with their guns, and far too few to attempt to board it. A few boats later advanced on the *Preble*, but even here they made a lackluster showing. Their Canadian militia crews were blamed, although Lt. Raynham's deserting to avoid answering questions in regard to his conduct demonstrated that more than just the militia was at fault. The failure of the gunboat flotilla to seize the *Ticonderoga* has traditionally been overshadowed by the northern portion of the battle, but in retrospect it was a key blow to Captain Downie's plan, and ironically, one of the elements of his overall strategy with a fair chance of success. There were nearly six hundred men in twelve vessels, more than five times the crew of the *Ticonderoga*, with a total number of guns on par with the schooner. A coordinated attack by so many vessels from multiple angles certainly would have called the American warship's fate into question, and with the *Ticonderoga* in British hands early in the battle, the fate of Macdonough's victory as well.

Prevost, seeing the naval battle lost, stunned his commanders and ordered a retreat back to Canada. There would be no more talk of using this avenue to strike at the Americans. Lake Champlain was from that point on, an American lake.[48]

SEVEN

A New Lake

MACDONOUGH'S VICTORY AT CUMBERLAND BAY HAD SECURED Lake Champlain for the American cause, and with little in the way of threats before him the recently promoted Macdonough sent the *Saratoga*, *Ticonderoga*, *Confiance*, and *Linnet* to winter quarters at Skenesborough in mid-October. The remainder of the fleet, consisting of ten gunboats and the sloops *Montgomery*, *Preble*, *Eagle*, and *Growler* (the latter now reverting back to its original name), he kept at Plattsburgh to counter any movements the British gunboats might entertain toward the waterway. By mid-November Macdonough, who was preparing to travel to Washington, D.C., ordered Lt. Charles Budd to move these vessels to Skenesborough as well.

Macdonough would return to Lake Champlain later in December when reports of a British winter expedition aimed at burning the American fleet at Skenesborough surfaced. Measures were instituted to deal with such possibilities, but no attack ever came.[1]

Prevost had entertained thoughts toward a winter expedition on Lake Champlain, but the American forces stationed at Plattsburgh coupled with the limited chances of actually reaching Skenesborough brought an end to the matter. Instead, efforts were focused on rebuilding the British fleet at Ile aux Noix. In January 1815 a contract was signed with master shipbuilder John Goudie for the construction of two brigs and three thirty-six-gun frigates at the island. In addition to these vessels, Goudie was to build eleven new gunboats and a flat-bottomed transport to support fleet operations on the lake.[2]

News of the Peace of Ghent in late February 1815, however, ended hostilities on the lake. For the British the news, just as in 1783, triggered a massive reduction in the Lake Chaplain fleet. Of the twelve recently constructed gunboats, three were launched for sea trials while the rest, including the older ones, were hauled ashore and covered. The forces on Ile aux Noix were reduced as well. The new complement was to be sixty-five sailors to man a handful of gunboats, and sixty-five marines to garrison the fort and man its artillery.[3]

A similar fate befell the American Lake Champlain fleet. The major vessels, the *Confiance*, *Saratoga*, *Eagle*, *Linnet*, and *Ticonderoga*, were stripped of their equipment, covered, and laid up in floating storage along the west bank of the channel just north of Skenesborough. The other larger vessels in the fleet, the converted merchantmen *Preble*, *Montgomery*, *President*, *Chub*, and *Finch* along with all the galleys, went onto the action block in late June 1815. The converted merchantmen all sold quickly, in some cases to their former owners who soon had them back to their original tasks. The four smaller gunboats sold, but the six gunboats built by Noah Brown, all of which were less than a year old, went for such a trifling amount that the new American commander on the lake, Captain James Leonard, did not carry through with the sale. Instead Leonard placed the vessels into storage by sinking them along the banks of the lake at Skenesborough. The galley *Allen* was raised a few years later and patrolled the lake for a time, but even this was short lived.[4]

The major vessels of Macdonough's fleet languished over the intervening years, and in January 1820 the ravages of time claimed the first of them, the *Confiance*. The frigate sank, settling in six feet of water along the bank of the channel. In anticipation of the maritime traffic that would be generated by the opening of the Champlain Canal, the decision was made to move the fleet. The *Ticonderoga, Linnet,* and *Eagle* were moved to the mouth of the Poultney River about a mile north of their old location. The leaky *Saratoga*, which had been converted into a barracks, was towed to the new sight a few months later as was the *Confiance* once it was raised and pumped out. The work made it clear to Captain Leonard that the fleet's days were numbered. "The decay of the vessels on this lake," he wrote the Navy Department on August 29, 1821, "and the consequent increase of leaks, will make it necessary, to either let them go down (as one or two of the smaller vessels already have), or to increase the men for the purpose of freeing them and keeping them afloat. The situation at the present moorings is very suitable, and the hulls are cleared out....The Saratoga which leaks considerably. . . may be placed so as to lodge on the bottom, well merged in water, & continue as quarters without inconvenience."[5]

It soon did not matter. In an effort to cut costs it was agreed to close the naval station at Whitehall, which manned by seventeen officers and men, cost the navy almost $10,000 per year to operate. An 1824 report characterized the vessels stored at Whitehall as "Entirely decayed" and "recommended to dispose of them, break them up, and transport the stores to New York, or dispose of them, as may be most advantageous." The *Confiance* would not even last this long. In July 1824 it shifted into the river's main channel. A navigation hazard, the wreck was hauled off and dismantled.

In June 1825 the remaining vessels were put up for auction under the proviso that the winning bid was also responsible for removing the derelict hulks. After this failed to generate any interest, the vessels were put back on the block without the condition that they be removed from their present location. This time the venture proved successful, and for years to come the remains of Macdonough's fleet proved sporadic work for salvagers, until what was left of them was either hauled away or consumed by the lake.[6]

It was a signal that a new era had come to the lake. In the fall of 1817 work began on a plan to link Whitehall to the Hudson River via a canal. Six years later the Champlain Canal opened to traffic. When the canal boat *Gleaner* passed through the locks to Fort Edward, New York, it ushered in a wave of commerce that washed away any thoughts of the past conflicts. Transportation lines were quickly formed and trade links between the towns on Lake Champlain and points south expanded. With the opening of the Chambly Canal in 1843 there now existed an all-water path from New York harbor to Montreal, further expanding trade connections north toward Canada. Steam vessels also began to ply the waters of the Champlain Valley in greater numbers, serving as passenger vessels, ferries, and later cargo haulers.[7]

A few military precautions still existed on the waterway. The British government undertook building Fort Lennox at Ile aux Noix in 1819. The project lasted ten years, and when it was finished the four-bastioned stone structure housed dozens of heavy cannons and a garrison of several hundred men. The opening of the Chambly Canal and the first railroad lines in the 1840s led to the decline of Fort Lennox. There was a brief rebirth of activity at the fort during the Canadian Rebellion in 1837 and during the American Civil War, but by 1870 the British government had decided to abandon the position.

The United States also built a fortification at Rouses Point near the exit of Lake Champlain. The first fort constructed, and never named, was an eight-sided stone structure started in 1816, and unfortunately due to a surveying error was accidentally built on the Canadian side of the border. The uncompleted fort was quickly abandoned. In 1842 the site of the first fort was ceded to the United States by treaty. Work then began on Fort Montgomery and continued for almost thirty years. When it was finished the stone structure boasted forty-eight-foot walls, a moat, and provisions for up to 125 cannons on three firing levels. Although the fort never held all of its complement of cannons or troops, it was manned until 1926 when the U.S. government sold it at public auction.

What armed vessels there were on Lake Champlain after the War of 1812 were confined to small boats equipped for police and revenue duties, but as fate would have it warships would once more take to the waters of the Champlain Valley. At the outbreak of World War II the Shelburne shipyards, operated by Donovan Contracting Company, won a bid to construct a pair of 110-foot wooden subchasers. Built over the summer of 1942, SC1029 and SC1030 slid into the waters of the lake with a great deal of local fanfare. The quality of workmanship put into the vessels was demonstrated when they were taken out onto the lake during a vicious chop stirred up by a stiff northern wind. The naval inspection staff was duly impressed by how well the subchasers handled the short period seven- to eight-foot waves, which were as punishing as long period thirty-foot swells on the ocean. The Shelburne shipyards would build torpedo lighters and tugboats over the next year and a half before finishing their navy wartime contracts with three more subchasers, SC1504 through SC1506, the last military vessels to ply the lake.[8]

The naval contest for the waters of the Champlain Valley lasted 150 years. Beginning with simple canoes, the struggle culminated in clashes between fleets led by ocean-going-size vessels. In reality these conflicts were better characterized as a series of naval arms

A subchaser on patrol near Cape Cod in August 1944.

races; the byproduct of necessity and the late realization of the strategic value of the waterways. The geography of the region led to natural shipbuilding centers, typically at opposite ends of the waterways to maximize security and to provide a safe anchorage for the fleet in being. In turn, the success of this arrangement hinged on two main elements; intelligence and logistics.

The first of these was crucial. Knowing the opposing fleet's strength not only dictated future shipbuilding efforts, but when to challenge for control of Lake Champlain.

At first, the sparse population of the region coupled with the distances involved led to faulty intelligence, and as a result, costly delays. Both Amherst's and Carleton's campaigns were undermined by this. To be fair, even though both British generals faced a late start, each managed to secure a position at one end of the lake, construct a fleet, and eventually establish British supremacy over the lake. In doing so however, each fell short of achieving the objectives of their respective campaigns.

Their adversaries, Laubaras and Arnold, both succeeded in sacrificing their fleets to obtain a year's respite for their respective causes, but to a large degree, this was only successful due to the faulty intelligence that undermined Amherst and Carleton. Amherst was convinced that the French fleet was larger and more powerful than anticipated, and as such, he delayed his advance down the lake until another sizable warship was completed. It was a miscalculation on both his part and the part of his senior naval officer, Joshua Loring, although one could argue an understandable one. Indeed, as time progressed, knowledge of the enemy's fleet and shipbuilding status became easier and easier to obtain. This was so much the case in the War of 1812 that it would have been difficult to imagine the American and British fleets meeting unless they thought themselves nearly equal.

The second element, logistics, was daunting. The practical considerations of constructing a fleet at the edge of civilization were the greatest obstacles. The physical means to construct the vessels had to be found, or in some cases, put into place. Naval supplies had to be located and transported to the shipyard, as well as shipwrights and carpenters. Defensive measures then had to be erected to protect the facilities. This in turn meant building fortifications and barracks to house the troops assigned to these defenses. All this had to be in place before the vessels were actually constructed and the sailors found to man them.

The task of constructing vessels aside, in the end control of the lake was dictated not by the vessels, but by the sailors aboard them. They were the final arbitrators of the fate of the waterways. From the poorly led and undermanned French fleet, to Arnold's undermanned inexperienced fleet, to the hastily put together crews of Downie's fleet, those who lost control of the waterway shared a common trait, and those who held control of the lake another.

Along Lake Champlain today there are but shadows of the waterway's naval past. Forts such as Ticonderoga, Chambly, and Amherst still remind visitors of the lake's turbulent past. Slowly the wrecks of the vessels from these days are giving up their secrets as well. The *Land Tortoise* and a number of bateaux from the time lie preserved in a hundred feet of water near the headwaters of Lake George, an underwater historic site. The sloop *Boscawen*, partially buried in the mud at Fort Ticonderoga, was examined closely in the 1980s, as have been Macdonough's warships the galley *Allen* and the brig *Eagle*. And recently one of Arnold's missing gondolas, the *Spitfire*, was discovered on the bottom of Lake Champlain. Perhaps the lake is simply reminding the visitors to its shores that it still has tales to tell.[9]

Maps

THE BATTLE OF VALCOUR ISLAND AND THE FLIGHT OF ARNOLD'S
FLEET

There are only a handful of maps detailing the Battle of Valcour Island
and the flight of Arnold's fleet over the next few days. Of these four
are considered, one of which was presented in chapter 4 of this text.
This version is certainly the most widely known map of the battle. It
was made in London, by William Faden, royal geographer to George
III, in late 1776 and was widely distributed as part of the British victory celebration. This map is in accord with the eyewitness testimonies
and reports. Unfortunately, beyond showing the path of Arnold's
escape it provides no further information about the fate of the
American fleet.

Another map that was released at the time was a modified version
of William Brasier's 1762 map of Lake Champlain. The battle at
Valcour Island and the scuttling of Arnold's ships were both added to
this older, but readily available map. The battle and fleet positions
around Valcour Island appear correct, but the portion of the map
detailing the scuttling of a major part of Arnold's fleet is incorrect, in
that Ferris Bay where Arnold burned his vessels is a good 10 miles
north (top of page) from the location pointed to on the map. It seems
likely that this mistake was the byproduct of Brasier's older map not
having detailed the various harbors along the east shore of the lake.

The next map is an anonymous map of Lake Champlain made in
1779. The map clearly shows Arnold scuttling a portion of his fleet at
"Faries" Bay, and the principle elements of the British fleet stationed

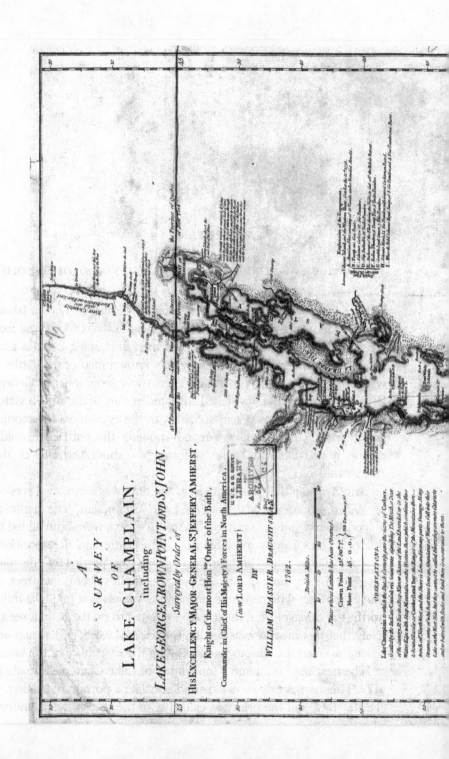

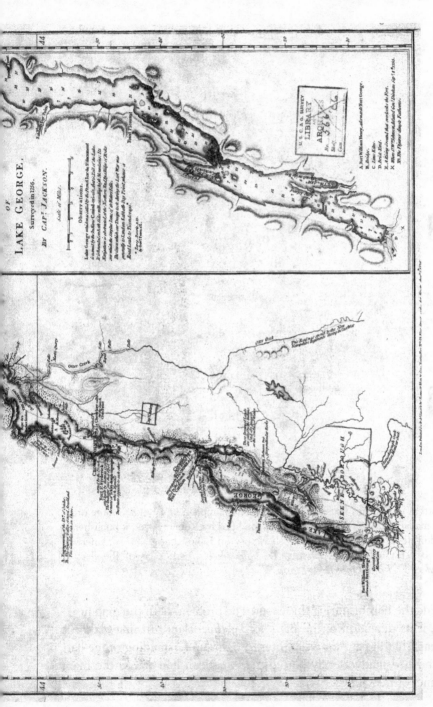

William Brasier's map of Lakes Champlain and George.

A portion of William Brasier's map of Lake Champlain and Lake George origi-
nally made in 1762. This map was later modified by Robert Sayer, a publisher in
London in 1776, to reflect the British victory on Lake Champlain. A. American
Line B. 21 Gunboats C. *Carleton* D. *Inflexible* E. Anchorage of the fleet F.
Thunderer G. *Loyal Convert* H. *Maria*

outside the harbor during this event. The problem with the map however, is its depiction of the Battle of Valcour Island. At first glance it
appears that the author was mistaken in his understanding of the battle and had inadvertently placed the American line across the main
channel of the lake.

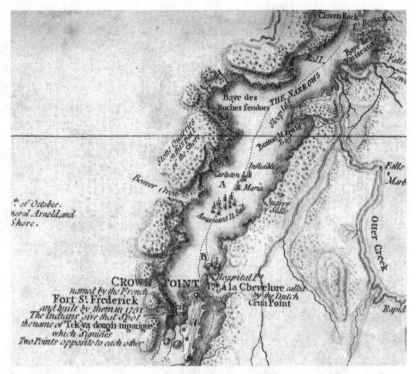

Another portion of Brasier's map showing the flight of Arnold's fleet, and his scuttling of the *Congress* and four gondolas in a small bay near Chimney Point.

Given all the accounts of the battle, such a gross mistake, particularly three years after the engagement, is difficult to believe. What seems more likely is the following; if the reader rotates the vessels on the map 180 degrees, placing the American line between Valcour Island and the west shore of the lake such that the *Royal Savage* is on the southwest point of Valcour Island, the vessel positions are in exact agreement with the eyewitness accounts. Indeed, with this alteration the anonymous map of 1779 proves one of the best diagrams of the Battle of Valcour Island. When viewed in this light it seems possible that the author of the map wanted to preserve the vessels' positions during the battle, but with no room to capture this on the map between Valcour Island and the New York shore, he elected to draw this information in where space permitted; that being the main channel of the lake.

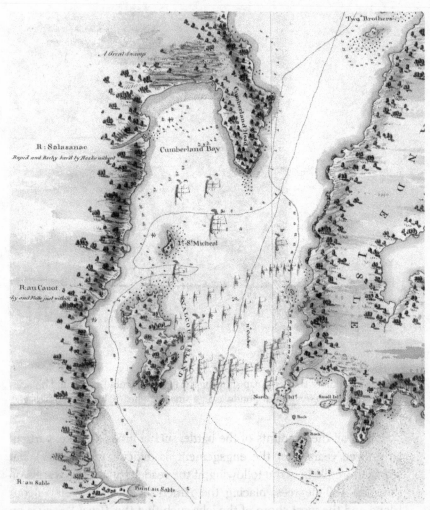

A portion of a 1779 map by an anonymous author showing the Battle of Valcour Island. The layout on the map is deceptive. At first glance it appears that the author has mistakenly placed the engagement in the lake's main channel and not in the channel between Valcour Island and the west (New York) shore of the lake. A. *Carleton* B. *Maria* C. *Royal Savage* D. *Inflexible* E. *Loyal Convert* F. *Thunderer* G. Gunboats.

The last map considered is from Lt. James Hadden who was an eyewitness and commanded a British gunboat during the battle. (Another example of this map can be found accredited to German

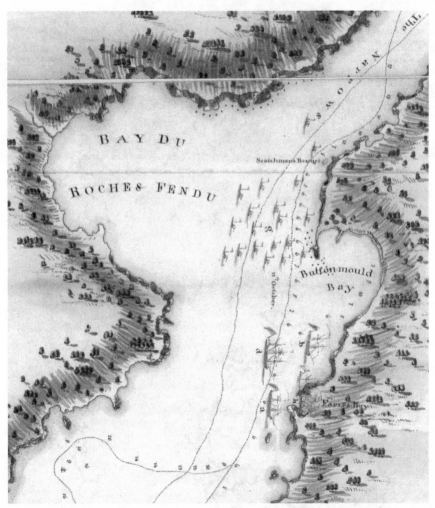

Another portion of an anonymous 1779 map showing Arnold's scuttling of the *Congress* and four gondolas in Faries (Ferris) Bay. A. *Carleton* B. *Maria* D. *Inflexible* G. Gunboats H. *Congress*.

captain Georg Pausch.) Hadden's map only details the Battle of Valcour Island, but it is in complete agreement with the contemporary accounts and the other maps of the battle, if one makes the necessary adjustments to the anonymous map of 1779. What is more interesting is that Hadden marks the position of the British fleet during the night

Lt. James Hadden's map of the Battle of Valcour Island. Hadden, an officer in the royal artillery, kept a journal of Burgoyne's campaign and commanded one of the British gunboats at the Battle of Valcour Island. A. The rebel line B. The line of gunboats C. *Royal Savage* D. Retreat of the rebels in the night. E. Anchored with the boats in the dotted line.

of October 11. This detail is supported by eyewitness accounts, and explains in part how the American fleet managed to slip by the British picket line.

THE BATTLE OF CUMBERLAND BAY

Maps of the Battle of Cumberland Bay are more numerous than those of Valcour Island. A quarter century of growth in the area and the general rise in literacy over the time period has much to do with this. Two of these maps are used in the text. The second of these, entitled "The Battle of Cumberland Bay," shows not only the vessels and their positions during the engagement, but with a bit of artistic license, several of the notable army participants in the foreground. This print was widely distributed as part of the American victory celebrations.

In addition to these maps, several others are presented below. The first is Commodore Macdonough's sketch of the engagement which he made some months after the battle. The map understandably concentrates on the north part of the engagement, which occupied Macdonough's attention. The layout of the American fleet is shown, as well as the position of the *Chub* after it drifted through the American line. The second map presented is from Benjamin Lossing's *Field Book of the War of 1812*. This map appears to represent the battle at its closing stages as shown by the position of the *Eagle* and the flight of the British gunboats. If this is the case however, then there are several inconsistences with the accounts of the battle and the map. Most pronounced is the facing of the *Confiance*, the *Linnet*, and the *Ticonderoga*. The second is the position of the *Preble*, which by its master's report, had let loose its anchor and moved inland for fear that the British gunboats would make an attempt to board it. Interestingly, the map calls out a British supply sloop which is likely the *Icicle*.

The third map is from Cooper's *History of the Navy of the United States*. This four-paneled map shows the approach of the British, the general engagement on both the north and south parts of the American line, and the final positions of the combatants. With the exception of the actual approach path of the *Finch* and the British gunboats, the map is in accordance with the narratives of the event. The next map in the series was widely distributed by naval historian Alfred Thayer Mahan. This map gives a better impression of the dis-

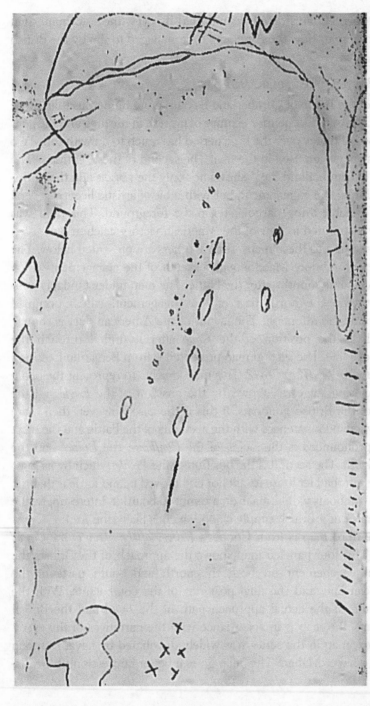

Commodore Macdonough's sketch of the Battle of Cumberland Bay. Understandably, Macdonough's work concentrates on the engagement to the north between the main elements of the two fleets. The diagram shows the *Eagle's* turning maneuver and the *Chub* having drifted through the American lines.

This map from Benjamin Lossing's *Field Book of the War of 1812*, depicts the Battle of Cumberland Bay at the end of the engagement. While the work is generally correct the *Linnet*, *Confiance* (show as *Confidence*), and *Ticonderoga* are shown pointed in the wrong direction, while the *Eagle* after performing her maneuver should be more to the starboard bow of the *Saratoga*.

tance between Crab Island and the southern portion of the American line. It also details the battle between the *Ticonderoga*, *Preble*, *Finch*, and the British gunboat flotilla. The map, and the movements depicted on it, are in complete accord with the testimony of the witnesses.

The last map presented is from a larger print in the Library of Congress. The map, drawn not long after the battle, is clearly incorrect, showing the American fleet too far east and too close to Cumberland Head. The work is of interest however, because unlike the others it details the approach of Captain Downey's fleet.

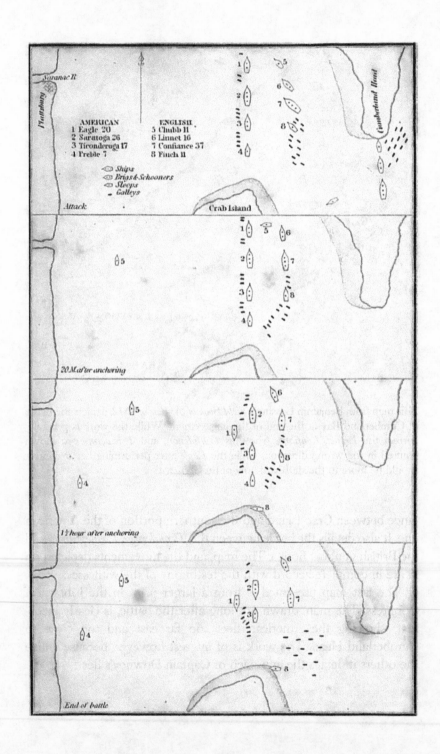

AMERICAN
1 Eagle 20
2 Saratoga 26
3 Ticonderoga 17
4 Preble 7

ENGLISH
5 Chubb 11
6 Linnet 16
7 Confiance 37
8 Finch 11

Ships
Brigs & Schooners
Sloops
Galleys

Attack

Crab Island

20 M after anchoring

1½ hour after anchoring

End of battle

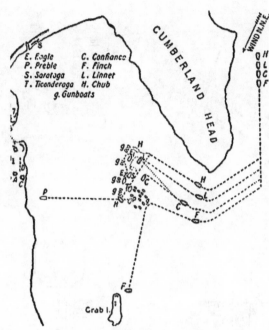

Opposite: The Battle of Cumberland Bay from James F. Cooper's *History of the Navy of the United States.* Cooper shows the engagement in stages from top to bottom. The positioning of the *Chub* is in question but more importantly the battle to the south involving the *Ticonderoga, Preble, Finch,* and the British gunboats is unclear as seen by the third diagram from the top which mistakenly shows the Preble in two locations. Above: A portion of Mahan's map of the Battle of Cumberland Bay. Mahan's work is in direct agreement with the witnesses and testimonials concerning the engagement.

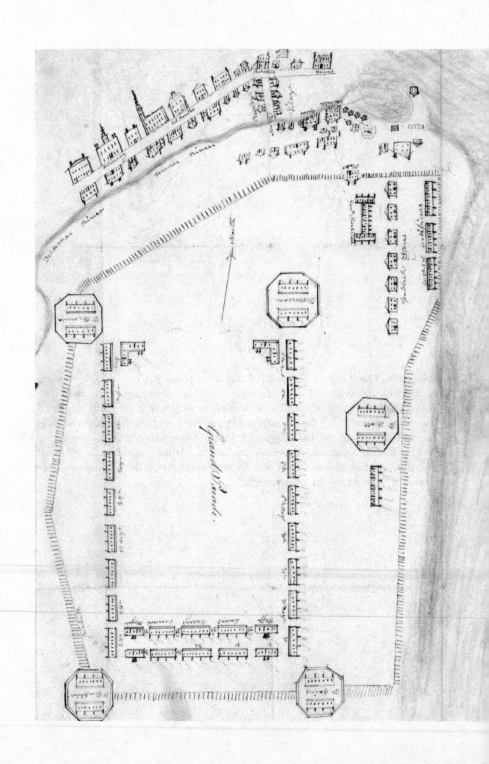

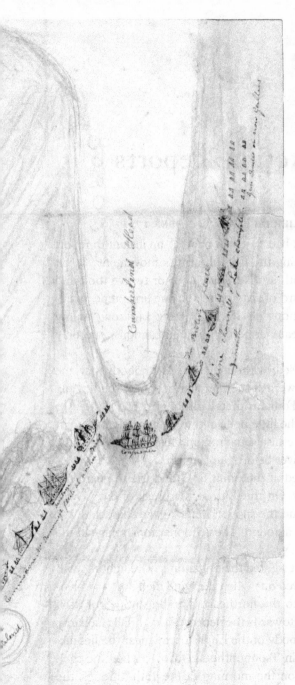

A portion of a manuscript map in the Library of Congress showing the approach of the British fleet and the American line in Cumberland Bay. Although the map shows the American and British too close to Cumberland Head it does raise an interesting question in regards to the British formation. The diagram shows six large British vessels. This would account for the *Confiance, Linnet, Chub,* and *Finch.* The *Icicle* was also present at the battle as well. This leaves the smallest of the six vessels shown unaccounted for, unless this vessel is the captured *Burlington Packet* which was lost by the retreating British near Grand Isle, or the tender *Canada.*

After Action Reports

BOURLAMAQUE TO CHEVALIER DE LEVIS, OCTOBER 17, 1759

17 October 1759. I have not had, my dear general, an instant to report to you until today concerning the English army's movements. It left St. Frederic on the 11th with around ten, eleven or twelve thousand men, preceded by a vanguard of sixty batteaux, one brigantine, twenty pieces of ordnance (canons de 18), one snow as strong as my schooner, and several batteaux armed with large cannons; one only carrying six de 24.

Our xebecs were surprised, without doubt, and nobody saw the vanguard pass them. They were at their regular post near the Iles aux Quatre Vents [now called Four Brothers], although I had written to their commander that, for the little he feared to be attacked, he ought to draw closer together his cruise squadron and his station, because it was essential to enter the river before the English.

The schooner was placed at the point of Grand Isle to guard the entrance to Missisquoi Bay. On the 12th at the break of day, it was greeted by the brigantine and the snow. The first gave chase and was about to take it when it ran aground. The schooner took refuge in the further end of Missisquoi Bay.

The xebecs, who had not sighted the brigantine, were fighting with the batteaux and had captured one when the wind died down suddenly and after that changed to the northeast. The brigantine got itself afloat again and went back towards the xebecs. At nightfall Laubaras, after having seen the main body of the English army near the Iles aux Quatre Vents, took refuge in Tsonnonthouans Cove, where he sank three ships, and marched, on the morning of the 13th, through the woods, having previously dispatched two long boats to warn me of the enemy's advance and give me an account of the prisoners.

The northeast wind, which continued violently for three days, prevented the enemy from approaching here; it could have advanced since yesterday morning and I believe them near the river.

The schooner, which emerged from the northeast of Missisquoi Bay, is opposite the end of Isle La Motte, near the north side, and has been waiting fruitlessly for three days for a southwest wind, the only one which can make [it] sail. The odds are ten to one that it is captured or burned by now. The loss of these ships is a great misfortune for the defense of the river.

I have asked for help from Vaudreuil, having too few men to hope to guard this frontier. I do not know what he will send me. My entrenchments have been finished for some time and I was in search of winter quarters; all is stopped; one must consider what is most urgent. If we are fortunate enough to repel or wear out the enemy, we will do what we can.

Source: H. R. Casgrain, *Lettres de Bourlamaque au Lévis*, 61–63.

JOSHUA LORING TO ROBERT LAMBERT, NOVEMBER 22, 1759

I beg the favor of you to acquaint their Lordships that agreeable to an order I received from his Excellency Major General Amherst, I have built a brigantine capable of carrying 6 and nine pounders, and a sloop of sixteen six pounders, but we have no larger guns here then six pounders, that on the 11th of October last, I received his Excellency's orders to proceed down Lake Champlain in quest of the enemy who had then three sloops carrying eight 4 pounders, and one of them had two brass twelve pounders, and a schooner that had ten 4 pounders, I accordingly sailed at six that evening and at 6 the next morning I saw the schooner standing out from behind an Island under her topsails. Immediately gave chase when she bore away behind two islands got her boats a stand her oars out, and made all the sail she possibly could, we come up with her very fast and expected to be onboard her in ten minutes, but was disappointed by running aground on a bar which extended across from island to island. She drawing less water then we did get over and escaped, we got off in a few hours without any damage to the vessels, at 3 in the afternoon saw three sloops bearing S. the wind then being NBE (north-by-east). Immediately gave chase when the enemy set their topsails, and crowded all the sail they could into a large bay we come up with them very fast & should have been alongside them before dark had not the wind failed, they run one of them on shore in the bottom of the bay, the other two they scuttled and sunk in five fathom water but close to the shore and made off by land to St. Johns they were in such a hurry that they left everything on board, we soon got that off that was run on shore, during this time the schooner got down to Isle aux Noix under the guns on that island, so that it was impossible to get at her, I returned to Crown Point fitted the two sloops in a proper manner for weighting those that was sunk and sent them down, they soon got them up and are now returned with them to this place where I am endeavoring to service them in the best manner I can for the winter, they are new vessels well found, so that we now have the entire command of the lake as the enemy has only that schooner that escaped which I believe will never venture out again. The two vessels I have built here are very fine vessels and sail extremely well we found on board the French sloops thirty six English muskets, 3 blunderbusses, one wall piece, and about two tons of musket balls and 16 thirteen inch shells sundry ten and eight. And about 100 32 pound shot.

For your most obedient & humble servant,

Joshua Loring

Source: "Joshua Loring to Robert Lambert, 22 November 1759," NAC, Admiralty Papers. Vol. 2048.

GENERAL ARNOLD TO GENERAL GATES: SCHUYLER'S ISLAND, OCTOBER 12, 1776

Dear General: Yesterday morning, at eight o'clock, the enemy's fleet, consisting of one ship mounting sixteen guns, one snow mounting the same number, one schooner of fourteen guns, two of twelve, two sloops, a bomb-ketch, and a large vessel (that did not come up), with fifteen or twenty flat-bottomed boats or gondolas, carrying one twelve or eighteen-pounder in their bows, appeared off Cumberland Head. We immediately prepared to receive them. The galleys and Royal Savage were ordered under way: the rest of our fleet lay at an anchor.

At eleven o'clock they ran under the lee of Valcour, and began the attack. The schooner, by some bad management, fell to leeward, and was first attacked; one of her masts was wounded, and her rigging shot away. The Captain thought prudent to run her on the point of Valcour, where all the men were saved. They boarded her, and at night set fire to her. At half past twelve the engagement became general, and very warm. Some of the enemy's ships and all their gondolas beat and rowed up within musket-shot of us. They continued a very hot fire with round and grape-shot until five o'clock, when they thought proper to retire to about six or seven hundred yards distance, and continued the fire till dark. The Congress and Washington have suffered greatly; the latter lost her First Lieutenant killed. Captain and Master wounded. The New-York lost all her officers except the Captain. The Philadelphia was hulled in so many places that she sunk about one hour after the engagement was over. The whole killed and wounded amounted to about sixty. The enemy landed a large number of Indians on the island and each shore, who keep an incessant fire on us, but do little damage. The enemy had, to appearance, upwards of one thousand men in batteaus prepared for boarding. We suffered much for want of seamen and gunners. I was obliged myself to point most of the guns on board the Congress, which I believe did good execution. The Congress received seven shot between wind and water; was hulled a dozen times; had her mainmast wounded in two places, and her yard in one. The Washington was hulled a number of times; her mainmast shot through, and must have a new one. Both vessels are very leaky, and want repairing. On consulting with General Waterbury and Colonel Wigglesworth, it was thought prudent to return to Crown-Point, every vessel's ammunition being nearly three-fourths spent, and the enemy greatly superiour to us in ships and men. At seven o'clock Colonel Wigglesworth, in the Trumbull, got under way; the gondolas and small vessels followed; and the Congress and Washington brought up the rear. The enemy did not attempt to molest us. Most of the fleet is this minute come to an anchor. The wind is small to the southward. The enemy's fleet is under way to leeward, and beating up. As soon as our leaks are stopped, the whole fleet will make the utmost dispatch to Crown-Point, where I beg you will send ammunition, and your further orders for us. On the whole, I think we have had a very fortunate escape, and have great reason to return our humble and hearty thanks to Almighty God for preserving and delivering so many of us from our more than savage enemies.

I am, dear General, your affectionate, humble servant,

B. Arnold.

P. S. I had not moved on board the Congress when the enemy appeared, and lost all my papers and most of my clothes on board the schooner. I wish a dozen batteaus, well manned, could be sent immediately, to tow up the vessels in case of a southerly wind. I cannot, in justice to the officers in the fleet, omit mentioning their spirited conduct during the action. B. A.

Source: American Archives, Series 5, vol. 2, 1038–1039.

GENERAL ARNOLD TO GENERAL SCHUYLER: TICONDEROGA, OCTOBER 15, 1776

Dear General: I make no doubt before this you have received a copy of my letter to General Gates of the 12th instant, dated at Schuyler's Island, advising of an action between our fleet and the enemy the preceding day, in which we lost a schooner and a gondola. We remained no longer at Schuyler's Island than to stop our leaks, and mend the sails of the Washington. At two o'clock, P. M., the 12th, weighed anchor with a fresh breeze to the southward. The enemy's fleet at the same time got under way; our gondola made very little way ahead. In the evening the wind moderated, and we made such progress that at six o'clock next morning we were about off Willsborough, twenty-eight miles from Crown-Point. The enemy's fleet were very little way above Schuyler's Island; the wind breezed up to the southward, so that we gained very little by beating or rowing, at the same time the enemy took a fresh breeze from the northeast, and by the time we had reached Split-Rock, were alongside of us. The Washington and Congress were in the rear, the rest of our fleet were ahead except two gondolas sunk at Schuyler's Island. The Washington galley was in such a shattered condition, and had so many men killed and wounded, she struck to the enemy after receiving a few broadsides. We were then attacked in the Congress galley by a ship mounting twelve eighteen-pounders, a schooner of fourteen sixes, and one of twelve sixes, two under our stern, and one on our broadside, within musket-shot.

They kept up an incessant fire on us for about five glasses, with round and grape-shot, which we returned as briskly. The sails, rigging, and hull of the Congress were shattered and torn in pieces, the First Lieutenant and three men killed, when, to prevent her falling into the enemy's hands, who had seven sail around me, I ran her ashore in a small creek ten miles from Crown-Point, on the east side, when, after saving our small-arms, I set her on fire with four gondolas, with whose crews I reached Crown-Point through the woods that evening, and very luckily escaped the savages, who waylaid the road in two hours after we passed. At four o'clock yesterday morning I reached this place, exceedingly fatigued and unwell, having been without sleep or refreshment for near three days. Of our whole fleet we have saved only two galleys, two small schooners, one gondola, and one sloop. General Waterbury, with one hundred and ten prisoners, were returned by Carleton last night. On board of the Congress we had twenty-odd men killed and wounded. Our whole loss amounts to eighty-odd. The enemy's fleet were last night three miles below Crown-Point; their army is doubtless at their heels. We are busily employed in completing our lines, redoubts, which I am sorry to say are not so forward as I could wish. We have very few heavy cannon, but are mounting every piece we have. It is the opinion of Generals Gates and St. Clair that eight or ten thousand Militia should be immediately sent to our assistance, if they can be spared from below. I am of opinion the enemy will attack us with their fleet and army at the same time. The former is very formidable, a list of which I am favoured with by General Waterbury, and have enclosed. The season is so far advanced, our people are daily growing more healthy. We have about nine thousand effectives, and if properly supported, make no doubt of stopping the career of the enemy. All your letters to me of late have miscarried. I am extremely sorry to hear by General Gates you are unwell. I have sent you by General Waterbury a small box containing all my publick and private papers, and accounts, with a considerable sum of hard and paper money, which beg the favour of your taking care of.

I am, dear General, your most affectionate, humble servant,

B. Arnold.

Source: American Archives, Series 5, vol. 2, 1079–1080.

CAPTAIN THOMAS PRINGLE TO MR. STEPHENS, SECRETARY OF THE ADMIRALTY: ON BOARD THE Maria, OFF CROWN-POINT, OCTOBER 15, 1776

It is with the greatest pleasure that I embrace this opportunity of congratulating their Lordships upon the victory completed the 13th of this month, by his Majesty's fleet under my command, upon Lake Champlain. Upon the 11th I came up with the Rebel fleet, commanded by Benedict Arnold; they were at anchor under the Island Vallcour, and formed a strong line, extending from the island to the west side of the continent. The wind was so unfavourable, that for a considerable time nothing could be brought into action with them but the gun-boats. The Carleton schooner, commanded by Mr. Dacres, who brings their Lordships this, by much perseverance, at last got to their assistance; but as none of the other vessels of the fleet could then get up, I did not think it by any means advisable to continue so partial and unequal a combat; consequently, with the approbation of his Excellency General Carleton, who did me the honour of being on board the Maria, I called off the Carleton and gun-boats, and brought the whole fleet to anchor in a line as near as possible to the Rebels, that their retreat might be cut off; which purpose was however frustrated by the extreme obscurity of the night; and in the morning the Rebels had got a considerable distance from us up the lake. Upon the 13th, I again saw eleven sail of their fleet making off to Crown-Point, who, after a chase of seven hours, I came up with in the Maria, having the Carleton and Inflexible a small distance astern; the rest of the fleet almost out of sight. The action began at twelve o'clock, and lasted two hours, at which time Arnold, in the Congress galley, and five gondolas ran on shore, and were directly abandoned and blown up by the enemy, a circumstance they were greatly favoured in by the wind being off shore, and the narrowness of the lake. The Washington galley struck during the action, and the rest made their escape to Ticonderoga. The killed and wounded in his Majesty's fleet, including the artillery in the gun-boats, do not amount to forty; but from every information I have yet got, the loss of the enemy must indeed be very considerable. Many particulars which their Lordships may wish to know I must at present take the liberty of referring you to Mr. Dacres for; but as I am well convinced his modesty will not permit him to say how great a share he had in this victory, give me leave to assure you that during both actions nothing could be more pointedly good than his conduct. I must also do the justice the officers and seamen of this fleet merit, by saying that every person under my command exerted themselves to act up to the character of British seamen.

Source: *American Archives*, Series 5, vol. 2, 1069–1070.

GOVERNOR SIR GUY CARLETON TO LIEUTENANT GENERAL JOHN BURGOYNE: ON BOARD THE Maria OFF ISLE VALCOUR OCTOBER [OCTOBER 12 TO OCTOBER 15]

Sir,

We found the Rebel fleet Yesterday morning behind the Island of Valcour apparently, and as we hear since from Prisoners, unaprized either of our force or motions. One of their Vessells perceived us only a little before we came abreast of the Island, and our van got to the Southward of it time enough to stop them just as they were making off. They then worked back into the narrow part of the passage between the Island and main, where they anchored in a line. Their principal vessell, the *Royal Savage*, one of the first endeavouring to get out, in her confusion, upon finding our ships before her, ran upon the south end of the Island, and our Gun boats got possession of her. Upon finding she could not get off she was afterwards set fire to, and she blew up. Her crew except Twenty who were made prisoners, got on shore. After we had, in this manner, got beyond the enemy and cut them off, the wind which had been favourable to bring us there, - however entirely prevented our being able to bring our whole force to engage them, as we had a narrow passage to work up, Ship by Ship, exposed to the fire of their whole line. The Gun boats and *Carleton* only got up, and they sustained every unequal cannonade of several hours, and were obliged to be ordered to fall back, upon our finding that the rest of the fleet could not be brought up to support them. We then Anchored in a line opposite the Rebels within the distance of Cannon shot, expecting in the morning to be able to engage them with our whole fleet, but, to our great mortification we perceived at day break, that they had found means to escape us unobserved by any of our guard boats or cruizers, thus an opportunity of destroying the whole rebel naval force, at one stroke, was lost, first by an impossibil-

ity of bringing all our vessels to action, and afterwards by the great diligence used by the enemy in getting away from us. We have been attempting to get up with part of them, which is still in our sight, this morning, but the wind blowing very strong from the southward we have been obliged to give over the chace for the present: The Enemy however is retarded as well as us. We have had one Gun boat which was served by the Hessian Artillery, sunk; and about thirty men sailors and Artillery have been killed and wounded. 14th Octor just as I had finished the above, and I could not but be very dissatisfied, the wind sprung up fair and enabled us, after a long chase, Yesterday to get up to the Rebels, and, in our second action, we have been, much more successfull; only three of their Vessels, as you will see by the list enclosed having escaped. Their second in command Mr [David] Waterbury struck to us in the *Washington* Galley, But Arnold run that he was on board of on shore, and set fire to her and several others of his Vessels. This success cannot be deemed less than a compleat victory; but considering it was obtained over the kings subjects, that, which in other circumstances ought to be a proper cause of publick rejoicing, is, in these, matter only of great concern; and therefore tho' it may be right to communicate it to the Troops, yet I dare say they think with me, that we should suppress all signs of triumph on the occation. The Rebels upon the approach of the shattered little remains of their fleet, set fire to all the buildings in and about Crown Point, abandoning the place and retired precipitately to Ticonderoga. The sooner Frasers Brigade with all the matter I wrote about yesterday arrive the better; I shall then be able to see what is to be done.
I am &c
Guy Carleton
Source: *Naval Documents of the American Revolution*, vol. 6, 1272–1274.

COMMODORE THOMAS MACDONOUGH TO SECRETARY OF THE NAVY WILLIAM JONES: U.S.S. Saratoga, PLATTSBURGH BAY, SEPTEMBER 13, 1814
SIR,
I have the honour to give you the particulars of the action which took place on the 11th instant, on this lake. For several days, the enemy were on their way to Plattsburgh by land and water, and it being well

understood that an attack would be made at the same time, by their land and naval forces, I determined to await, at anchor, the approach of the latter. At eight A. M. the look-out boat announced the approach of the enemy. At nine, he anchored in a line ahead, at about 300 yards distance from my line; his ship opposed the Saratoga, his brig to the Eagle, captain Robert Henley; his gallies, thirteen in number, to the schooner, sloop, and a division of our gallies; one of his sloops assisting their ship and brig, the other assisting their gallies. Our remaining gallies with the Saratoga and Eagle. In this situation, the whole force on both sides, became engaged, the Saratoga suffering much, from the heavy fire of the Confiance. I could perceive at the same time, however, that our fire was very destructive to her. The Ticonderoga, lieutenant commandant Cassin, gallantly sustained her full share of the action. At half past 10 o clock, the Eagle not being able to bring her guns to bear, cut her cable, and anchored in a more eligible position, between my ship and the Ticonderoga, where she very much annoyed the enemy, but unfortunately, leaving me exposed to a galling fire from the enemy's brig. Our guns on the starboard side being nearly all dismounted, or not manageable, a stern anchor was let go, the bower cut, and the ship winded with a fresh broadside on the enemy s ship, which soon after surrendered. Our broadside was then sprung to bear on the Brig, which surrendered in about 15 minutes after. The sloop that was opposed to the Eagle, had struck some time before, and drifted down the line; the sloop which was with their gallies having struck also. Three of their gallies are said to be sunk, the others pulled off. Our gallies were about obeying with alacrity, the signal to follow them, when all the vessels were reported to me to be in a sinking state; it then became necessary to annul the signal to the gallies, and order their men to the pumps. I could only look at the enemy's gallies going off in a shattered condition, for there was not a mast in either squadron that could stand to make sail on; the lower rigging being nearly shot away, hung down as though it had been just placed over mast heads. The Saratoga had 55 round shot in her hull, the Confiance 105; The enemy's shot passed principally just over our heads, as there were not 20 whole hammocks in the nettings at the close of the action, which lasted, without intermission, two hours and twenty minutes. The absence and sickness of lieutenant Raymond

Perry, left me without the services of that excellent officer; much ought fairly to be attributed to him for his great care and attention in disciplining the ship's crew, as her first lieutenant. His place was filled by a gallant young officer, Leutenent Peter Gamble, who I regret to inform you, was killed early in the action. Acting lieutenant Vallette worked the 1st and 2d division of guns with able effect. Sailing master Brum's attention to the springs, and in the execution of the order to wind the ship, and occasionally at the guns, met my entire approbation: also captain Youngs, commanding the acting marines, who took his men to the guns. Mr Beaie, purser, was of great service at the guns, and in carrying my orders throughout the ship, with midshipmen Montgomery. Master' s mate, Joshua Justin, had command of the 3d division; his conduct during the action, was that of a brave officer. Midshipmen Monteath, Graham, Williamson, Platt, Thawing, and acting midshipman Baldwin, all behaved well, and gave evidence of their making valuable officers. The Saratoga was twice set on fire, by hot shot from the enemy's ship. I close, sir, this communication, with feelings of gratitude, for the able support I received from every officer and man attached to the squadron which I have the honour to command.

I have the honour to be, &c.

T. MACDONOUGH

Source: John Brannan (ed.), *Official Letters of the Military and Naval Officers of the United States during the war with Great Britain in the Years 1812, 13, 14, & 15.* Washington, 1823.

COMMANDER DANIEL PRING, R.N. TO COMMODORE SIR JAMES L. YEO, R.N.

United States Ship *Saratoga*

Plattsburg Bay, Lake Champlain

12th September 1814.

Sir,

The painful task of making you acquainted with the circumstances attending the capture of His Majesty's Squadron yesterday, by that of the American under Commodore McDonough, it greaves me to state, becomes my duty to perform, from the ever to be lamented loss of that worthy and gallant Officer Captain Downie who unfortunately fell early in the Action. In consequence of the earnest Solicitation of His Excellency Sir George Prevost, for the Co-operation of the Naval Force on this Lake, to attack that of the Enemy, who were placed for the support of their Works at Plattsburg, which it was proposed should be Stormed by the Troops at the same moment the Naval Action should commence in the Bay, Every possible Exertion was used to accelerate the Armament of the New Ship, that the Military movements might not be postponed at such an advanced Season of the Year-longer than was absolutely necessary. On the 3d Inst I was directed to proceed in Command of the Flotilla of Gun Boats to protect the left Flank of our Army advancing towards Plattsburg and on the following day, after taking possession and paroling the Militia of Isle la Motte, I caused a Battery of 3 Long 18 Pounder Guns to be constructed for the support of our position abreast of little Chazy where the supplies for the Army were ordered to be landed. The Fleet came up on the 8th Instant but for want of Stores for the Equipment of the Guns could not move forward until the 11th- At daylight we weighed and at 7 were in full view of the Enemy's Fleet, consisting of a Ship, Brig, Schooner and one Sloop, moored in line, abreast of their encampment, with a Division of 5 Gun Boats on Each Flank;- at 7.40 after the Officers Commanding Vessels and the Flotilla had received their final instructions, as to the plan of attack; we made sail in order of Battle, Capt. Downie had determined on laying his Ship athwart hawse of the Enemy's, directing Lieut. McGhee of the *Chub* to support me in the *Linnet*, in engaging the Brig to the right, and Lieut. Hicks of the *Finch* with the flotilla of Gun Boats, to attack the Schooner & Sloop on the left of the Enemy's line. At 8 the Enemy's Gun Boats and smaller Vessels commenced a heavy and galling fire on our Line, at 8.10 the *Confiance* having two Anchors shot away from her Larboard Bow, And the wind baffling was obliged to anchor (though not in the situation proposed) within two Cables length of her Adversary. The *Linnet* and *Chub* soon afterwards took their allotted Stations, something short of that distance, when the Crews on both sides cheered and commenced a spirited and close Action, a Short time however deprived me of the valuable services of Lieutenant McGhee who, from having his Cables, Bowsprit and Main Boom shot away drifted within the Enemy's line and was obliged to surrender. From the light airs and the smoothness of the water, the Fire on each side proved very destructive from the commencement of the Engagement, and with the Exception of the Brig, that of the Enemy, appeared united against the *Confiance*. After two hours severe Conflict with our opponent; she cut her cable, run down, and took Shelter between the Ship and Schooner which enabled us to direct our fire against the Division of the Enemy's Gun Boats, and Ship, which had so long annoyed us, during our close Engagement with the Brig, without any return on our part: At this time, the fire of the Enemy's Ship slackened considerably, having several of her Guns dismounted-when she cut her Cable, and winded her Larboard Broadside to bear on the *Confiance* who, in vain endeavoured to effect the same Operation, at 10.30 I was much distressed to observe the *Confiance* had struck her Colours- The whole attention of the Enemy's Force then became directed towards the *Linnet*, the shattered and disable state of the Masts sails, rigging and Yards, precluded the most distant hope of being able to effect an Escape by cutting the Cable, the result of doing so, must in a few minutes have been her drifting alongside the Enemy's Vessels, Close under our Lee-but in little hope that the Flotilla of Gun Boats who had abandoned the object assigned them would perceive our wants and come to our assistance, which would afford a reasonable prospect of being towed clear, I determined to resist the then destructive Cannonading of the whole of the Enemy's Fleet, and at the same time dispatched Lieutenant W. Drew to ascertain the state of the *Confiance*. At 10.45 I was apprized of the irreparable loss she had sustained by the Death of her brave Commander (whose merits it would be presumption in me to Extol) as well as the great Slaughter which had taken place on board, and observing from the Manoeuvres of the Flotilla, that I could enjoy no further expectation of relief; the situation of my gallant Comrades, who had so nobly fought, and even now fast falling by my side, demanded the surrender of His Majesty's Brig entrusted to my Command, to prevent a useless waste of valuable lives, and, at the request of the surviving Officers & Men, I gave the painful orders for the Colours to be Struck. Lieutenant Hicks of the *Finch* had the Mortification to strike on a reef of Rocks, to the Eastward of Crab Island, about the Middle of the Engagement; which prevented his rendering that assistance to the Squadron that might from an Officer of such ability have been expected. The misfortune which this day befell us by Capture, will, Sir I trust Apologize for the lengthy detail, which injustice to the Sufferers, I have deemed it necessary to give of the particulars which led to it; And when it is taken into consideration that the *Confiance* was Sixteen days before, on the Stocks, with an unorganized Crew, comprized of several Drafts of Men; who had recently arrived from different ships at Quebec, many of whom only joined the day before, and were totally unknown either to the Officers or to each other, with the want of Gun Locks as well as other necessary appointments, not to be procured in this Country; I trust you will feel satisfied of the decided advantage the Enemy possessed, Exclusive of their great superiority in point of force, a comparative Statement of which I have the honor to annex.- It now becomes the most pleasing part of my present duty, to notice to you, the determined skill and bravery of the Officers and men in this unequal Contest, but it grieves me to State, that the loss sustained in Maintaining it, has been so great; that of the Enemy, I understand amounts to something more than the same number.- The fine style in which Captain Downie conducted the Squadron into Action admidst a tremendous fire, without returning a Shot, until secured, reflects the greatest credit to his Memory, for his judgment and coolness as also on Lieuts. McGhee & Hicks so strictly attending to his Example and instructions, their own accounts of the Capture of their respective Vessels, as well as that of Lieutenant Robertson, who succeeded to the Command of the *Confiance*, will, I feel assured, do ample Justice to the Merits of the Officers and Men serving under their immediate Command, but I cannot omit noticing the individual Conduct of Lieutenants Robertson, Creswick and Hornby, and Mr. Bryden Master, for their particular Exertion in Endeavouring to bring the *Confiance's* Starboard side to bear on the Enemy, after most of their guns were dismounted on the other. It is impossible for me to Express to you, my Admiration of the Officers and Crew serving under my personal Orders, their coolness and steadiness, the effect of which was proved by their irresistible fire, directed towards the Brig opposed to us, claims my warmest acknowledgements, but more particularly for preserving the same, so long after the whole strength of the Enemy had been directed against the

Linnet alone, my 1st Lieutenant Mr. William Drew, whose merits I have before had the honor to report to you, behaved on this occasion in the most exemplary manner. By the death of Mr. Paul, Acting 2nd Lieutenant the Service has been deprived of a most Valuable and brave Officer, he fell early in the Action, Great Credit is due to Mr. Giles, Purser, for Volunteering his Services on deck, to Mr. Mitchell, surgeon for the Skill he evinced in performing some amputations required at the moment as well as his great attention to the Wounded during the Action, at the close of which the Water was nearly a foot above the lower Deck, from the number of shot which struck her, between Wind and Water.- I have to regret the loss of the Boatswain Mr. Jackson, who was killed a few minutes before the Action terminated. The assistance I received from Mr. Muckle the Gunner and also from Mr. Clarke, Master's Mate, Messrs. Fouke and Sinclair, Midshipmen, the latter of whom was wounded on the head and Mr. Guy my Clerk, will, I hope, recommend them, as well as the whole of my gallant little Crew, to Your Notice. I have much Satisfaction in making you acquainted with the humane treatment the wounded have received from Commodore McDonogh. They were immediately removed to his own Hospital on Crab Island, and were furnished with every requisite. His generous and polite attention also to myself, the Officers and Men, will ever hereafter be gratefully remembered. Enclosed I beg leave to transmit you the statement of the different Commanding Officers of Vessels relative to the circumstances attending their capture, also the Return of killed & Wounded, and I have honor to be [&c.]

(Signed) Dan. Pring

Captain

late of H.M. Sloop *Linnett*

Source: Wood, *Select British Documents*, vol. 3, 368–373.

Ship Types

Ships were typically referred to by their rigging type, or primary propulsion type as in the case of a radeau or galley. Warships, however, under the British rating system were also officially classified by number of gun decks, number of guns, and size regardless of their sail plan. This rating system is shown below.

Type	Rating	Guns	Gun Decks	Men	Tonnage
Ship-of-the-Line	1st	100 to 120	3	850–875	2,500
	2nd	90 to 98	3	700–750	2,200
	3rd	64 to 80	2	500–650	1,750
	4th	50 to 60	2	320–420	1,000
Frigate	5th	32 to 44	1	200–300	700–1,450
	6th	24 to 28	1	140–200	340–450
Sloop-of-War	none	16 to 18	1	90–125	380
Brig, Sloop, Cutter, or Schooner	none	4 to 14	1	20–90	220 or less

The Fleets

THE FRENCH LAKE CHAMPLAIN FLEET 1742–1760

OVERVIEW

The French Lake Champlain Fleet 1759–1760

Vessel	Crew	Gun Complement (lb)					Totals
		18	12	9	4	2	
Vigilante	30				10		10
Brochette	50				6		6
Esturgeon	50				6		6
Musquelongy	50		2		8		10
Grand Diable	60	3					3
Little One	45				4		4
Gabare	10					4	4
Jacobs[a]	90			6			6
Totals							
Crew[b]	385						
Guns		3	2	6	34	4	49
Metal weight (lb)		54	24	54	136	8	276

a. Reports also exist claiming that the "Jacobs" carried 12 pounders or 11 pounders.

b. Bourlamaque gives the total crew complement of the *Vigilante*, *Brochette*, *Esturgeon*, and *Musquelongy* as 82 sailors and 96 regulars or militia acting as marines. In contrast Bougainville gives his naval personnel as 37 sailors and marine officers at the siege of Ile aux Noix. Although detachments of regulars and volunteers were used to supplement this force, it is clear that Bougainville's fleet was severely undermanned. While in British service Loring listed the wartime crew complement for the three xebecs as 30 sailors and 20 marines.

Sources: Casgrain, *Bourlamaque Letters*, 17; Casgrain, *Lettres de Divers Particuliers*, 147; "Loring to Amherst, 23 Feb. 1760," WO34/64; "Return of Guns, Ammunition & Stores, found on board the Three French Sloops, taken on Lake Champlain," CO5/57; *Knox Journal*, II, 140; *The Journal of Jeffery Amherst*, 157; "News from America," *London Magazine*, Dec. 1759 reprinted in *FTMB*, VI, no. 33 (Jan. 1942), 108–111.

VESSELS

Name: *Vigilante*
Nationality: French
Type: Topsail Schooner
Launched: 1757
Place: St. Jean (St. Johns)
Armament: 10 x 4 pdrs
Crew: 30
Background: Constructed by French colonial shipbuilder René-Nicolas Levasseur, the 70-ton *Vigilante* was the largest vessel in the French Lake Champlain fleet. Commanded by lake veteran Joseph Payan *dit* St. Onge, the *Vigilante*'s primary task was to keep Forts St. Frédéric and Carillon supplied. Given that it was not employed as a warship its crew complement was kept down to a dozen or so, although this was later increased when English operations on the lake and at Ile aux Noix placed the vessel at more risk. Having only fired its guns in self-defense a few times during its short life, the *Vigilante* and its crew were captured at the siege of Ile aux Noix in 1760. The topsail schooner served briefly under a British flag in the years following the conclusion of the last French and Indian War, but unnecessary, and unable to deal with the expenses surrounding its upkeep, its new owners allowed it to decay until it was eventually consumed by the lake a few years later.

Sources: "List of the Vessels on the Different Lakes . . . November, 1762," WO34/65; Gabriel de Maurès, de Malartic, *Journal des campagnes au Canada de 1755 à 1760 par le comte de Maurès de Malartic* (Paris: E. Plon, Nourrit, et Cie, 1890), 108; Levasseur to Minister, 1 November 1756 and 1 November 1757, NAC, MG1-C11A, vol. 101, fol. 318–319 and vol. 102, fol. 223–224.

Name: *Brochette, Esturgeon,* and *Musquelongy*
Nationality: French
Type: Xebec
Launched: 1759
Place: St. Jean (St. Johns)
Armament: *Brochette* and *Esturgeon,* 6 x 4 pdrs; *Musquelongy,* 2 x 12 pdrs, 8 x 4 pdrs
Crew: 50
History: The fifty- to sixty-foot *Brochette, Esturgeon,* and *Musquelongy* were built over the winter of 1758 and spring of 1759 by Pierre Levasseur, the son of colonial shipbuilder René-Nicolas Levasseur. The selection of the vessel type is odd, and although often referred to as xebecs, contemporary accounts point to a hybrid vessel known as a polacre-xebec, where a square main sail and small topsail are flown on the main mast while the other two masts carried the traditional lateen sails associated with a standard xebec. In any case, the trio of vessels proved to be poor sailers and without accommodations for oars, difficult to navigate amidst the confines of the Richelieu River, making them vulnerable to attack whenever they operated in this waterway. Even the vessels' armament was a compromise. René-Nicolas Levasseur wrote that he had intended to mount six four-pound cannon and two twelve-pound brass cannon on each, but although such guns were difficult to come by in war-weary New France, questions as to the vessels' ability to handle heavy guns may also be one explanation. A fourth vessel was planned, but was later abandoned when General Charles Bourlamaque confiscated the completed hull and transformed it into a floating battery to guard the west channel of Ile aux Noix. The *Brochette, Esturgeon,* and *Musquelongy* were all raised and incorporated into the British fleet after being scuttled by their crews in October 1759. The *Brochette* and *Esturgeon* were used sporadically by the British after the conclusion of hostilities under the names *Brochet* and *La Chigan.* In constant need of repairs, the pair were eventually abandoned to the lake sometime after 1767. Ironically, the French flagship *Musquelongy* was the last operating vessel from the French and Indian War. The vessel underwent a major overhaul in 1765 to replace its rotting deck and upper works, and in 1767 John Blackburn, an English merchant, entered into a contract

A ten gun xebec entering a Mediterranean port.

with the army to use this vessel to maintain the supply routes between the posts on Lake Champlain and the upper Richelieu River. It continued to see use until 1771, when it was deemed so unfit that the seventy-ton sloop *Betsy* was built at Fort St. Johns to replace her. Sometime later that year, the crew of the *Musquelongy* stripped it of anything valuable and scuttled it, making it one of a handful of warships in history to be intentionally sunk by two different nations.

Sources: "Return of Guns, Ammunition & Stores, found on board the Three French Sloops, taken on Lake Champlain," CO5/57; "List of the Vessels on the Different Lakes . . . November, 1762," WO34/65; "Contract between John Blackburn and Lords of Treasury, 5 May 1767," NAC, Haldimand Papers, B27; Carter, *Correspondence of General Thomas Gage*, 1:258, 301, 2:427, 466; "Burton to Gage, 2 May 1765," Gage Papers, vol. 35, William Clements Library; *The Journal of Jeffery Amherst*, 156–157, 182–185, 191–192.

Name: *Grand Diable*
Nationality: French
Type: Tartane/Row Galley
Launched: 1760

Place: St. Jean (St. Johns)
Armament: 3 x 18 pdrs (two in prow and one firing astern)
Crew: 60
History: French sources refer to the *Grand Diable* as a tartane, as it no doubt carried a rig that bore a close resemblance to the type of vessel commonly encountered in Mediterranean seaports. But in essence, the *Grand Diable* was a row galley, employing between forty and sixty oars according to contemporary accounts. The reliance on oar power versus sail power was no doubt dictated by the loss of French naval control on Lake Champlain, which confined the *Grand Diable*'s operations to the Richelieu River, where oar power was far more useful and reliable. It carried a large crew, not only to man the oars, but to protect itself from being boarded in the narrow riverway, and although no mention is made of it, the vessel likely carried a large number of swivel guns to augment its firepower. The *Grand Diable* was captured after a brief fight at Ile aux Noix in 1760, and was pressed into British service shortly thereafter, tasked with carrying supplies first from Ticonderoga to Ile aux Noix, and then from Fort Ticonderoga to the newly constructed Fort Amherst at Crown Point. British commander-in-chief General Jeffery Amherst, who sailed on the *Grand Diable* from Crown Point to Ticonderoga in the fall of 1760, was not impressed by the craft, saying, "I think it not near so good as our Row Galleys." On the night of October 22, 1761, loaded down with 150 barrels of flour, the *Grand Diable* tripped its anchor in a gale and staved its hull in against the rocks near Crown Point.

Sources: *The Journal of Jeffery Amherst*, 261–262; Col. John Young to Amherst, 23 October 1761, WO34/51; Haviland to Amherst, 17 November 1760 and 4 June 1761, ibid.; Elliot to Amherst, 21 November 1761, ibid.

Name: *Little One*
Nationality: French
Type: Tartane/Row Galley
Launched: 1759
Place: St. Jean (St. Johns)
Armament: 4 x 4 pdrs
Crew: 35
History: The *Little One*, as it was simply referred to, was a smaller ver-

sion of the *Grand Diable* designed to employ twenty-four oars and a small tartan sail arrangement. Like its larger cousin it was captured at the siege of Ile aux Noix and was soon pressed into transport duties by the British for the next few years. With the war's official conclusion in 1763, however, and the reduced garrisons that followed, it quickly outlived its usefulness and was allowed to decay until it eventually sank or was broken up.

Sources: Examination of Prisoners aboard the *Duke of Cumberland*, 20 June 1760, WO34/51; Charbonneau, *Fortifications of Île aux Noix*, 331–336; *Pennsylvania Gazette*, 11 September 1760.

Name: Unnamed gabare
Nationality: French
Type: Sailing Barge
Displacement: 30 tons
Launched: 1758
Place: St. Jean (St. Johns)
Armament: Four small cannon probably 1 to 2 pdrs
Crew: 8–10
History: This vessel was probably similar in size to an early vessel constructed on the lake which would place it somewhere around fifty feet in length and displacing some thirty-five tons. It was an unwieldy box-like vessel which the British would classify as a radeau, and today would be called a sailing barge. It was a fair-weather sailer, likely employing a single square sail, but appears to have been put to good use on the lake first in supplying Forts St. Frédéric and Carillon, and then in ferrying Bourlamaque's retreating garrisons north in 1759. It was captured at the siege of Ile aux Noix and was quickly pressed into transport duties by the British. From there, however, there are no more records of it actually being employed, implying that it either was broken up or found a home beneath the cold lake waters.

Sources: Malartic, *Journal*, 114, 117, 195; Abbé Charles-Nicolas Gabriel, *Le Maréchal de camp Desandrouins, 1729–1972*, 2 vols. (Verdun: Renvé-Lallement, 1887), 1:286.

Name: *Jacobs*
Nationality: French

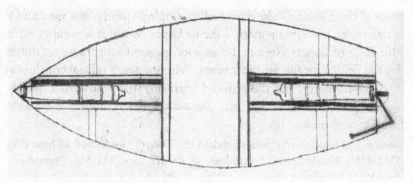

The French gunboat *Jacobs*.

Type: Gunboat
Displacement: 1 to 4 tons
Launched: 1757–1760
Place: various
Armament: 1 x 9 pdr or 1 x 12 pdr, mounted on prow and 1 to 2 swivel guns.
Crew: 15–18
Background: These vessels were basically fifteen- to twenty-foot bateaux modified to accept a forward-firing cannon, and often equipped with a swivel gun or two on their stern. Lieutenant Louis-Thomas Jacau de Fiedmont of the French Royal Artillery is credited with their creation and hence the vessels were referred to as "Jacobs" in his honor. A French deserter reported in August 1758 that there were "six ten oared boats each carrying a 12 ponder in their bow" at the outlet of Lake George. These gunboats had escorted Montcalm's army south during the siege of Fort William Henry in 1757, before being carried back over to Lake Champlain later that year. The "Jacobs" were employed in escort and reconnaissance duties over the last few years of the French and Indian War. The vessels proved useful in this role, particularly when it came to operations along the Richelieu River during these years, but burdened by their main armament their operations were subject to the will of the weather, reducing their overall effectiveness.

Sources: Charbonneau, *The Fortifications of Ile aux Noix*, 335–336; "Deposition of Charles de Lorme," 31 Aug, 1758, WO34/75; *Pouchot Journal*, 291–292.

THE BRITISH LAKE GEORGE AND LAKE CHAMPLAIN FLEETS, 1758–1760

OVERVIEW

The British Lake George Fleet 1759–1760

Vessel	Crew	Gun Complement (lb)				Totals
		24	12	6	4	
Land Tortiose[a]	100			7		7
Earl of Halifax	100			8	6	14
Invincible	100	6				6
Totals						
Crew	300					
Guns		6		15	6	27
Metal weight (lb)		144		90	36	270

The British Lake Champlain Fleet 1759–1760

Vessel	Crew	Gun Complement (lb)				Totals
		24	12	6	4	
Ligonier[b]	50	6				6
Boscawen	112			4	12	16
Duke of Cumberland	132			6	12	18
3 Gunboats	45		3			3
Totals						
Crew	339					
Guns		6	3	10	24	43
Metal weight (lb)		144	36	60	96	336

a. The *Land Tortoise*'s guns were never installed aboard her. Its crew was large enough to handle a variety of guns. For lack of any evidence the author has listed the armament as 7 six-pounders. Built in the fall of 1758 the *Land Tortoise* was purposely sunk not long after it was launched. It could not be recovered the next year and still lies at the bottom of Lake George.
b. At least three other smaller radeaus were built during the summer of 1760, although it is unclear how or if all of these vessels were armed. At least one of these unnamed craft did mount guns and was damaged in the opening shots of the siege of Ile aux Noix. In addition to the vessels shown above, the British fleet also employed the captured French xebecs *Brochette*, *Esturgeon*, and *Musquelongy* during the campaign of 1760.

Sources: *The Journal of Jeffery Amherst*, 158, 174, 179–180; "List of the Vessels on the Different Lakes . . . November, 1762," WO34/65; "Loring to Amherst, 23 Feb. 1760," WO34/64.

VESSELS

Name: *Land Tortoise*
Nationality: British
Type: Radeau
Launched: 1758
Place: Fort George
Armament: 7 guns
Crew: 100
History: The *Land Tortoise* was a 52-foot-long, 18-foot-wide radeau built by Captain Samuel Cobb in the late summer of 1758. The vessel employed 26 oars and offset gun positions on both sides, although no guns were ever placed on it. In the fall of 1758, not long after it was commissioned, the vessel was sunk for the winter to prevent French raiders from burning it. When the British army returned to Lake George the following spring, the *Land Tortoise* and the sloop *Halifax* would be raised, pumped out, and refloated. Unfortunately Loring had inadvertently sunk the *Land Tortoise* in 105 feet of water, making any recovery out of the question. Henry Champion, a Connecticut captain, left an account of this unusual vessel in his October 7, 1758, journal entry.

> A large floaty thing has been building about three weeks, looks as if it would be done in one week more. It is 51 feet in length, about 16 or 18 wide, straight flat bottom, flaring waist about 5 feet high, then turns with an elbow or timber and covers over ye top all but a streak about 8 or 9 feet wide, ye sides and ends are according to this plan. . . . The outside planck 4 inches thick, ye ceiling 3 inches ditto.

Sources: *Champion Genealogy*, 431; Cobb's Journal, 117–121; Glasier's Journal, 81.

Name: *Earl of Halifax*
Nationality: British
Type: Sloop
Launched: 1758

Place: Fort George
Armament: 14 x 6 pdrs and 4 pdrs, 20 swivels
Crew: 100
History: Built by Captain Samuel Cobb, the sloop *Earl of Halifax* was launched on September 11, 1758. It carried a company of marines in addition to a crew of 50 to sail and man its 18 six- and four-pound cannons. As it was, the *Earl of Halifax* was only to remain afloat for a few months. When Abercromby withdrew from Lake George in the fall of 1758 the decision was reached to sink the sloop and raise it in the spring.

In June 1759 Loring and the British army returned to Lake George to stage another attack on Fort Carillon. The commodore and his men quickly set to work on raising the *Earl of Halifax*, but there were problems. The vessel had been sunk the previous fall by drilling holes in the hull through which ropes were run. These ropes were tied to nets filled with rocks, which were in turn pushed off the pontoon boats that flanked the vessel, sending the craft to the bottom. To recover the sloop Loring's divers had to find the vessel. This they did, but the *Earl of Halifax* was in deeper water than thought. This made cutting the nets free and attaching lines to the freed ropes very difficult. With effort, all the nets were freed and the attached lines hauled to the surface. With the cables running through the vessel's hull now attached to recovery vessels on either side, the sunken vessel was slowly raised by winching on these lines. When enough of the vessel appeared above the water, the recovery craft towed it to shore where it could be pumped out. "Capt. Loring got the sloop a little above water and hawled her to the wharf so that I hope she will be soon ready," General Jeffery Amherst wrote in his journal a week and a half after Loring started salvage operations.

The *Earl of Halifax* was refitted, and escorted Amherst's army down Lake George. With the capture of Fort Carillon the sloop took on the function of transport. It experienced crew troubles not long after. Colonel James Montressor of the Royal Engineers wrote in his journal, "The Draughts put on board, the sloop mutinied which occasioned my sending a Captain & 20 men to take the ring leaders & put them in a Batoe to keep with the sloop and deliver to the Commanding officer at the landing place."

A view of the 8-gun radeau *Invincible* (left) and the 14-gun sloop *Halifax* at the head of Lake George, 1759.

The sloop continued its duties until it was broken up sometime after the fall of Montreal in 1760.

Sources: Loring to —, Aug 19, 1758, Chatham Fonds MG23-A2, vol 8; Knox Journal, I, 378, 382, 386; *The Journal of Jeffery Amherst*, 127–133; Cobb's Journal, 117–121; *The Journals of Col. James Montresor*, 92; Spicer Diary, 402; Glasier's Journal, 77, 80–81.

Name: *Invincible*
Nationality: British
Type: Radeau
Launched: 1759
Place: Fort George
Armament: 8 x 24 pdrs
Crew: 100
History: The radeau *Invincible* was built in the early summer of 1759 to replace the *Land Tortoise*, which was sunk the previous fall in deep water and could not be recovered. Captain Thomas Ord of the royal artillery oversaw the construction of the vessel. Amherst left a small criticism of the vessel: "A little mistake in the height of the Port Holes of the Radeau, but she will do. Fired every gun out of her to try." With the capture of Ticonderoga in 1759 the *Invincible* was relegated to transport duties. It was broken up upon the conclusion of hostilities.

Source: *The Journal of Jeffery Amherst*, 132–133, 138, 141.

Name: *Ligonier*
Nationality: British
Type: Radeau
Launched: 1759
Place: Crown Point
Length: 84´
Beam: 20´
Armament: 6 x 24 pdrs
Crew: 120
History: The *Ligonier* was built in
the summer of 1759 by Royal
Artillery major Thomas Ord in
response to the threat posed by

The *Ligonier* under sail, 1760.

the French fleet operating on Lake Champlain. Ord had built a similar vessel on Lake George the previous spring, and thus was able to pursue the construction of this vessel without interfering with Loring's efforts to build a brigantine at Ticonderoga. When its guns were tested the first time the *Ligonier* proved an excellent firing platform, but its sailing performance was directly tied to the mood of the lake. Its boxlike hull made it nearly impossible to handle in even moderate weather, forcing its crew to turn to its oars more often than they would have liked to. On good days, however, the vessel was capable of making excellent time over the lake. The vessel does not show up in a list of British ships at Ticonderoga in the fall of 1762, implying that it was either broken up or purposely abandoned before this date. Ord built at least three additional smaller versions of the *Ligonier* for the campaign against Ile aux Noix in 1760. None of these vessels seem to have been named nor are they referenced in future correspondence, leading one to believe that they were either dismantled shortly after the surrender of Montreal, or simply abandoned to the lake.

Sources: *The Journal of Jeffery Amherst*, 158, 174, 178; "News from America," *London Magazine*, Dec. 1759, reprinted in *FTMB*, VI, no. 33 (Jan. 1942), 108–111.

Name: *Boscawen*
Nationality: British
Type: Sloop
Displacement: 115 tons

Length: 75´
Beam: 25´
Launched: 1759
Place: Ticonderoga
Armament: 4 x 6 pdrs, 12 x 4 pdrs, 22 swivels
Crew: 112
History: Built at Ticonderoga during the fall of 1759 to counter the threat posed by the French Lake Champlain fleet, the 115-ton *Boscawen* was a typical sloop design, employing fore and aft sail plan. Examination of the wreck in the early 1980s pointed to the haste in which Loring was forced to construct it. Many finishing touches were never applied to the vessel, and it carried a smaller sail plan than was typical for its size with the belief that it would lead to easier operations on the lake. It was used by Lt. Alexander Grant to support raids by Rogers' Rangers into the Richelieu Valley and patrol the lake throughout the summer of 1760. After the war the *Boscawen* was used to ferry supplies between the forts along Lake Champlain and St. Johns. It was either left to sink of its own accord at the Ticonderoga shipyard, or more likely, was purposely sunk before the winter of 1762, which was a common form of vessel storage when arrangements did not exist to pull the vessel out of the water. Although it stayed on the official list of British Lake Champlain vessels for the next dozen years, no attempt was ever made to raise it.

Sources: "News from America," *London Magazine*, Dec. 1759, reprinted in *FTMB*, VI, no. 33 (Jan. 1942), 108–111; "List of the Vessels on the Different Lakes . . . November, 1762," WO34/65; *Knox Journal*, II, 140–141; *The Journal of Jeffery Amherst*, 164, 174, 179; Loring to Amherst, 14 Sept. 1759," WO34/65; "Joshua Loring to Robert Lambert, 22 November 1759," NAC, Admiralty Papers, vol. 2048.

Name: *Duke of Cumberland*
Nationality: British
Type: Brigantine
Displacement: 155 tons
Length: 100´
Beam: 30´
Launched: 1759

Place: Ticonderoga
Armament: 6 x 6 pdrs, 12 x 4 pdrs, 22 swivels
Crew: 132
History: The brigantine *Duke of Cumberland* was the first of two vessels built at Ticonderoga during the summer of 1759. Its construction was plagued by delays and difficulties. The retreating French garrison at Fort Carillon had destroyed the sawmills on the La Chute River. These were repaired, but frequently broke down in part because they were overtaxed by requests for wood for building vessels, repairing Fort Carillon, and the building of Fort Amherst. Just as much of a problem for Loring, was securing naval supplies and cannons to outfit his ship. As a result the planned armament of eighteen six and nine pound cannons never materialized. Even so, the resulting two-masted 155 ton brigantine carried an armament greater than half that of the French fleet. The *Duke of Cumberland* was laid up shortly after the war and like the *Boscawen* was purposefully sunk. A report by Loring in 1762 makes mention to the brigantine, but no attempt was ever made by the British to raise her.

Sources: "News from America," *London Magazine*, Dec. 1759, reprinted in *FTMB*, VI, no. 33 (Jan. 1942), 108-111; "List of the Vessels on the Different Lakes . . . November, 1762," WO34/65; "Amherst to Loring, 10 Aug., 23 Aug., & 27 Aug. 1759, and Loring to Amherst, 28 Aug. and 31 Aug. 1759," WO34/64; "Joshua Loring to Robert Lambert, 22 November 1759," NAC, Admiralty Papers, vol. 2048; "The Revenge (The Hull of the Duke of Cumberland)," *FTMB*, I, no. 4 (July 1928), 6; *Knox Journal*, II, 140-141. *The Journal of Jeffery Amherst*, 179-181.

Name: Unnamed gunboats
Nationality: British
Type: Gunboat
Launched: 1759-1760
Place: Crown Point/Ticonderoga
Armament: Single cannon from 4 to 12 pounds
History: These vessels were essentially the British version of the Jacobs. Several were made, with those carrying smaller ordinance proving more capable of taking on the rigors of the lake. Amherst employed several of these vessels in his advance up the lake in the fall of 1759. The gunboat approach, which offered speed of deployment

for minimal effort, would become a mainstay in naval confrontations on the lakes of North America for another fifty years.

Source: The Journal of Jeffery Amherst, 179–180.

THE AMERICAN LAKE CHAMPLAIN FLEET, 1776–1777

OVERVIEW

The American Lake Champlain Fleet 1776

Vessel	Crew	Gun Complement (lb)						Totals
		18	12	9	6	4	2	
Royal Savage	60			6	4		10	10
Enterprise	50					10		10
Lee	45	1		1		4		6
Philadelphia	45		1	2				3
Boston	45		1	2				3
New Haven	45		1	2				3
Providence	45			3				3
Spitfire	45			3				3
New Jersey	45		1	2				3
Connecticut	45			3				3
New York	45		1	1	2			4
Revenge	35					4	4	8
Congress	70	2	2		4			8
Trumbull	70	1	1		2	2		6
Washington	70	1	3		4			8
Liberty[a]	35					2	6	8
Totals								
Crew[b]	795							
Guns		5	11	19	18	26	10	89
Metal weight (lb)		90	132	171	108	104	20	625

a. *Liberty* was not present at the Battle of Valcour Island.
b. Arnold frequently complained that he was in want of men. Although some of this deficit was remedied, it seems that he was still short from 100 to 200 men at the Battle of Valcour Island. More important, his actual numbers have to be tempered by the fact that many of his men had little or no sailing experience.

Sources: *American Archives*, series 5, vol. 2, 1039–1041, 1178–1179; *Digby's Journal*, 162–164; *NDAR*, VI, 1258, 1344; "A Journal of Carleton's and Burgoyne's Campaigns," *FTMB*, XI, 5 (Dec. 1964), 256–258.

The American Lake Champlain Fleet 1777

Vessel	Crew	Gun Complement (lb)						Totals
		18	12	6	4	3	2	
Enterprise	15			8		4		12
New York	11					1		1
Revenge	7							
Trumbull	24	2		2	6	4		14
Gates	40		2		6	4		12
Liberty[a]	12							
Totals								
Crew[b]	109							
Guns		2	2	2	20	1	12	39
Metal weight (lb)		36	24	12	80	3	24	179

a. Both the *Revenge* and the schooner *Liberty* had been stripped of their guns and converted to dispatch and supply vessels.

b. By way of comparison, the crew numbers for these same six ships the previous year amounted to 305.

Sources: *NDAR*, 9: 174–175; "A Journal of Carleton's and Burgoyne's Campaigns," *FTMB*, XI, 6 (Sept. 1965), 321.

VESSELS

Name: *Royal Savage*
Nationality: American
Type: Schooner
Displacement: 70 tons
Launched: 1775
Place: St. Johns
Armament: 6 x 6 pdrs, 4 x 4 pdrs, 12 swivels
Crew: 60
History: The *Royal Savage* was a fifty foot, two-masted schooner built by the British at St. Johns during the fall of 1775. "She is a vessel of between 70 & 80 tuns burden, very long and something flat bottom'd–

elegantly built & finish'd oft–
'mounts 14 brass 6 pounders
besides a number of swivels–&
has a strong net work on each side
from her bow to her Quarter rail
to secure her from being boarded.
On the whole she is a very hand-
some elegant vessel, & when, she
lay riding on the Lake made a
very warlike appearance," one
American witness wrote about the
schooner during the siege of Fort
St. Johns. Later, this same witness
would note that, "We shot so

The American schooner *Royal Savage*.

many Balls thro her that next morning she lay careen'd so low that the
water ran into her port holes."

The *Royal Savage* was raised and repaired shortly after the British
surrender of the fort, and by late December it was in winter quarters
at Fort Ticonderoga. For a short time it went under the name *Yankee*,
but it did not stick. For almost a year after this it spent time shuttling
troops and supplies north to sustain the American advance into
Canada, and acting as a powerful deterrent toward Carlton's advance
on Fort Ticonderoga once Fort St. Johns was recaptured by the
Governor-General in June 1776. It was badly damaged and run
aground early in the Battle of Valcour Island. The British captured the
stranded vessel late in battle and burned it.

Sources: "The Journal of Major Henry Livingston," *PMHB*, XXII, 17, 29; Trumbull,
Benjamin, "Journal of the Principle Movements towards St. John's," *Collections of
the Connecticut Historical Society*, VII (1899), 156; *American Archives*, series 4, vol. 3,
468, 738; "The Royal Savage," *FTMB*, XII, no. 2 (Sept. 1966), 128–150.

Name: *Liberty*
Nationality: American
Type: Schooner
Launched: 1774
Place: Skenesborough (Whitehall)
Arrmament: 2 x 4 pdrs; 6 x 2 pdrs; 6 swivels
Crew: 35

History: The forty-ton *Liberty* began life under the name *Katherine*. Built by former British major Philip Skene in 1771, it was seized by Captains Eleazer Oswald and John Brown the same day Arnold and Allen captured Fort Ticonderoga. It received its new name shortly thereafter, when after being fitted with cannon at Ticonderoga, it became the first vessel in the American Lake Champlain fleet. Rigged as a ketch the forty-one-foot shallow-draft vessel was a noted poor sailer, especially within a few points of the wind. Arnold used the *Liberty* to seize the *Betsy* from the British garrison at Fort St. Johns in 1775, and it was also at this post when General Richard Montgomery laid siege and captured the fort on November 2. Barely a fighting vessel, the *Liberty* occupied most of its time shuttling supplies and messages across the lake in support of the American advance into Canada. It was not present at the Battle of Valcour Island in October 1776, but was captured the following summer when General John Burgoyne attacked Skenesborough as part of his advance on Saratoga. In April 1780 Captain William Chambers wrote Governor Haldimand of the *Liberty*'s decaying condition, saying that it would be cheaper to build a new schooner than repair the vessel.

Sources: American Archives, series 4, vol. 2, 686, 891; "Philip Skene to Lt. Thomas Gamble, 26 April, 1771," *FTMB*, VI, 35 (Jan. 1943), 163; "A Journal of Carleton's and Burgoyne's Campaigns," *FTMB*, XI, 6 (Sept. 1965), 321; *Report on the Canadian Archives, 1887*, 493, 497.

Name: *Enterprise*
Nationality: American
Type: Sloop
Displacement: 50 tons
Launched: 1771
Place: St. Johns
Armament: 2 x 6 pdrs (as *Betsy*); 10 x 4 pdrs, 12 swivels (as *Enterprise*)
Crew: 50
History: The *Enterprise* was originally the British *Betsy* built in 1771 to replace the decaying *Musquelongy*, which had been used to transport supplies across the lake for over a decade. Arnold captured the *Betsy* in the spring of 1775 and renamed it *Enterprise*, in what would turn out to be the first in a long line of famous American vessels. The *Enterprise* and *Liberty* patrolled Lake Champlain for the next few months. In

August 1775 the ship's new captain, James Smith, arrived at Crown Point. After looking over the vessel Smith reported to Schuyler that it was "of Very Little use to the Service," and in his estimation "could be taken by four bateau with a swivel gun and ten men each." Nonetheless, *Enterprise* was busy over the next year shuttling supplies and patrolling the lake. One passenger traveling from Isle La Motte to Crown Point in the late fall of 1775 recounted a harrowing voyage in the vessel.

The American sloop *Enterprise*.

> As soon as daylight appeared we weighed anchor, and under a very heavy Gale & but a rag of the Mainsail hoisted stood up the Lake, snowing very fast all the time, we no sooner lost sight of the Isle of Mott but we were lost, and not a man on board knew where we was till 3 in the afternoon when we were just by the 4 Brothers 30 miles perhaps from where we set off. In running this distance we were often in great danger, running often but a few rods from the rocky shores of Islands we never saw before to remember again. Once between a couple of those Islands we sounded and found the depth of water but 2 1/2 fathom. As our vessel ran very fast and the sea went high, if we had struck a rock, or even sand, our old crazy sloop must have gone to pieces.

The *Enterprise* was used as a hospital ship at the Battle of Valcour Island in 1776, and was one of the few American vessels to escape the British attack and pursuit. To avoid capture by General Burgoyne's advancing forces it was run aground and burned by its crew the next summer near Skenesborough.

Sources: *NDAR*, I, 503–504, 589, 797, 1044, VI, 1306–1307; "The Journal of Major Henry Livingston," *PMHB*, XXII, 31–32; "Journal of Jahiel Stewart," *Vermont History*, 64, no. 2 (Spring 1996), 92–94; *American Archives*, series 4, vol. 2, 686; "A Journal of Carleton's and Burgoyne's Campaigns," *FTMB*, XI, 6 (Sept. 1965), 321.

Name: *Lee*
Nationality: American
Type: Cutter
Displacement: 48 tons
Launched: 1776
Place: Skenesborough (Whitehall)
Armament: 1 x 12 pdr, 1 x 9 pdrs, 4 x 4 pdrs
Crew: 45
History: Although referred to in contemporary records as a gondola, the *Lee* was different than the other gondolas constructed at Skenesborough during the summer of 1776. This was because it was based on a partially completed British frame captured at St. Johns in the fall of 1775. Before Arnold put Fort St. Johns to the torch in July 1776, he had this frame dismantled and shipped south to Skenesborough, where it was eventually used to construct the cutter. Displacing some forty-eight tons, the forty-four-foot *Lee* participated in the Battle of Valcour Island, but was run aground along the west shore of the lake and abandoned by its crew in the ensuing British pursuit. The British repaired the *Lee* and continued to use it throughout the conflict, primarily as a transport. It was reported afloat in October 1783, but sometime in the years following it was either broken up or left to be claimed by the lake.
Sources: Chapelle, 103–104, 107; *Report on the Canadian Archives*, 1887, 512; *American Archives*, series 5, vol. 2, 185, 353, 1039.

Name: *Philadelphia, Boston, New Haven, Providence, Spitfire, New Jersey, Connecticut*, and *New York*
Nationality: American
Type: Gondola
Launched: 1776
Place: Skenesborough (Whitehall)
Armament: 1 x 12 pdr, 2 x 9 pdrs, 8 swivels
Crew: 45
History: The *Philadelphia* was representative of the eight gondolas built at Skenesborough during the summer of 1776. At fifty feet long and fifteen feet abeam, these squat utilitarian vessels could be propelled by sweeps or raise a sail on a single mast. Schuyler's original

plan was to build more sleek Delaware-style row galleys, but work was forced to proceed without a shipwright familiar with the Delaware design when Schuyler's pleas for a naval architect went unanswered. Slow sailers, the vessels certainly raised moments of doubt among a number of observers, especially when the weather soured on the lake, but although uninspiring they proved capable vessels. The British captured several of these vessels and later employed them as transports.

Sources: Chapelle, 101–112; for details about the construction of the gondolas and the salvaging of the *Philadelphia* see Bratten, *The Continental Gondola Philadelphia* (Ph.D. thesis).

Name: *Revenge*
Nationality: American
Type: Topsail Schooner
Launched: 1775
Place: St. Johns
Armament: 4 x 4 pdr, 4 x 2 pdr, 10 swivels
Crew: 35
History: The *Revenge* started life as an unnamed, partially completed British schooner that was captured by the Americans at St. Johns in the fall of 1775. Major Henry Livingston of the 3rd New York Continentals left a brief description of the vessel during the siege of Fort St. Johns; "The Row Galley is abt 25 tuns burden neatly built, & was intended for a sloop. She carried a 24 pounder of Brass in her Bow & on each side 1, 4 pounder, besides swivels–& conveniences for 16 oars to row on a side." By late November the row galley was at Ticonderoga. The following summer a number of carpenters under Colonel Jeduthan Baldwin converted the vessel to its originally intended schooner form. A good sailer, the *Revenge* escaped the Battle of Valcour Island and the devastating British pursuit, only to be blown up by its crew the following year during the British attack on Skenesborough.

Sources: "The Journal of Major Henry Livingston," *PMHB*, XXII, 17–18, 29; *American Archives*, series 4, vol. 3, 468; "A Journal of Carleton's and Burgoyne's Campaigns," *FTMB*, XI, 6 (Sept. 1965), 321.

Name: *Congress, Washington, Trumbull, Gates*
Nationality: American
Type: Galley
Displacement: 128 tons
Length: 72'4"
Beam: 19'7"
Draft: 7'
Launched: 1776
Place: Skenesborough (Whitehall)
Armament: 2 x 18 pdr, 2 x 12 pdr, 4 x 6 pdr, 10 swivels
Crew: 70
History: The *Congress* and its sister ships *Trumbull, Washington,* and *Gates,* were often referred to as Spanish-style row galleys. The four vessels were constructed at Skenesborough in the late summer and early fall of 1776. Measuring some seventy-three feet in length and displacing a little over 120 tons, these vessels could be propelled by twenty sweeps (oars) and/or a pair of lateen-rigged sails on two masts. Arnold had originally planned to arm the ships with a pair of twenty-four-pound cannons firing fore and aft, and a pair of eighteen-pound cannons, a pair of nine-pound cannons, and four four-pound cannons mounted amidships. Although the four-pounders called for were upgraded to six-pound guns, the twenty-four-pound cannons could not be procured nor could enough eighteen-pound guns be found, which led to a compromise in the vessels' final armament. Arnold had also originally wanted eight galleys for his fleet, but sickness and attrition among the shipwrights and carpenters at Skenesborough reduced the number to four. It is questionable given the naval supply and manpower shortages faced by Arnold that he could have employed more of these vessels, even if they had been constructed. There were no major complaints about the vessels in regards to their sailing qualities, but as it turned out this was never really put to the test, at least under American control.

The *Congress,* which served as Arnold's flagship, the *Trumbull,* and the *Washington* all participated in the Battle of Valcour Island, while the *Gates* remained at Ticonderoga awaiting the final elements of its rigging. The British captured the *Washington,* while Arnold burned the *Congress.* The *Trumbull* was captured the following year at

Skenesborough, while the *Gates* was burned by its crew during the attack.

Both the *Trumbull* and the *Washington* saw service with the British Lake Champlain fleet. Major General Riedesel recorded a harrowing late October voyage from Point au Fer to Crown Point on the *Washington*.

The *Washington* was the same vessel which had been taken on the 13th from the Americans. At the present time it was loaded with provisions for the garrison at Crown Point. The voyage up Lake Champlain was very stormy. The main mast broke, and the ship ran aground upon a sand bank, in which situation it was forced to remain the entire night. Away from all human help, and lashed by the angry waves, it was in constant danger of becoming a total wreck. Nor was it until morning that some boats, coming to its assistance, succeeded in getting it afloat. It then continued its voyage up the lake with a favorable wind.

The general's luck was no better on his return voyage. On the passage he again encountered a storm, and the vessel was once more in danger of being wrecked. The captain was obliged to cast anchor off the Isle aux Quatres Vents. The misfortunes of the ship, however, were not yet at an end. The day after resuming its voyage it ran aground near the River la Colle.

With the British withdrawal from Ticonderoga, Ile aux Noix and St. Johns became the port of call for the *Washington* and the *Trumbull*. The former was seldom used, and was fitted out for service in the spring of 1782 for the last time. The latter was regularly employed on the lake. In the fall of 1779 it struck bottom and sank in the shallow waters along the banks of the Richelieu River, but not long after Captain William Chambers, who was busy putting the fleet into winter quarters at St. Johns, was able to report, "She has been raised and repaired and is now laid up with the rest." The *Trumbull* was busy the next few years transporting troops, loyalist families north, and eventually American prisoners south, but with the official conclusion of hostilities in 1783 it was dismantled as part of the British naval reductions on Lake Champlain.

Sources: *NDAR*, VII, 830–831; "A Journal of Carleton's and Burgoyne's Campaigns," *FTMB*, XI, 6 (Sept. 1965), 321; *Riedesel Journal*, 78, 80; *Report on the*

Canadian Archives, 1887, 492, 496–500, 502–504, 510; *American Archives*, series 5, vol. 2, 1039.

THE BRITISH LAKE CHAMPLAIN FLEET, 1776–1777

OVERVIEW

The British Lake Champlain Fleet, 1776

Vessel	Crew	Gun Complement (lb)						Totals
		24	12	9	6	8″ hwt	5.5″ hwt	
Maria	45				14			14
Loyal Convert	35			7				7
Thunderer	130	6	6				2	14
Carleton	45				12			12
Inflexible	120		18					18
10 Gunboats	210	2	8			2		12
16 Gunboats	320				12		4	16
1 Gunboat	20		1					1
Totals								
Crew	925[a]							
Guns		8	33	7	38	2	6	94
Metal weight (lb)		192	396	63	228	84	78	1041[b]

a. Captain Charles Douglas lists the sailors and seamen present at the Battle of Valcour Island as 670 seamen, 8 officers, and 19 petty officers. The remainder of the crew complements would be filled out by marines and detachments of German and British artillerymen.

b. If the howitzers mounted on the vessels in the fleet are excluded from the gun totals, the result is 86 guns with a weight of metal of 879 pounds.

Sources: *NDAR*, VI, 883–884, 955, 1244–1245, 1343–1345; *American Archives*, series 5, vol. 2, 1178–1179.

The British Lake Champlain Fleet, 1777

Vessel	Crew	Gun Complement (lb)					Totals
		24	12	9	6	3	
Maria	45				16		16
Loyal Convert	35 (7)			8			8
Thunderer	90 (15)	18					18
Carleton	35				14		14
Royal George	130 (15)		20		6		26
Lee	30 (7)				6		6
Inflexible	100 (12)			18		4	22
Washington	80 (9)				16	4	20
New Jersey	30 (5)			5			5
Commissary[a]	5						
Receipt	5						
Delivery	5						
Ration	5						
Camel	5						
28 Gunboats[b]	440 (196)	2			12		14
Totals							
Crew[c]	1040 (371)						
Guns		20	20	31	70	8	149
Metal weight (lb)		480	240	279	420	24	1443

a. The *Commissary, Receipt, Delivery, Ration,* and *Camel* were small transport sloops ranging from 30 to 50 tons in size. After the capture of Ticonderoga the *Camel* was turned into a floating magazine at the fort.

b. Only 14 of the 28 gunboats in the British fleet were armed with cannons larger than swivel guns. Two of the gunboats were converted to dispatch vessels, and four others were converted into tenders.

c. The manpower totals for the British fleet are given for full crew complements, and in parentheses, for vessels equipped as transport vessels. Captain Skiffington Lutwidge's fleet was certainly far short of the numbers required to man every vessel with its complete complement, although during the advance on Fort Ticonderoga and Skenesborough much of this deficiency was overcome by drawing on Burgoyne's soldiers, particularly when it came to manning the gunboats. Even so, it seems likely that the *Loyal Convert, Lee, Washington,* and *New Jersey* were manned as supply vessels from the onset. The *Thunderer, Royal George,* and

Inflexible were converted to transports in late July, and at the same time the gunboat crew numbers were reduced. A report in late July 1777 placed the naval manpower requirements on Lake Champlain, Lake George, and the Hudson River at 521, with 349 present for duty exclusive of the detachments from the HMS *Viper* and HMS *Triton*, which added perhaps another 100 men to the total. In September when Colonel John Brown's forces threatened Fort Ticonderoga and the British posts on Lake George, Lieutenant John Starke informed Governor Carleton that "the *Maria* & *Carleton* which are station'd for the Defence of Mount Independance must certainly fall into the hands of the Rebels should the Garrison be obliged to capitulate or surrender. . . . If it should be thought necessary to have the other Vessels mann'd and arm'd, to maintain the Lake, and prevent an Invasion of Canada, more Seamen & also Officers will be wanted there. The Vessels as to themselves are all in proper repair & fit for Service only their Guns are landed." Carleton responded to Starke's report by sending additional naval detachments from the British warships in the St. Lawrence basin, and rearming several of the vessels assigned to transport duty. By mid-October Captain Richard Pearson, now in command on Lake Champlain, reported that there were 435 men assigned to naval operations on Lake Champlain and Lake George with almost a fifth of these reported as sick or unfit for duty.

Sources: *NDAR*, VII, 955–956, VIII, 986, IX, 331–333, 934–935, X, 140–142; Pell, Joshua, "Diary of Joshua Pell Junior, 1776–1777," *Magazine of American History*, II (1878), 107; *American Archives*, series 5, vol. 3, 788.

VESSELS

Name: *Maria*
Nationality: British
Type: Topsail Schooner
Displacement: 129 tons
Length: 66´
Beam: 21´6″
Draft: 8´2″
Launched: 1776?
Place: Quebec?
Armament: 14 x 6 pdr, 6 swivels
Crew: 45
Background: The *Maria* was originally a provincial schooner captured by the Americans during their advance on Montreal in late November 1775. It was used by the American's during their siege of Quebec in late 1775 and early 1776, but was captured when the lead elements of the British relief force under Captain Charles Douglas arrived in early

May. "This moment a fine arm'd schooner taken by the *Surprize*, and *Martin*, carrying four six pounders, and six three pounders, is come down the River," Douglas wrote of the incident. Douglas gave command of the *Maria* to Lt. John Starke of HMS *Lizard*, and ordered him to refit the vessel with fourteen six-pound cannons. Starke's new command was ready not long afterward, and conducted General Carleton up the St. Lawrence as the governor launched a counter-offensive against the American Army of Canada.

Attempts were made to move the *Maria* by land around the Chambly rapids, but in the end the vessel was partially disassembled, and moved by wagon to St. Johns, where it was reassembled. The *Maria* acted as the British flagship throughout its long career on Lake Champlain. It survived the post-war cuts that dismantled the British fleet at Ile aux Noix and St. Johns, and was a frequent visitor to Lake Champlain in the years that followed the conflict, often causing some nervousness among American merchant ships doing business north.

The *Maria* was still on the official list of active vessels on Lake Champlain in 1793, although its actual sailing state was questionable. The next year the last surviving vessel of the Battle of Valcour Island was decommissioned and broken up with the launching of its replacement, the *Royal Edward*.

Sources: NDAR, IV, 1432, 1454, 1456, V, 86, 100, 197, 595–596, 957, VII, 830–831; Hadden's Journal, 53.

Name: *Carleton*
Nationality: British
Type: Topsail Schooner
Displacement: 96 tons
Length: 59'2"
Beam: 20'
Draft: 6'6"
Launched: 1776?
Place: Quebec?
Armament: 12 x 6 pdr, 6 swivels
Crew: 45
Background: The *Carleton* was a provincial schooner taken from the Americans during the British advance up the St. Lawrence Valley in

A depiction of the Battle of Valcour Island published in London, December 1776. The three vessels in the foreground are, from left to right, the *Maria, Carleton,* and *Inflexible.* Interestingly, the image is incorrect. Although the *Carleton* was heavily engaged, the bulk of the battle was fought and won by the British- and German-led gunboats. It is likely that this depiction was an attempt to promote the capital ships in Pringle's fleet, and thereby shift more of the glory toward the Royal Navy officers who commanded these vessels.

the spring and early summer of 1776. Like the *Maria* and the *Loyal Convert,* it was partially disassembled and transported by wagon to St. Johns where it was reassembled. The schooner was heavily damaged in the Battle of Valcour Island, and suffered almost half the total British casualties in the engagement. The *Carleton* continued to operate on the lake throughout the American Revolution, often in the rescue of loyalist families who would travel to the shores of the lake in search of refuge in Canada. The schooner was laid up upon the naval reductions that followed the Peace of Paris.

Sources: *NDAR,* V, 1168, VII, 830–831; *Hadden's Journal,* 53; *Digby's Journal,* 148, 151–152.

Name: *Loyal Convert*
Nationality: British
Type: Gondola
Displacement: 108 tons
Length: 62′10″

Beam: 20´3˝
Draft: 3´7˝
Launched: 1775
Place: Skenesborough
Armament: 7 x 9 pdr, 6 swivels
Crew: 35
Background: The *Loyal Convert* started life under the name of either *Hancock* or *Schuyler*. Built during the summer of 1775, these vessels were captured by the British during the lifting of the siege of Quebec. The *Loyal Convert* was rearmed and carried around the St. Jean rapids in the summer of 1776, and later that year was present at the Battle of Valcour Island. The *Loyal Convert* served with the Burgoyne flotilla the next year, but primarily as a transport vessel. It was active as late as 1783 carrying "bullocks" north from Crown Point as a gift to the governor-general. Although the vessel was to have been broken up upon the conclusion of hostilities, a 1790 report speaks to the gondola as the last member of the British Lake Champlain fleet still afloat.

Sources: *NDAR*, IV, 1456, VII, 830–831; *American Archives*, series 4, vol. 4, 585; *Report on the Canadian Archives, 1887*, 510, 512.

Name: *Thunderer*
Nationality: British
Type: Radeau
Displacement: 422 tons
Length: 91´9˝
Beam: 23´4˝
Draft: 6´8˝
Launched: 1776
Place: St. Johns
Armament: 6 x 24 pdr, 4 x 12 pdr, 2 x 8 in. howitzers, 2 x 5.5 in. howitzers
Crew: 90
Background: At almost ninety-two feet in length, and thirty-three feet in breadth this flat-bottomed box-like craft was a modified version of the vessels built by Ord and Amherst a generation before. Fitted with oars, a pair of short masts, and rigged as a ketch, the *Thunderer* was not the most elegant sailer to ever try the northern lake, although in

a favorable wind it was more than capable, having once sailed from Crown Point to Ile aux Noix in nine hours. Its sailing qualities aside, with nearly 90 sailors, marines, and gunners onboard, and a complement of six twenty-four-pound cannon, four twelve-pound cannon, two eight-inch howitzers, and two five-and-a-half-inch howitzers it was certainly the most heavily armed vessel to try the lake. A German officer described the craft in his journal of Burgoyne's expedition. "Next to this the 'Radeau,' or floating battery (The *Thunderer*) was anchored. It was built in a square of strong rafters, fitted, however, with masts, sails, wheel and a cabin, like a ship, and carried six 24 pound mortars, six 12 pounds cannon and 2 howitzers."

The *Thunderer* was present at the Battle of Valcour Island but was not involved in the action or chase of the American fleet. It participated in the brief advance and siege of Fort Ticonderoga in 1777, but shortly after the fort's capture Burgoyne had it stripped of its guns and turned into a transport vessel–a duty it was well suited for. With the British withdrawal from Ticonderoga the bulky vessel was seldom used, and was eventually broken up upon the conclusion of hostilities.

Sources: Chapelle, 104–106; *NDAR*, VII, 830–831; *Journal of Du Roi the Elder*, 87; *Pausch Journal*, 81.

Name: Gunboats
Nationality: British
Type: Gunboat/Galley
Length: 35´
Beam: 16´
Launched: 1776
Place: St. Johns
Dimensions:
Armament: 1 x forward firing gun from 4 to 24 pdrs or 1 x 8 in. or 5.5 in. howitzer
Crew: 18 to 22 sailors and gunners
Background: In response to a request from Canadian governor Carleton in 1775 these utilitarian vessels were designed and constructed in England specifically for Lake Champlain. Ten of these disassembled craft arrived at Quebec with a relief squadron in the summer of 1776. They were further supplemented by at least 16 more built in

Canada. Propelled by 10 oars, or when the weather cooperated, sporting a sloop rig, these vessels carried a wide assortment of bow mounted cannons.

The gunboats proved a perfect match for Lake Champlain and Lake George. Cheap, easy to produce, and small enough to transport around rapids, a fleet of these craft successfully engaged Arnold at Valcour Island, destroyed the remnants of the American fleet at Skenesborough, and were involved in patrol duties on Lake Champlain and Lake George. Lt. James Hadden of the Royal Artillery spent time aboard one of these vessels and described the cramped accommodations and the measures taken by the crew to protect themselves from the elements.

> The situation of one Gentleman in a space of 35 Feet by 16 F and 18 Soldiers or Sailors does not appear the most eligible or comfortable as they cannot always be restrained nor wou'd one wish it: the experience of last year taught us to make several little conveniences particularly a kind of seperate Tilt over the Magazine in the Stern of the Boat. This space, about 6 Feet by 5–was sufficient to contain a small Table & your Baggage &c and cou'd be kept constantly cover'd when not Rowing against the Wind, that being necessary the Cover was removed and the necessary Sticks remain'd bent & standing: in Wet weather this was a very considerable inconvenience. Soldiers meet with many and temporary reliefs are all he can hope in this kind of War. When at an Anchor the Men & Officer put up each their cover and except one Sentry went to rest. The Men put up two lashed Oars at each end and by means of a Fifth communicating with these spread the Sail over them, which proved a sufficient defence against most Rains.

The gunboats remained active on Lake Champlain and the Richelieu River until the conclusion of the conflict, shortly after which they were ordered to be dismantled as part of a force and cost reduction along the border.

Sources: *Hadden's Journal*, 53, 56; *Pausch Journal*, 64–65, 75, 84; Chapelle, 93–95.

An eighteenth-century brigantine (foreground) followed by a ship rigged vessel and a sloop.

Name: *Royal George*
Nationality: British
Type: Ship
Displacement: 383 tons
Length: 96'6"
Beam: 30'6"
Draft: 10'
Launched: 1777
Place: St. Jean (St. Johns)
Armament: 20 x 12 pdrs, 6 x 6 pdrs, 10 x swivel
Crew: 130
Background: Built at St. Jean over the winter of 1775–1776 the *Royal George* exceeded the *Inflexible* in size and power. The *Royal George* led Burgoyne's fleet during the general's advance on Fort Ticonderoga, but after the fall of the fort it was converted to a transport vessel. With the British withdrawal from Fort Ticonderoga the *Royal George* was rearmed and used to patrol the lake over the remaining years of the war. The *Royal George* was decommissioned after the war and eventually broken up.

Sources: NDAR, X, 140; *Warships of the Great Lakes*, 34–37; *Digby's Journal*, 201; *Report on the Canadian Archives, 1887*, 358, 485, 499, 504.

Name: *Inflexible*
Nationality: British
Type: Ship
Displacement: 203 tons
Length: 80′1″
Beam: 23′10″
Draft: 9′
Launched: 1776
Place: Quebec
Armament: 18 x 12 pdrs, 10 swivels
Crew: 100
Background: The three-masted ship rigged *Inflexible* was Captain James Douglas's answer to the American fleet on Lake Champlain. With news of the growing American fleet reaching him, Douglas decided to launch a vessel onto the lake that would be beyond anything that the Americans could build. To accomplish this he ordered the 204-ton *Inflexible*, recently finished at the Quebec shipyards, to be dismantled, and transported to St. Johns, where it would be reassembled and outfitted. In an impressive display of skill the disassembled vessel was transported to St. Johns and reconstructed in less than a month. The work impressed Captain Skeffington Lutwidge of HMS *Triton* who would command the British fleet on Lake Champlain in 1777. "*Inflexible* is a better kind of Vessel than one cou'd expect," he wrote a friend after sailing the frigate. The *Inflexible* participated in the Battle of Valcour Island, and Burgoyne's advance up the Champlain Valley the following year. It was operational for the next few years, at one point without sails being used as a guard ship at Ile aux Noix. The vessel was ordered to be dismantled shortly after the Treaty of Paris concluded the conflict.

Sources: NDAR, V, 1184, VI, 45–47, 54, 136, 1193–1194, VII, 830–831, VIII, 1001; *Report on the Canadian Archives, 1887*, 485, 488, 490, 503–504, 507, 521–522.

AMERICAN MERCHANTMEN ON LAKE CHAMPLAIN, 1790–1814

The Lake Champlain Merchant Fleet 1790–1814[a]

Name	Built for	Launched	Builder	Ton.	Year
Unknown	B. Boardman	Burlington	Wilcox	30	1790
Dolphin	G. King	Burlington	Wilcox	30	1793
Burlington Packet	J. Boynton	Burlington	Wilcox	30	1793
Burlington Packet	B. Smith	Burlington	Wilcox	30	1796
Lady Washington	R. Jones	Burlington	Wilcox	30	1795
Maria	G. King	Burlington	Fittock	30	1795
Unknown	G. King	Burlington	Fittock	30	1800
Union	J. Boynton	Burlington	Fittock	30	1800
Elizabeth	D. Ross	Essex, N.Y.	Eggleston	40	1800
Jupiter	G. King	Essex, N.Y.	Eggleston	40	1802
Juno	G. King	Essex, N.Y.	Wilcox	40	1802
Unetta	E. Boynton	Essex, N.Y.	Eggleston	30	1803
Independence	S. Boardman	Essex, N.Y.	Eggleston	35	1805
Privateer	G. King	Burlington	Wilcox	40	1807
Hunter	G. King	Burlington	Wilcox	50	1809
Emperor	H&A Ferris	Barber's Pt.	Young	50	1810
Rising Sun	E. Boynton	Essex, N.Y.	Eggleston	50	1810
Eagle	S. Boardman	Whitehall	Eggleston	60	1810
Essex	G. King	Essex, N.Y.	Eggleston	50	1810
Boston	G. King	Burlington	Wilcox	30	1810
Saucy Fox[b]	G. King	Essex, N.Y.	Eggleston	50	1810
Gold Hunter	E. Boynton	Whitehall	Young	50	1811
President	J. Boynton	Essex, N.Y.	Eggleston	75	1812
Fair Trader	J. Boynton	Essex, N.Y.	Eggleston	75	1812
Morning Star	S. Boardman	Whitehall	Eggleston	50	1812
Jacob Bunker	Has'l & Chit'n	Burlington	Bay	65	1812
Richard	G. King	Essex, N.Y.	Eggleston	60	1812
Leopard	J. Boynton	Essex, N.Y.	Eggleston	50	1813
Boxer	G. King	Essex, N.Y.	Eggleston	60	1813
Paragon	G. King	Burlington	Eggleston	75	1814[c]

a. Although no definitive evidence exists, indications are that the majority, if not all, of the above vessels were sloops.

b. The *Saucy Fox* was registered under the Spanish flag as part of a scheme to facilitate illegal trade between Canada and the United States.

c. The above list is not all inclusive. Accounts of Murray's raid claim that the British seized or destroyed the vessels *Mars* 34 tons, *Enterprise*, 44 tons, and a number of smaller vessels, which might not have made the above list because of their size.

Sources: *Vermont Historical Gazetteer*, I, 670, "The British Attack on Burlington," *Vermont History*, XXIX, 2 (April 1961), 83.

THE AMERICAN LAKE CHAMPLAIN FLEET, 1814

OVERVIEW

The American Lake Champlain Fleet 1814

Vessel	Crew	Gun Complement (lb)							Totals
		Carronade		Long				Columbiad	
		42	32	24	18	12	9	18	
Saratoga	210	6	12	8					26
Ticonderoga	110		5		4	8			17
Eagle	120		12		8				20
Preble	30						7		7
6 Gunboats[a]	246			6				6	12
4 Gunboats[b]	104					4			4
Montgomery	50						6		6
President[c]	50					4		6	10
Totals									
Crew[d]	920								
Guns		6	29	14	12	16	13	12	102
Weight of metal (lb)		252	928	336	216	192	117	216	2257

a. The six larger gunboats were the *Allen, Borer, Burrows, Centipede, Nettle,* and *Viper.*

b. The *Alwyn, Ludlow, Ballard, Wilmer.*

c. The *Montgomery* and the *President* were not present at the Battle of Cumberland Bay.

d. There is no doubt that Macdonough was short on men, given that some of the galleys were manned by army troops. There seems, however, to have been a difference of opinion as to his actual staffing needs and his numbers.

Sources: *Vermont Antiquarian*, I, 3 (March 1903), 81–93; *The Naval War of 1812*, II, 606, *III*, 430–431, 542; *Life of Macdonough*, 143–144, 153, 163–165; *Letter from the Secretary of the Navy . . . Relating to the Capture of the British Fleet on Lake Champlain*, 15–16; *The Battle of Plattsburgh*, 10.

Vessels

Name: *Saratoga*
Nationality: American
Type: Sloop-of-war
Displacement: 734 tons
Length: 143´
Beam: 36´6″
Draft: 14´6″
Launched: 1814
Place: Vergennes
Armament: 6 x 42 pd carronade, 12 x 32 pd carronade, 8 x 24 pdrs
Crew: 210
Background: The *Saratoga* was built at Vergennes by Noah Brown in February–March of 1814. The 180 foot by 36 foot sloop-of-war was originally called the *Jones*, but was quickly changed to the *Saratoga* by the secretary of the navy. Launched in 35 days from its keel being laid, the 734-ton vessel was the largest American made warship to ply the lake, carrying a weight of metal more than Arnold's entire fleet. "I find the *Saratoga* a fine Ship, she sails & works well," Macdonough wrote the secretary of the navy after his flagship's first voyage.

The *Saratoga* anchored the American position at the Battle of Cumberland Bay, and as a result sustained a tremendous beating. The ship was struck in the hull over fifty times, its rigging was shredded, and every gun on the starboard side was disabled. Over half the casualties suffered by Macdonough's fleet during the engagement came from the *Saratoga*.

The *Saratoga*, along with the other major elements of the U.S. Lake Champlain fleet, were placed in floating storage near Whitehall upon the conclusion of hostilities. The decayed hulk of Macdonough's former flagship was sold to salvagers in 1825.

Sources: *The Naval War of 1812*, III, 396–397, 428–429, 431, 461, 482, 505; *The Navy of the United States*, 20; Crisman, *The Eagle*, 18–19; *Warships of the Great Lakes*, 122; "Statement of Noah Brown," *Journal of American History*, #8 (1914), 103–108; *The Battle of Plattsburgh: What Historians Say About It*, 10; *Letter from the Secretary of the Navy . . . Relating to the Capture of the British Fleet on Lake Champlain*, 7, 11–16.

Name: *Eagle*
Nationality: American
Type: Brig
Displacement: 520 tons
Length: 117´
Beam: 34´9´
Launched: 1814
Place: Vergennes
Armament: 12 x 32 pd carronades, 8 x 18 pdrs
Crew: 120
Background: Reports of British shipbuilding efforts at Ile aux Noix spurred a decision to build a 20-gun brig in the summer of 1814. The *Eagle* was the last vessel built at Vergennes by the Brown brothers, with Adam leading this effort. In an impressive performance, Brown and his crew of over 200 shipwrights and carpenters launched the vessel in 25 days. Commodore Macdonough had originally intended to arm the *Eagle* with long 18-pound cannons, but the scarcity of quality 18-pound guns caused him to substitute part of the *Eagle*'s gun complement with 32-pound carronades. The *Eagle* was in the thick of the fighting at the Battle of Cumberland Bay, suffering some 33 casualties as well as significant damage during the course of the battle. Along with the other major elements of the fleet it was placed in storage at Whitehall upon the conclusion of hostilities. The decayed *Eagle* was sold in 1825, and after being salvaged for anything of value, it was abandoned, eventually sinking along the banks of the Poultney River. The brig was rediscovered and examined in the early 1980s.

Sources: Crisman, *The Eagle*, 26–47, 113–135, 168–169; *Letter from the Secretary of the Navy . . . Relating to the Capture of the British Fleet on Lake Champlain*, 11–16. *The Naval War of 1812*, III, 507, 538–539.

Name: *Montgomery*
Nationality: American
Type: Sloop
Launched: 1812–1814
Displacement: 80
Place: Unknown
Armament: 7 x 9 pdrs; 2 x 18 pd columbiad
Crew: 50

Background: The *Montgomery* was one of several merchant vessels purchased by Commodore Macdonough after the loss of the *Growler* and *Eagle*. While two of the converted merchant vessels were sold back to their original owners, the *Montgomery* was retained in service. It was down gunned to six 9-pounders and used as a dispatch vessel and tender in the spring of 1814. The *Montgomery* was in Burlington during the Battle of Cumberland Bay, busy taking on troops to be transported to the threatened American position at Plattsburgh. It was sold at auction for $1,900 in 1815.

Sources: *Naval War of 1812*, II, 514–515, 606, III, 431, 482, 542, 643; *Life of Macdonough*, 153, 162, 165; Crisman, *The Eagle*, 99–100; *The Navy of the United States*, 20.

Name: *Frances*
Nationality: American
Type: Sloop
Launched: Unknown
Displacement: est. 40 tons
Place: Unknown
Armament: 3 x 12 pdrs
Crew: 30
Background: The *Frances*, like the *Wasp*, was a merchant ship pressed into service by Commodore Macdonough during the summer of 1813. Unable to take more than a few cannons, and poor sailers, both vessels were used as armed tenders until Macdonough returned them to their owners when the American fleet went into winter quarters in late 1813.

Source: *Naval War of 1812*, II, 606.

Name: *Wasp*
Nationality: American
Type: Sloop
Launched: Unknown
Displacement: 40 tons
Place: Unknown
Armament: 3 x 12 pdrs
Crew: 30

Background: The *Wasp* was a merchant ship pressed into service by Commodore Macdonough after the loss of the *Eagle* and *Growler* in mid-1813. The vessel proved too small to take anything more than a trio of 12-pound cannons. As a stopgap measure, Macdonough informed the secretary of the navy in December 1813 that, "The sloop *Wasp* is a small vessel & sails badly, I took her last summer from a Merchant of this place and promised to pay him what she should be appraised at, this however being little I suspect her owner will take her again & will be satisfied for the time I have had her by the repairs done to her I shall endeavour to make this arrangement as the sloop is not fit for the service." Macdonough would later use the guns from the *Wasp* and *Frances* to help arm the *Ticonderoga*.

Sources: *Naval War of 1812*, II, 606; *Life of Macdonough*, 144.

Name: *President*
Nationality: American
Type: Sloop
Launched: 1812
Displacement: 75 tons
Place: Essex, N.Y.
Armament: 6 x 18 pd columbiad; 4 x 12 pdrs
Crew: 50
Background: The *President* began its career as an Essex, N. Y.-based merchant ship. The vessel was purchased by the U.S. government in the summer of 1812, and after being modified to carry a complement of 10 cannons, served as Macdonough's flagship for the next few years. By the winter of 1813 it was clear that the *President* was incapable of performing its duties, and as such it was converted to a tender, a role in which it would serve out the remainder of the conflict. "In disarming two of my Sloops," Macdonough informed the secretary of the navy of the changes to the *Montgomery* and *President*, "I have got rid of two heavy dull Sailers, vessels that would have retarded (if sailing in squadron) the whole force." The longest serving member of Commodore Macdonough's fleet, the *President* was sold at auction for $1,750 upon the conclusion of hostilities.

Sources: *Naval War of 1812*, I, 326, II, 606, III, 430–431; *Vermont Historical Gazetteer*, I, 669–670; Crisman, *The Eagle*, 99–100; *The Navy of the United States*, 20.

Name: *Preble*
Nationality: American
Type: Sloop
Launched: 1810
Displacement: 80 tons
Place: Essex, N.Y.
Armament: 7 x 9 pdrs
Crew: 30
Background: The *Preble* began its career as the *Rising Sun*, built in 1810 by Elijah Boynton in Essex, N.Y. This was one of the vessels purchased by Macdonough after the capture of the *Growler* and *Eagle* in 1813. Macdonough reworked the vessel to carry a broadside of three nine-pound guns, and mounted another nine-pounder on a circle mount. It was a stopgap measure, and in this role it performed admirably. Taking on more of a supporting role in Macdonough's rebuilt 1814 fleet, the *Preble* nonetheless stood up well against the larger British vessels at the Battle of Cumberland Bay. The *Preble* was sold at auction in 1815 for $2,340.
Sources: *Vermont Historical Gazetteer*, I, 669–670; *Naval War of 1812*, II, 514–515, 606; Crisman, *The Eagle*, 99–100; *The Navy of the United States*, 20.

Name: *Ticonderoga*
Nationality: American
Type: Topsail Schooner
Displacement: 350 tons
Length: 125′
Beam: 24′
Launched: 1814
Place: Vergennes
Armament: 5 x 32 pd carronade, 4 x 18 pdrs, 8 x 12 pdrs
Crew: 110
Background: The *Ticonderoga* began life as a steamboat, being built at Vergennes in early 1814 by the newly chartered Lake Champlain Steamboat Company. Macdonough purchased the 125-by-24-foot hull of what was to be the steamboat *Providence* from the company, and converted the vessel into a 17-gun schooner. Consideration was given to commissioning the first steam-powered gunboat. Such a ves-

An early nineteenth century topsail schooner with a
pivot mount amidships.

sel offered a number of advantages. It provided for the maneuvering
of a galley, with the ability to carry a much larger number of guns. In
the end, the decision not to use the *Providence*'s steam engines was
based more on reliability and the nonexistent supply of spare parts.

The completed 350-ton topsail schooner was ready for service in
May 1814 after having taken on its armament and crew. "The
Schooner is also a fine Vessel & bears her metal full as well as was
expected," Macdonough wrote the secretary of the navy after the
ship's first voyage down the lake to Plattsburgh. The *Ticonderoga* was
commanded by Lt. Stephen Cassin at the Battle of Cumberland Bay,
where it successfully warded off a British attempt to board the vessel
with their gunboat flotilla. At the conclusion of the war the schooner,
along with a number of other vessels, was stripped down and placed
in floating storage, or "ordinary," as it was called. Eventually abandoned, the hulk sank along the shore of the Poultney River. In 1958
what remained of the vessel's hull was retrieved and now rests in a
local museum.

Sources: Vermont Historical Gazetteer, I, 687–688; *The Naval War of 1812*, III,
396–397, 429–431, 480–483, 505, 542, 692; Crisman, *The Eagle*, 113–135.

Name: Gunboats
Nationality: American
Type: Gunboat/Galley
Displacement: 70 tons (larger gunboats), 40 tons (smaller gunboats)

Launched: 1814
Place: Vergennes (6), Burlington (2), Plattsburgh (2)
Armament: 1 x 24 pdr, 1 x 18 pd columbiad (larger gunboats); 1 x 12 pdr (smaller gunboats)
Crew: 40 (larger gunboats), 26 (smaller gunboats)
Background: The larger gunboats in the American fleet–*Allen, Borer, Burrows, Centipede, Nettle,* and *Viper*–were 75-foot-long row galleys built by Noah Brown at Vergennes in early 1814. Propelled by up to 40 oars and a pair of lateen sails, these vessels carried an 18-pound columbiad in their bow, and a long 24-pound cannon in their stern. The smaller gunboats–*Alwyn, Ballard, Ludlow, Wilmer*–mounted roughly half the number of oars and a single 12-pound gun in their prow.

With a low silhouette, the ability to maneuver against the wind, and a swallow draft which gave these vessels the ability to move up rivers or into tricky bays, both the American and British naval commanders on Lake Champlain initially considered an all-gunboat navy. They were supported in this judgment by the performance of the British gunboats at the Battle of Valcour Island in 1776, and Skenesborough the following year. The failure of the approach, however, was based in firepower and crew requirements. Manpower shortages plagued almost every fleet built on the Lake Champlain waterway, and galleys required too many men for the number of guns that they could bring to bear. The converted sloop *Preble*, for instance, carried 7 nine-pound cannons with a smaller crew complement, and, as it was, Macdonough's fleet was no exception to the manpower shortages. As such it seems that most of the galleys were actually undermanned, and often were forced to draw upon army troops to supplement their ranks.

These vessels performed admirably at the Battle of Cumberland Bay and were instrumental in towing off some of the more badly damaged ships in the aftermath. Upon the conclusion of the war the ten gunboats in the Lake Champlain fleet went up for sale, but they fetched such a miserable price that the decision was made to pull them from the auction. Instead the vessels were purposely sunk for storage and never recovered. The *Allen* was later raised in 1817 and used for patrol duty on the lake until it was abandoned in 1825.

Sources: *Warships of the Great Lakes*, 122–124; *Letter from the Secretary of the Navy . . . Relating to the Capture of the British Fleet on Lake Champlain*, 15–16; "Statement of Noah Brown," *Journal of American History*, #8 (1914), 103–108; *The Naval War of 1812*, 393–395, 424.

BRITISH LAKE CHAMPLAIN FLEET, 1814

OVERVIEW

The British Lake Champlain Fleet 1814

Vessel	Crew	Carronade 32	Carronade 24	Carronade 18	Long 24	Long 18	Long 12	Long 6	Columbiad 18	Totals
Confiance	270	4	4		27					35
Linnet	120						16			16
Chub	41			10		1				11
Finch	41			6				6	1	13
Icicle	5									
3 Gunboats	180		3		3					6
1 Gunboat	60	1				1				2
1 Gunboat	60			1				1		2
4 Gunboats	140	4								4
3 Gunboats	105					3				3
Totals										
Crew	1027									
Guns		9	7	17	30	5	16	7	1	92
Weight of metal (lb)		288	168	306	720	90	192	42	18	1824

Sources: *Vermont Antiquarian*, I, 3 (March 1903), 81–93; *Letter from the Secretary of the Navy . . . Relating to the Capture of the British Fleet on Lake Champlain*, 15–16; *The Battle of Plattsburgh: What Historians Say About It*, 11; *Warships of the Great Lakes*, 122–124.

VESSELS

Name: *Linnet*
Nationality: British
Type: Brig
Displacement: 350 tons
Length: 82´6˝

Beam: 27′
Draft: 6′8″
Launched: 1814
Place: Ile aux Noix
Armament: 16 x 12 pdrs
Crew: 120
Background: The 16-gun brig *Linnet* was built by master carpenter William Simmons in response to the naval arms race that developed on Lake Champlain in 1814. When it was launched in April its addition gave temporary naval superiority to the British, which they used to launch an unsuccessful attack on the American works at Point Cassion. Macdonough when he saw the vessel for the first time referred to it in his reports as "First class, a remarkably fine looking vessel." Recent archaeological evidence supports the naval commander's opinion, showing that the *Linnet* was constructed in a more careful manner than many of the other warships rushed into service on the lake. After the *Linnet*'s capture at Cumberland Bay it was sent to Whitehall, where at the conclusion of the war it was placed in floating storage until sold for its fittings in 1825. Decay caught up with the *Linnet*, and it sank along the west shore of the Poultney River sometime thereafter. An attempt to raise the vessel in 1949 broke what remained of the British brig in two, one half of which drifted downriver. The rest of the vessel settled back onto the bottom where it still rests today.

Sources: *Naval War of 1812, III*, 390–391; Woods, *British Documents of the Canadian War of 1812*, III, part 1, 343–344, 351, 366, 467; Crisman, *The Eagle*, 97–110; Lewis, *British Naval Activity on Lake Champlain*, 12–18, 46–47.

Name: *Chub*
Nationality: British
Type: Sloop
Length: 60′
Beam: 19′
Displacement: 90 tons
Launched: 1810
Place: Essex, N.Y.
Armament: 10 x 18 pd carronades, 1 x 6 pdr

Crew: 41

Background: The *Chub*, which began life as one of the American War Department's purchase of six commercial sloops, was destined to be one of the principal warships on Lake Champlain throughout the War of 1812. It was also destined to carry more names than any other vessel used on these waters. It began life as the *Fox*, built in Essex, N.Y., by Gideon King in 1810. As the name failed to meet a warship's criteria it was renamed the *Bull Dog*, and then in keeping with the canine scheme, it quickly thereafter was christened the *Growler*. Macdonough initially mounted two twelve-pounders, four six-pounders, and one long eighteen-pound gun on the vessel, the latter being in a circular pivot mount. In the winter of 1812, looking for a way to mount more guns on the *Growler* and the *Eagle*, Macdonough modified the quarterdeck to allow the ship to take on two more guns a side. He then replaced all of the guns on the vessel with recently arrived eighteen-pound carronades, moving some of the replaced guns over to the *Eagle*. The vessel was captured by the British in June 1813 and was promptly put into service under the new name *Shannon*, which like *Bull Dog* did not last. By 1814 the Admiralty had directed that it be renamed the *Chub*, its fifth name in two years. It was badly damaged and captured by the American fleet during the Battle of Cumberland Bay on September 11, 1814. Almost a year later, with the war officially over, it was sold at auction for $835.

Sources: *Vermont Historical Gazetteer*, I, 687–688; *Naval War of 1812*, I, 325–326, 370–371, II, 403–404, 424–425, 488–492, 519, III, 390–391; Woods, *British Documents of the Canadian War of 1812*, III, 422–428; Crisman, *The Eagle*, 99–100; *The Navy of the United States*, 20; *The Plattsburgh Republican*, April–June, 1815.

Name: *Finch*
Nationality: British
Type: Sloop
Length: 64´
Beam: 20´4˝
Draft: 6´
Displacement: 90 tons
Launched: 1810
Place: Whitehall

Armament: 6 x 18 pd carronades, 4 x 6 pdrs, 1 x 18 pd columbiad
Crew: 41
Background: The *Finch* began its life as the merchantman *Hunter*. It was obtained from Gideon King as part of the initial purchase of six merchant vessels by the War Department in 1812. Briefly renamed the *Bulldog*, it was finally given the name *Eagle*. Macdonough originally armed it with 6 six-pound cannons in the fall of 1812, but in early 1813 the American commander had the quarterdeck of the vessel reworked to increase its gun count to eleven. Along with the *Growler*, the *Eagle* was captured near Ash Island a few months later. Nearly intact, it was taken to St. Johns to be repaired and refitted, and within a week was flying a British banner under the name *Broke*. When the British Admiralty department took over responsibility for the lake establishments in 1814 it was renamed *Finch* to prevent the duplication of names within the British service. The *Finch* participated in every major action along Lake Champlain during the War of 1812 before being recaptured by the Americans at the Battle of Cumberland Bay. When the war ended in 1815 the *Finch*, along with many other elements of the American Lake Champlain fleet, went up for public auction. It was purchased by none other than its original owner, Gideon King, for $805.

Sources: *Naval War of 1812*, I, 325–326, 370–371, II, 403–404, 424–425, 488–492, 519, III, 390–391; Crisman, *The Eagle*, 99–100; *The Navy of the United States*, 20; *The Plattsburgh Republican, April–June, 1815*; Woods, *British Documents of the Canadian War of 1812*, III, 482–484, 495–497.

Name: *Confiance*
Nationality: British
Type: Frigate
Length: 147´5˝
Beam: 37´2˝
Draft: 8´
Displacement: 1,200 tons
Launched: 1814
Place: Ile aux Noix
Armament: 27 x 24 pdrs, 4 x 32 pd carronades, 4 x 24 pd carronades
Crew: 270

Background: In response to American naval control of Lake Champlain during the summer of 1814 British governor George Prevost ordered the construction of a vessel that would dominate anything it encountered. The result was the 35-gun, fifth-rate frigate *Confiance*, the largest warship to ever sail on the lake. Named after Commodore James Yeo's first command, a French privateer he captured at Muros Bay, the three-masted warship was built at Ile aux Noix by William Simons in the late summer of 1814. To keep his timetable concerning the planned invasion of upper New York, in August Governor Prevost ordered all industries associated with the construction of the frigate to make this project their number-one priority. Even so, Prevost's planned invasion of upper New York was ultimately delayed by the construction of this vessel. It slid into the east channel of the island on August 27, 1814, very much a rushed ship. Numerous complaints would arise as to the unfinished state of the vessel when it participated in the Battle of Cumberland Bay a few weeks after its launch. Its sailing master, Robert Brydon, later testified that "the Guns in general worked very heavy, owing to the Decks being rough scraped, and a quantity of Pitch on them." The ship's carpenter, Henry Cox, was more critical. "She had only one Pump fit for Service, and the other I had to finish during the time she was in Action, some of the Bolts in the Sides (breaching Bolts) were not perfectly cinched neither was there a Cleat or belaying Pin, fit to belay a Rope to, and the Ship was in an unfinished State altogether."

Several officers, Captain Pring among them, believed that the vessel required more time before being put into combat. This feeling stemmed as much from the state of the crew as the engineering deficiencies in the frigate. To man the *Confiance* Prevost had ordered drafts to be made among the warships and transports in the St. Lawrence. This approach had been used for many years to man naval expeditions on Lake Champlain. Carleton had used this method with success, as had Prevost in the past in organizing Murray's Raid. In these instances, however, the drafted sailors that manned the lake vessels typically came from the same crew, which since all the hands had worked together in the past allowed for a smoother transition to the new vessel. The complement of the *Confiance*, however, dwarfed the normal demands for seamen. As such the 270-man crew was taken from the following:

From	Number	From	Number
Officers	20	*Montreal*	2
Leopard	58	Lake Establishment	12
Ceylon	26	Transports	25
Ajax	10	Impressed	4
Warspite	12	Prison	1
Virgo	1	Volunteers	2
Indian	7	Royal Marines	65
Linnet	1	Royal Artillery	3
Royal Sovereign	2	Royal Marine Artillery	8
Cornelia	1	39th Regiment	10

The diverse complement in and of itself would not have been so detrimental if the crew had been given sufficient time to integrate themselves into a team, but as it was, the first elements of the *Confiance*'s crew did not reach the ship until September 6 and the last elements arrived September 9, two days before the Battle of Cumberland Bay.

If the disorganization of its crew was faulted in the battle, the ship itself could not be blamed. It proved a solid vessel, standing before the combined fire of the *Eagle*, the *Saratoga*, the forward guns of the *Ticonderoga*, as well as a number of gunboats for over two hours. The warship had been hulled 105 times and had three and a half feet of water in its hold when it finally surrendered. It likely would have sunk were it not for the shifting of its guns to starboard which kept the damaged port planks out of the water. Its days as a warship, however, were over. After several weeks at Plattsburgh while damage was repaired, the *Confiance*, along with the captured *Linnet*, the *Saratoga*, and the *Ticonderoga*, were sent to winter quarters at Whitehall. With the conclusion of the war it was stripped down to its main masts, covered, and placed in floating storage at Whitehall along with a number of other warships. In 1820 the *Confiance* had decayed to such a point that it sank on even keel in six feet of water along the west bank of the Poultney River, clear of the main channel. Four years later the rains washed the wreck into the main channel. The vessel was partially dismantled to clear the channel, but apparently portions of the hull remained. In 1873 what remained of the *Confiance* was destroyed by explosives to remove any threat to navigation.

Sources: Woods, *British Documents of the Canadian War of 1812*, III, part 1, 475–481; Malcomson, *Warships of the Great Lakes, 1754–1834*, 131–133; Crisman, *The Eagle*, 97–110; Chapelle, *The American Sailing Navy*, 299.

Name: *Yeo, Prevost, Blucher* . . .
Type: Gunboat/Galley
Launched: 1812–1814
Displacement: 40 to 50 tons
Place: Ile aux Noix
Armament: see below
Crew: 25–41
Background: Twelve of these row galleries, typically rigged as cutters, were either built at Ile aux Noix, or elsewhere in Canada and then transported around the St. Jean rapids to Ile aux Noix. A list of these vessels along with their specifics is shown below.

Name	Length (feet)	Beam) (feet)	Carronades (no./size)	Long-guns (no./size)	Crew
Beckwith	57	12.5		1–18	33
Beresford	46	11	1–32		25
Blucher	57	12.5	1–32	1–18	41
Brock	46	11	1–32		25
Drummond	62	12		1–18	33
Murray	62	12		1–18	33
Popham	46	11	1–32		25
Prevost	64	12	1–32	1–24	41
Simcoe	32	7.5	1–32		25
Wellington	53	12	1–18	1–18	35
Yeo	62	12	1–32	1–24	41

The British gunboat flotilla stationed at Ile aux Noix was employed with mixed success. Vessels of this flotilla successfully captured the USS *Eagle* and *Growler* near Ash Island in 1813, and were at the heart of a number of successful raids along the shores of the lake. The weaknesses of the flotilla, however, showed at the Battle of Cumberland Bay when a large portion of the British gunboats did not execute the command to advance and board the enemy schooner *Ticonderoga*.

Given the level of training, and the need to draw upon militia troops to man large portions of the flotilla, it is perhaps understandable. The idea of attacking a vessel armed with 32-pound carronades loaded with grapeshot and backed by broadsides of 18- and 12-pound long guns, any one of which could cripple a gunboat with a single hit, was a daunting task for trained crews much the less militia crews. A handful of the British gunboats did advance on the schooner *Ticonderoga*, but they were too few in number to seriously threaten the warship.

Although all of the British gunboats escaped the Battle of Cumberland Bay, they were ordered to be disassembled at the conclusion of hostilities. Of an order for twelve gunboats placed with shipbuilder John Goudie, three were armed and launched at Ile aux Noix and served with the garrison there after the war.

Sources: Lewis, *British Naval Activity on Lake Champlain*, 17–18, 46–48; *Naval War of 1812*, III, 703–704; *Warships of the Great Lakes*, *1754–1834*, 136–137; Chapelle, 303–304.

Name: *Canada, Icicle*
Nationality: British
Type: Tender
Canada
Length: 44´
Beam: 14´
Displacement: 34 tons
Icicle
Length: 32´
Beam: 11´4˝
Displacement: 20 tons
Launched: 1814
Place: Ile aux Noix
Armament: none
Crew: 5
Background: These vessels were small tenders used to supply the British operations on Lake Champlain. The *Canada* was the former merchantman *Mars*, taken by the British during Murray's Raid in the summer of 1813, and it is likely that the *Icicle* is either the *William Maid* or *Federal Victory*, both of which were captured during the same raid. Several other captured American merchant vessels were also

employed in this role. One, the *Burlington Packet*, sank near Grand
Island during the British retreat from the Battle of Cumberland Bay
and was later recovered by the Americans.

Sources: "The British Attack on Burlington," *Vermont History*, XXIX, 2 (April 1961),
83; Irving, L. Homfrey, *Officers of the British Forces in Canada during the War
1812-15*, 223-224. Woods, *British Documents of the Canadian War of 1812*, III, part
1, 400; *Plattsburgh Republican* 3, Dec. 1814. The captured *Burlington Packet* was
raised in November (*Niles Weekly Register*, VII, 192); Lewis, *British Naval Activity
on Lake Champlain*, 16, 46.

U.S. NAVY VESSELS CONSTRUCTED ON LAKE CHAMPLAIN,
1942–1945[a]

Vessel	Type	Length (ft.)	Launched	Comment
SC 1029[b]	Subchaser	110	16 Nov. 1942	to Free French 1944, CH 123
SC 1030	Subchaser	110	16 Nov. 1942	to Free French 1944, CH 136
YFT3[c]	Torpedo Lighter	85	1943	
YFT4	Torpedo Lighter	85	1943	
YFT5	Torpedo Lighter	85	1943	
YT297[d]	Yard Tug	66	1943–44	later YTL 297
YT298	Yard Tug	66	1943–45	later YTL 298
YT299	Yard Tug	66	1943–46	later YTL 299
YT300	Yard Tug	66	1943–47	later YTL 300
SC 1504	Subchaser	110	31 May 1944	to USSR 1944, BO-228
SC 1505	Subchaser	110	29 June 1944	to USSR 1944, BO-234
SC 1506	Subchaser	110	21 July 1944	to USSR 1944, BO-241

a. All built at Shelburne Shipyards by Donovan Contracting.
b. The subchasers built at the Shelburne Shipyard were armed with a 75mm cannon (forward) and a pair of twin .50-caliber machine guns mounted amidship.
The vessels also carried depth charges and a crew complement of 22. Maximum
speed was 20 knots.
c. These unarmed vessels were used for torpedo transportation during harbor
resupply operations.

d. These were small tugboats used for harbor or river operations.

Sources: *From Steamboats to Subchasers*: A History of the Shelburne Shipyard, Red Barn Books, 2012; also "Shipyard Index: Shelburne Shipyard, Shelburne Vermont." at Shipbuilders.com.

GLOSSARY

*Abaft of aft–*Those sections of the ship that lay toward the stern or near the stern.

*Abeam–*Perpendicular to the center point of the hull: "the schooner was lying abeam of us."

*Abreast–*Side by side. For two vessels sailing abreast, their sides would be parallel to one another.

*Acting Lieutenant–*A warrant officer's position below that of lieutenant. In the Royal Navy the term was later replaced with that of sub-lieutenant.

*Aloft–*A term referencing the mast tops or rigging above the deck.

*Amidships–*Pertaining to the middle or center of the ship.

*Anchor–*There are several types of anchors. The main or bower anchor is the vessel's primary anchor used when the vessel is at rest or in a holding position. Another type of anchor carried by the small lake vessels was a kedge anchor. These anchors, of which several might be carried, were lighter than the main anchor, but could be deployed to limit a vessel's turning radius or for warping.

*Athwart–*Crossing the vessel's bow.

*Avast–*An order to stop or desist from a task.

*Backstays–*These are ropes attached to the top of the vessel's mast(s) that are anchored to the deck or sides of the ship aft of the mast. These ropes help support the mast against the force exerted on it by the wind pushing on its sails.

*Between wind and water–*This is the area of a ship's hull that is exposed when the vessel tacks to one side or from the simple rolling of waves. A ship damaged in this area would take on water, particularly if it attempted to tack to the damaged side.

Blocks–The wooden portions of pulley arrangements over which ropes are passed to give mechanical advantage and allow for the lifting of heavy loads.

Boarding Netting–Angled nets secured to the sides of the ship to prevent boarding by enemy sailors.

Bomb–A mortar round. This short range exploding ordinance required the fuse on the round to be lit before the gun's charge was fired, which (usually) launched it at the intended target.

Boom–A long spar extending from a mast, or in the case of the bowsprint the vessel's prow, to hold or extend the foot of a sail. The term is also used to describe a barrier composed of a chain and/or floating logs which is deployed to obstruct water passage.

Bow–Pertaining to the front part of the ship or in the direction of the front of the ship.

Bowsprit–A boom extending from the bow of the ship which is used to anchor the jib and stay sails.

Breeching–A rope used to restrict, or limit the recoil of a cannon.

Brigantine–A brigantine is a two-masted vessel where the main (forward) mast is square sail rigged and the rear mast is inline rigged.

Cable–A large rope. In the time period in question if the cable were made of chain it is typically distinguished from rope and referred to as a chain cable.

Cannon–Cannons of the eighteenth and early nineteenth centuries were scaled based on the weight of shot they fired. Hence, a six-pound cannon, or a six-pounder, as it would have been called, fired a round shot weighing six pounds. The range of cannon scaled in this fashion spanned from diminutive three-pound guns to thirty-two- and forty-eight-pound behemoths that were reserved for the strongest fortresses and ships-of-the-line. Cannons below two or three pounds were typically classified as swivel guns.

Capstan–A machine employing mechanical advantage to haul up anchors.

Captain–A commissioned officer's rank above commander, and usually associated with the command of a frigate-sized or larger vessel.

Carronade–A short-barreled wide-mouth cannon designed for engaging an opponent at close range. Carronades offered two advantages. First, they were significantly lighter than comparable long guns, meaning that more guns could be carried, and second, they required smaller gun crews to operate. Both of these advantages translated to more firepower, especially for small vessels like those operating in the Champlain and Richelieu valleys, where weight and the shortage of experienced gunners were always an important consideration.

Casemates–Chambers under the forts ramparts or walls used for storage and cover for the garrison during a bombardment. These were sometimes referred to as bomb-proofs.

Chain Shot–This round consisted of smaller round-shot linked together by a length of chain. The purpose of the round was to damage an opponent's sails and rigging, thereby reducing their maneuverability. A variation on chain shot is bar shot, where the larger ends are connected by an iron bar instead of a chain.

Close Hauled–A vessel is close hauled when it is beating into the wind. That is, its sails are rigged to impart as much forward motion as possible, while sailing a zigzag pattern against the wind. There is a practical limit to how close a vessel could sail into the wind without risking not having enough wind in its sails to maintain its forward motion. To be able to sail close to the wind was a desirable trait for vessels on the confines of Lake George, Lake Champlain, and the Richelieu River, where tricky winds could make headway along the waterways difficult.

Commander–A commissioned officer's rank originally entitled "master and commander" in the Royal Navy, until it was shortened to just commander in the early 1800s.

Commodore–Commissioned officer's rank above captain, typically involving the command of several vessels.

Cordage–A general term for the running rigging of a ship or the rope that is used to maintain and operate the vessel's sails.

Ensign–The flag used to denote the vessel's nation of origin; also an army rank being that before lieutenant. The rank would later become associated with naval operations on par with the army rank of second lieutenant.

Fathom–A nautical unit of distance measuring six feet.

Fouled–Pertaining to a line, such as the anchor cable, that is twisted or wrapped around another object in an undesired fashion.

Furling–Wrapping or rolling up a sail in a cylindrical fashion such that it is secured close to its yardarm.

Gaff–A spar attached to the mast in a fore-and-aft sail plan which is used to extend the upper edge of a sail.

Grapeshot–Used for close range encounters, grapeshot consisted of a load of large musket balls prepackaged in a cloth bag that would disintegrate upon firing. The range of a gun firing grapeshot was drastically reduced, but at close quarters the effects could be devastating upon exposed enemy crews, as well as their vessel's rigging. An extension of this idea was the canister, a prepackaged cartridge that fired a large number of smaller musket balls.

Haul–A nautical expression implying to pull on a single rope such as to haul-down, haul-in, etc.

Helm–The term helm pertains to the parts of the ship that control its direction. The physical components involved consist of three parts, the rudder, the tiller, and the wheel. Note that on small vessels a wheel is typically not used.

Knot–The measurement of a vessel's speed, being nautical miles (1.15 statute miles) per hour.

Lanyard–Ropes used for various purposes on a ship such as the buoy lanyard, among others.

Larboard–The port side.

Leeward–The side of the ship away from, or sheltered from the wind; the side of the ship not in first contact with the wind.

Lieutenant–The lowest commissioned officer rank aboard a vessel.

Master–The master or sailing master of the vessel was responsible for the sailing and navigation of the vessel. The position was also a senior warrant officer rank, below that of lieutenant.

Master Commandant–An early U.S. naval rank between lieutenant and captain. The rank would eventually be changed to commander.

Midshipman–This was an officer candidate who occupied a position between the crew and those ranking as warrant officers.

Mortar–A broad wide-mouthed cannon designed to launch explosive rounds. Mortars were classified by the diameter of the "bomb" they could fire. Their range was much shorter than that of typical cannon, but the arching trajectory of their fire meant that mortars could drop their rounds over enemy fortifications and walls.

Oakum–A substance used to caulk the seams of a vessel.

Petty Officer–A petty officer was a seaman specialized in a rating, or technical art required either to run the vessel or operate its guns. Such positions were the senior ranking seamen among the crew.

Port–The left side of the vessel.

Ratlines or Ratlings–Rope ladders that lead from the deck to the mastheads.

Redoubt–An earthen field fortification that is sometimes reinforced by timbers.

Rigging–A term that encompasses all the ropes and lines required to operate the sails of a vessel.

Round-Shot–A cannonball, the size and weight of which was determined by the poundage of the cannon.

Sail Plan–The sail plan of a vessel refers to how the sails are laid out, what type of sails are employed, and what number of sails are present. Sail plans fall into several broad categories, inline sail plans, like a sloop and a schooner where the mains sails were swung on booms to catch the wind, square rigged vessels, like a frigate where the main sails are fixed across yards attached perpendicularly to the masts, combinations of the two such as a brigantine, or cutter, and lateen rigged vessels with large triangular sails, like xebecs. Galleys, gondolas, and radeaux being viewed as rowed vessels were not classified by sail plan although all three carried various types of sailing rigs.

Schooner–A two-masted vessel with an inline sail plan. Some would employ a small square sail at the top of the main mast, and hence were referred to as topsail schooners.

Ship–A three-masted vessel, square-sail rigged.

Ship types–Ships were typically referred to by their rigging type, or primary propulsion type as in the case of a radeaux or galley. Warships however, under the British rating system were also officially classified by number of gun decks, number of guns, and size regardless of their sail plan. This rating system is shown in Appendix C.

Shrouds–These are lines strung from the ship's masts secured to the side of the vessel. These lines are typically net arrangements in larger ship rigged vessels, and are seen in two sets, a topmast shroud and a lower shroud. (see image no. 1)

Sloop–A single-masted vessel employing an inline sail plan. These vessels were favored for their ability to get under way in light or variable winds, such as are often encountered on the lakes and rivers of the Champlain Valley.

Starboard–The right side of the vessel.

Swivel guns–Small cannons mounted on a pivot or swivel arrangement along a ship's deck rails. These small guns could fire round-shot or grapeshot, with the early guns of this type being designed to fire small stone projectiles.

Tacking–Technically, tacking is the act of turning the vessel's bow through the direction in which the wind is blowing. Often however, it is used in the sense of beating to windward or beating upwind, where the vessel makes a zigzag course so that the angle in which the wind strikes the sails imparts a forward and lateral motion to the vessel, which makes up the legs of the zigzag pattern.

Tackle–As in a block-and-tackle pulley arrangement used aboard sailing vessels to lift heavy loads.

Warping–The movement of a vessel by which the vessel is winched to its anchor. A small boat would deploy the ship's anchor some distance ahead, upon which the ship would pull itself to the anchor. Given the contrary winds, the current, and the limited room to tack, warping was popular on the Richelieu River.

Weather gauge–The weather gauge is the status of the prevailing winds. More often the term is encountered in the form of "having the weather gauge," meaning having the wind in one's favor or having the ability to maneuver. Not having the weather gauge would imply a lack of maneuvering options given the status of the wind.

Windward–The side of the ship which is facing the wind.

Xebec–A small three-masted vessel with a shape similar to that of a galley. These vessels typically employed large triangular sails, the tops of which were attached to a yardarm that was set at an angle to the mast. This lateen sail arrangement made xebecs fast and very maneuverable, but tricky to handle especially when running before the wind. Built for speed rather than fighting, this was the vessel of choice among the Mediterranean raiders of the day.

Yards–Long cylindrical spars hung to the masts of a craft in a perpendicular fashion to allow for the deployment of the vessel's sails.

NOTES

ABBREVIATIONS

Amherst Journal	Webster, ed., *The Journals of Jeffery Amherst*
CO5	Colonial Office Records, American and West Indies, London
DCB	*Dictionary of Canadian Biography*
DHSNY	O'Callaghan, ed., *Documentary History of the State of New York*
EIHC	*Essex Institute Historical Collections*
FTMB	*Fort Ticonderoga Museum Bulletin*
NAC	National Archives of Canada, Ottawa
NDAR	Clark et al., eds., *Naval Documents of the American Revolution*
NEHGR	*New England Historical and Genealogical Register*
NY Col. Doc.	O'Callaghan, ed., *Documents Relative to the Colonial History of the State of New York*
NYHSC	*New-York Historical Society Collections*
RAPQ	*Rapport de l'Archiviste de la Province de Québec*
WO	War Office Records, London

CHAPTER 1: THE CHAMPLAIN WATERWAY

1. *NY Col. Doc.*, IX, 17–19, 52–54; *Jesuit Relations*, vol. 50, 141–145, 199–203; Marshall, *Word from New France*, 321–325; *DHSNY*, I, 74–78.

2. Marshall, *Word from New France*, 330. A storm during Tracy's return voyage down Lake Champlain accounted for the only losses in the expedition when two canoes where swamped and their eight occupants drowned (*Jesuit Relations*, vol. 50, 147).

3. Colden, *History of the Five Nations*, I, 17–18; *Jesuit Relations*, vol. 50, 209–211. The treaty concluded Tracy's and the Carignan–Salières regiment's task in Canada, but given the previous dealings with the Mohawk it was deemed unwise to call for their immediate return to France. Tracy and the two La Colonel companies departed for France in late 1667, but the bulk of the regiment and the Marquis de Salières were to remain in Canada manning and consolidating the defensive works along the Richelieu River for another year. When the regiment finally did embark for France in 1668, over 400 officers and men chose to accept the king's offer of land and money and stay in Canada. (Verney, *The Good Regiment*, 116–117).

4. *NY Col. Doc,* III, 771–772, 800–805, IV, 193–196, IX, 466–469, 842–843; *DHSNY,* I, 285–306, II, 279–288; Whitehead, *Contributions to the Early History of Perth Amboy,* 87–89; "Catastrophe in the Wilderness," 441–456. *Calender American & West Indies Papers, Vol. 24 (1708–1709),* 488–496; Vaudreuil to Ministre, Nov. 12, 1712, MG1-C11A, vol. 33, fols. 15–37; Mémoire de M. de Lery–Fort de Chambly, Oct. 26, 1720, MG8-A1 serie 3, vol. 7, 741–744.

5. Roy, *Hommes et Choses du Fort Saint-Frédéric,* 20–21; Plan du Terrain de la Pointe a la Chevelure, Oct. 25, 1731, MG1-C11A, vol. 54, fols. 346–346v; Conseil de Marine à M. Rocbert de Morandière, April 22, 1732, MG1-B, vol. 57, fol. 644; *NY Col. Doc.,* IX, 1034, 1037. For the initial colonial reaction to the French fort see *Calender American & West Indies Papers, Vol. 38 (1731),* 312–314, 331–332. At this time Pointe-a-la-Chevelure or Scalp Point referred to the peninsulas on both sides of the lake today known separately as Crown Point and Chimney Point. The English and Dutch also did not distinguish between the two sides of the lake at this time referring to the whole region as Crown Point, with the term "crown" referring to the top of one's head.

CHAPTER 2: THE FIRST FLEETS

1. Beauharnois to Minister, 13 October 1735, National Archives of Canada (NAC), MG1-C11A, vol. 63, fol. 73–103; Hocquart to Minister, 3 October 1741, ibid., vol. 75, fol. 28–33.

2. Projet de dépense pour la construction et armement d'une gabare ou bateau plat . . . à faire naviguer dans le lac Champlain, NAC, MG1-C11A, vol. 73, fols. 21–22; Beauharnois and Hocquart to Minister, 5 November 1740, ibid., vol. 73, fols. 46–48v; Rogers, *Journals,* 21; Hamilton, ed., *Adventure in the Wilderness,* 65; Extrait des registres des magasins . . . la présente année 1746 (31 December 1746), NAC, MG1-C11A, vol. 88, fols. 214–245; État de la dépense . . . du fort Saint-Frédéric . . . 1744, ibid., vol. 84, fols. 113–114; État de la dépense . . . du fort Saint-Frédéric pendant l'année 1746 (15 October 1747), ibid., vol. 88, fols. 246–246v; Kalm, *Travels into North America,* 3: 42.

3. Beauharnois and Hocquart to Minister, 5 October and 5 November 1740, NAC, MG1-C11A, vol. 73, fol. 19–20v, 46–48v; Projet de dépense pour la construction et armement d'une gabare ou bateau plat . . . à faire naviguer dans le lac Champlain, NAC, MG1-C11A, vol. 73, fols. 21–22; Extrait des registres des magasins . . . la présente année 1746 (31 December 1746), NAC, MG1-C11A, vol. 88, fols. 214–245; État de la dépense . . . du fort Saint-Frédéric . . . 1744, ibid., vol. 84, fols. 113–114; État de la dépense . . . du fort Saint-Frédéric pendant l'année 1746 (15 October 1747), ibid., vol. 88, fols. 246–246v; Kalm, *Travels into North America,* 3: 42.

4. "Journal of Chaussegros de Léry," *FTMB* (July 1942), 143–144; "Meloizes Journal"), 11; Rogers, *Journals,* 21–22; Casgrain, ed., *Lettres du Marquis de Vaudreuil,* 25. Ile aux Têtes is known today as Ash Island.

5. Malartic, *Journal*, 108; Levasseur to Minister, 1 November 1756 and 1 November 1757, NAC, MG1-C11A, vol. 101, fols. 318–319 and vol. 102, fols. 223–224.

6. A difficult proposition given the thirty-seven-foot waterfall a few miles upstream.

7. Joshua Loring, *DCB*, IV. Officers on half pay were equivalent to active reservists.

8. "Loring to Admiralty, 16 September, 1756," Admiralty Papers, I, vol. 2046.

9. *NY Col. Doc.*, X, 542–544, 551, 576; Casgrain, *Montcalm's Journal*, 159–160; "Relation de M. Poularies," 47–48; Casgrain, *Relations et Journaux* . . . , 81–82; Eyre to Loudoun, 20, 24, and 25 March 1757, CO5/48; "Journal of an Attack made on Fort William Henry," WO34/101.

10. Kimball, *The Correspondence of William Pitt*, I, 15, 18, 39–40, 53; Pargellis, *Lord Loudoun in North America*, 232–235, 244–246; Webb to Loudoun, 5 Aug. 1757, CO5/48; *Collections of the New-York Historical Society for the Year 1881: Montresor Journals*, 37.

11. "Father Pere Roubaud's Letter," *Jesuit Relations*, vol. 70, 106–107; *NY Col. Doc.*, X, 594, 599; Webb to Loudoun, 1 Aug. 1757, CO5/48.

12. Hamilton, *Bougainville Journals*, 140–141; Casgrain, *Levis Journal*, 85–86; *NY Col. Doc.*, X, 591.

13. Hamilton, *Bougainville Journals*, 142–143; Casgrain, *Levis Journal*, 86–87; "Roubaud's Letter," 119–123; *NY Col. Doc.*, X, 591, 594; *Supplement to the New York Mercury*, 1 Aug. 1757; Webb to Loudoun, 1 Aug. 1757, CO5/48; *Colden Papers*, V, 163–164.

14. *Supplement to the New York Mercury*, 1 Aug. 1757; "Roubaud's Letter," 119–123; *NY Col. Doc.*, X, 591; Webb to Loudoun, 1 Aug. 1757, CO5/48. Webb stated that fifty or so of Parker's men returned with him and that another fifty made their way back a few days later. The rest were listed as missing. The accounts in the Colden Papers and the *New York Mercury* give slightly higher numbers stating that seventy or so returned with Parker and that another sixty to seventy found their way back later. Roubaud gave specific numbers, 157 taken prisoner and 131 killed. Montcalm's numbers were much higher. In a letter to Vaudreuil on the incident he claimed that 160 or so of the English were killed in the attack while he had taken 160 prisoners, including five officers. As he had access to the official returns, Webb's numbers hold the most weight, which implies that both Montcalm and Roubaud overestimated the actual number of English killed in the attack.

15. Casgrain, *Levis Journal*, 87; Webb to Loudoun, 1 Aug. 1757, CO5/48; Loudoun to Holdernesse, 16 Aug. 1757, CO5/48.

16. *NY Col. Doc.*, X, 604–605, 617–618, 621–626, 631; *Bougainville Journals*, 175–178; "Relation of M. Poularies," 65–66; "A Journal Kept During the Siege of Fort William Henry," 149–150.

17. Loring to --, Aug. 19, 1758, Chatham Fonds MG23-A2, vol 8.

18. Choate (ed.), "Journal," 117–119; Knox, *Historical Journal*, I, 378, 382, 386.

19. Choate, "Journal," 119–121; Trowbridge, *The Champion Genealogy*, 431; Abbass, *Plan View of the Land Tortoise Radeau.*

20. Choate, "Journal," 121–122; Trowbridge, *The Champion Genealogy*, 433.

CHAPTER 3: THE DESTRUCTION OF THE LAKE CHAMPLAIN FRENCH FLEET

1. *Amherst Journal*, 153.

2. For the details behind Amherst's campaign and the capture of Forts Carillon and St. Frédéric the reader is directed to *Amherst Journal* as well as "Captain-Lieutenant Skinner's Journal," in Samuel, *The Seven Years War in Canada, 1756-1763*, Colonel William Amherst's Journal, CO5/56, and "Meloizes Journal," *RAPQ* (1928–1929).

3. *Amherst Journal*, 146–148.

4. Ibid., 156–157.

5. Ibid., 157–158, 163; Amherst to Loring, 23 and 27 Aug. 1759, and Loring to Amherst, 22, 28, 29 Aug., 19 and 23 Sept. 1759, WO34/64.

6. Amherst to Loring, 15 Sept. 1759, WO34/65; Loescher, *The History of Rogers' Rangers*, II, 52–55; "Wood Diaries," 190–191; "Meloizes Journal," 73. Although the expedition failed to burn the French sloop they were able to correctly identify the state of the vessel. "The Serjeant Who Commanded the Party," Amherst wrote Loring, "imagines the Enemy does not intend to rig her as She is laid across the Channel with Six guns run out on one Side two port holes shut up. Pickets Drove in the channel from the Island to opposite Shore to the Bow and Stern of the vessel." (Amherst to Loring, 15 Sept. 1759.)

7. *Amherst Journal*, 148, 153, 163, 167–168; Amherst to Loring, 23 and 27 Aug. 1759, and Loring to Amherst, 22, 28, and 29 Aug., 19 and 23 Sept. 1759, WO34/64.

8. Casgrain, *Lettres de Bourlamaque*, 10–17, 26–28; Levis to Bourlamaque, 23 May and 2 June 1759, NAC MG18-K9 vol. 3, 83–86, 91–94.

9. Casgrain, *Lettres de Bourlamaque*, 17, 21, 30–31; Webster, *Amherst Journal*, 156–157; "Meloizes Journal," 39, 80–81; *NY Col. Doc.* X, 1055; État de la dépense faite pour l'entretien du fort Saint-Frédéric . . . , 24 Oct. 1745, NAC MG1-C11A, vol. 84, 113–114; Rene Levasseur to Ministre, 1 Nov. 1757 and 30 Oct. 1758, NAC MG1-C11A, vol. 102, 223–224, vol. 103, 414–417; Return of Guns . . . found on board the Three French Sloops, CO5/57; Charbonneau, *The Fortifications of Ile aux Noix*, 331–336.

10. Olabaratz, *DCB*, V.

11. *Amherst Journal*, 178–179; "Sailing Orders for Captain Joshua Loring,"10 Oct. 1759, WO34/64.

12. Amherst to Pitt, 22 Oct. 1759, CO5/57; *Amherst Journal*, 179. As a point of comparison between the two fleets, based on what was believed according to information related by a previous French deserter (weight of metal–French fleet 180 lbs, Loring 156 lbs.; tonnage–French 265 tons, Loring 270 tons; manpower–

French 178, Loring 224) shows that Loring's two ships were easily on equal footing with the combined French squadron. In actuality the French fleet only possessed a 152 lb. weight of metal, less than the combined weight of Loring's sloop and brig.

13. *Amherst Journal*, 180–181; Loring to Admiralty, 22 Nov. 1759, NAC, Admiralty Papers I, vol. 2048; Casgrain, *Lettres de Bourlamaque*, 61; "Meloizes Journal," 80; Knox, *Journal*, II, 196.

14. *Amherst Journal*, 179–180. Casgrain, *Lettres de Bourlamaque*, 30, 61; Amherst to Pitt, 22 Oct. 1759, CO5/57; *NY Col. Doc.*, X, 1056. Amherst's convoy was protected by the *Ligonier* and three gunboats each mounting a 12-pound gun in their prow.

15. Loring to Admiralty, 22 Nov. 1759, NAC, Admiralty Papers vol. 2048; *Amherst, Journal*, 180–181. Amherst to Pitt, 22 Oct. 1759, CO5/57; Kimball, *Pitt Correspondence*, II, 200, 223–224; Casgrain, *Lettres de Bourlamaque*, 62, 65–66, 68; "Meloizes Journal," 80–81; *NY Col. Doc.*, X, 1056; Knox, *Journal*, II, 196–197; Casgrain, *Levis Journal*, 228. The French twelve-pound brass guns were recovered by divers in the 1960s. One of these short brass guns can be found on display at the Crown Point state museum. Ironically, it has English markings and may have been captured at Oswego in 1756. (*NY Col. Doc.*, X, 485).

16. Casgrain, *Lettres de Bourlamaque*, 65–68. In an impressive undertaking Lt. Grant managed to salvage all three French xebecs. By November 16 these vessels, which doubled the English naval presence on Lake Champlain, were safely anchored under the guns of Fort Ticonderoga. (*Amherst Journal*, 191; Kimball, *Pitt Correspondence*, II, 223–224.)

17. Casgrain, ed. *Lettres de Divers Particuliers*, 137–147; *NY Col. Doc.* X, 1101–1102; *Memoirs of the Chevalier de Johnstone*, 3: 68–69.

18. Casgrain, *Lettres de Divers Particuliers*, 148–149; Casgrain, *Levis Journal*, 288; "Mémoire sur la Frontière du Lac Champlain par M. le Chevalier de Bourlamaque," NAC, MG18–K9, vol. 6, 105–115; "Bourlamaque Instructions to La Valette, 24 Nov. 1759," NAC, MG18–K9, vol. 6, 129–132; Charbonneau, 331–336; *Pennsylvania Gazette*, 11 Sept. 1760.

19. Hastings, ed., *Orderly Book and Journal of Major John Hawks*; Jenks, "Journal"; "Amherst to Grant, 13 April 1760," WO34/65.

20. Rogers, *Journal*, 188–190; "Haviland's Journal, Aug. 11–15, 1760," WO34/77; Holden, "Journal of Sergeant David Holden," 396–397; "Diary of John Bradbury," in Lapham, *Bradbury Memorial*, 275–276.

21. Jenks, "Journal," 368; "Haviland's Journal, Aug. 16, 1760," WO34/77; Rogers, *Journal*, 190; *Col. John Whitcomb's Orderly Book for 1760*, MS at Lancaster Public Library, Lancaster, Mass.

22. "Haviland's Journal, Aug. 17, 1760," WO34/77; "Diary of John Bradbury," 276–277; Woodwell, ed., *The Diary of Thomas Moody*, 26.

23. Casgrain, *Lettres de Divers Particuliers*, 144–146. Haviland in his report on the island's defenses noted that, "The works are extensive and with a great garrison it

could not be taken, but it would require at least 6,000 men to fill it properly."
("Haviland to Amherst, Aug. 31, 1760," WO34/101).
24. "Haviland's Journal, Aug. 23–24, 1760," WO34/77; Jenks, "Journal," 370–371;
"Diary of John Bradbury" 278–279; Holden, "Journal of Sergeant David Holden,"
398; "Jacob Bagley's Journal," in Wells, *History of Newbury, Vermont*, 379–380;
Pennsylvania Gazette, Sept. 18, 1760.
25. "Haviland's Journal, Aug. 24–27, 1760," WO34/77; "Haviland to Amherst,
Aug. 31, 1760," WO34/101; Rogers, *Journal*, 190–191; Jenks, "Journal," 371–372;
Pennsylvania Gazette, 11 and 18 Sept. 1760; Casgrain, *Lettres de Divers Particuliers*,
148–149; *NY Col. Doc.*, X, 1103–1104. A number of English accounts claim that a
sloop was taken as well as the *Vigilante* and the *Grand Diable*. This was actually
the gabare. It should be noted small vessels such as this were commonly misclas-
sified. Loring, for instance, in a survey of the vessels at Fort William Henry in the
fall of 1756, refers to "two open lighters of about 25 tons each" as small sloops in
a list he presented to the Admiralty. ("Diaries Kept by Lemuel Woods," *Essex
Institute Historical Collections*, 20 [1883], 293; Jenks, "Journal," 371; *Pennsylvania
Gazette*, 11 Sept. 1760; "Loring to Admiralty, 29 Sept. 1756," NAC, Admiralty
Papers, vol. 2046.)
26. "Haviland's Journal, Aug. 24–27, 1760," WO34/77; "List of Prisoners Taken at
the Reduction of Ile aux Noix," CO5/59; *Pennsylvania Gazette*, 11 and 18 Sept.
1760.
27. "Haviland's Journal, Aug. 24–27, 1760," WO34/77; "Haviland to Amherst, Aug.
31, 1760," WO34/101; Rogers, *Journal*, 190–191; Jenks, "Journal," 371–372;
Pennsylvania Gazette, 11 Sept. 1760; Casgrain, *Lettres de Divers Particuliers*,
148–149; *NY Col. Doc.* X, 1104. With the abandonment of the island the English
seized the remaining elements of the French Lake Champlain fleet, namely, the
"little one" tartane, and the four Jacobs (*NY Col. Doc.*, X, 1103–1104; Jenks,
"Journal," 371). The importance placed on the French fleet's defense of the
Richelieu River below Ile aux Noix may be seen in a comment allegedly made by
St. Onge. The "Commodore," as the English styled him, was reputed to have
wished Darby "the joy of the country" upon his capture. Meaning simply, that
with this last obstacle cleared that New France was open for the taking.
(*Pennsylvania Gazette*, 11 Sept. 1760.)
28. "Bourlamaque Instructions to La Valette, 24 Nov. 1759," NAC, MG18-K9, vol.
6, 129–132; Casgrain, *Lettres de Bourlamaque*, 21–22; "Diary of John Bradbury," 281.
29. "Journal of Sergeant David Holden," 401; *Amherst Journal*, 245–247. The
Articles of Surrender are printed in *NY Col. Doc.*, X, 1107–1120.

CHAPTER 4: VALCOUR ISLAND

1. *Hadden's Journal*, 16–17; *Digby's Journal*, 150–153; Chapelle 75–76.
2. Carrington, *Battles of the American Revolution, 1775–1776*, 122–137; "Carleton to
Germaine, 14 May, and 20 June 1776," *American Archives*, series 4, vol. 6, 456–457,

1002–1003; *Lamb's Journal*, 109–110; *Enys Journal*, 16; NDAR, V, 20–21. Carleton's command in Canada when hostilities commenced was around 700 regulars, 300 militia, and perhaps 1,200 uncertain native warriors he could call upon (*American Archives*, series 4, vol. 3, 211–212).

3. "Advices from Canada," *American Archives*, series 4, vol. 6, 1089; "Carleton to Douglas, 21 June 1776," NDAR, V, 657; "Douglas to Stevens, 27 June, 1776," NDAR, V, 762–763; "Carleton to Douglas, 29 June 1776" and "Carleton to Pringle, 29 June, 1776," NDAR, V, 806–807.

4. *Hadden's Journal*, 56, *Digby's Journal*, 119–120; NDAR, II, 210, V, 762–763; *American Archives*, series 4, vol. 5, 1099.

5. *Journal of Du Roi the Elder*, 39–40; NDAR, V, 595–596, 889, 957–959, 1184–1185, VI, 54–55; *Digby's Journal*, 120.

6. NDAR, VI, 54–55, 883–884, 951, 1344–1345, 1437; *Digby's Journal*, 118–120; Chapelle, 75–76.

7. NDAR, VI, 45–47, 883–884, 1193–1194, 1257, 1340–1341; Enys's Journal, 16; *Wasmus Journal*, 25.

8. *Digby's Journal*, 153.

9. "Knox's Journal," *Vermont History*, 46, no. 3, 147–148; *Hadden's Journal*, 16–17; *Digby's Journal*, 148, 150–151, 153–157; *Lamb's Journal*, 110.

10. Randall, *Benedict Arnold*, 102–107; *American Archives*, series 4, vol. 2I, 485, 557, 584–585, 645–646, 686. The hastily organized raid was never intended to seize Fort St. Johns. Arnold simply did not possess the manpower or the mandate to hold the British fortification.

11. For accounts of the Canadian campaign and the failed siege of Quebec see Ward, *The War of the Revolution*, I; Randall's *Benedict Arnold*; Carrington, *Battles of the American Revolution, 1775–1776*, among others.

12. Wilkinson, *Memoirs of My Own Times*, I, 54–55; *American Archives*, series 4, vol. 6, 649, 796–797, 925–926, 930–931, 1107–1108.

13. Randall, 244; *American Archives*, series 5, vol. 1, 232–238, 375–376.

14. *American Archives*, series 5, vol. 1, 232–238, 375–376, 396–397.

15. *American Archives*, series 4, vol. 6, 581–582, 641, 758, 925, 1057–1058, 1071–1075; NDAR, V, 132, 680, 733.

16. NDAR, V, 730–731; *American Archives*, series 4, vol. 6, 1101–1108, series 5, vol. 1, 236.

17. *American Archives*, series 5, vol. 1, 207–209, 233, 375–376, 396–398, 559–563; Randall, 247–251.

18. *American Archives*, series 5, vol. 1, 423, 680–682, 1002–1003, 1051, 1073, 1083, 1187, 1218.

19. Ibid., series 5, vol. 1, 581–582, 656, 825–827, 988, 1096, 1123, vol. 2, 834.

20. Ibid., series 5, vol. 1, 1266–1267; "The Journal of Bayze Wells of Farmington," *Collections of the Connecticut Historical Society*, VII (1889), 270–277; NDAR, VI, 857–858, 925–926.

21. *American Archives*, series 5, vol. 2, 834–835, 860–861; "Wells's Journal," 280–282. Gates informed Arnold that the promised 200 New York sailors had not arrived and that he doubted that they ever would. Gates's ultimate answer to Arnold was, "Where it is not to be had, you and the princes of the earth must go unfurnished" (*American Archives*, series 5, vol. 2, 860).

22. "Wells's Journal," 283; "The October 1776 Journal of Jahiel Stewart," *Vermont History*, 64, no. 2 (spring 1996), 91. Also see Appendix D for the *Congress*.

23. "Wells's Journal," 283; *American Archives*, series 5, vol. 2, 1017.

24. "Dr. Robert Knox's Account of the Battle of Valcour Island," *Vermont History*, 46, 3 (summer 1978), 147–148; NDAR, VI, 1272–1274.

25. NDAR, VI, 1235–1237; "Journal of Jahiel Stewart," 92; "The Diary of Pascal De Angelis," *Vermont History*, 42, no. 3 (summer 1974), 198; NDAR, VII, 1294–1295; "Wigglesworth Journal," in Smith, *The History of Newburyport*, 357–358.

26. "Wigglesworth Journal," 358; "The Diary of Pascal De Angelis," 198; *American Archives*, series 5, vol. 2, 1038, 1224; NDAR, IX, 49–51; *Hadden's Journal*, 22–23.

27. *American Archives*, series 5, vol. 2, 440, 1038; NDAR, VI, 1272, IX, 49–51.

28. NDAR, VI, 1272–1275, IX, 49–51; *Digby's Journal*, 158–159; *American Archives*, series 5, vol. 2, 1038; Jones, *History of the Campaign for the Conquest of Canada in 1776*, 164–165.

29. *Journal of Du Roi, the Elder*, 54; Osler, *The Life of Admiral Viscount Exmouth*, 17–18.

30. *Pausch's Journal*, 83–84; *American Archives*, series 5, vol. 2, 1038; "Diary of Joshua Pell," *Magazine of American History*, II (1878), 46; *Hadden's Journal*, 22–24.

31. *American Archives*, series 5, vol. 2, 1038, 1224; *The Life of Admiral Viscount Exmouth*, 17–18; "Journal of Jahiel Stewart," 92.

32. "Wells's Journal," 283–284; *American Archives*, series 5, vol. 2, 1038; *The Life of Admiral Viscount Exmouth*, 17–18; NDAR, VI, 1272–1275; *Hadden's Journal*, 22–24; NDAR, IX, 49–50. Pringle was later criticized for not doing more to refloat and make a prize of the *Royal Savage*. (Ibid.)

33. One British officer claimed that two gunboats had been sunk, and that 10 men had been killed and 16 wounded ("Diary of Joshua Pell," 92), while another account stated that 8 artillery men were lost as well as another 22 sailors and regulars (NDAR, VII, 123). One of the casualties was almost Carleton. Standing on the quarterdeck of the *Maria* with Dr. Knox early in the battle, an eighteen-pound shot whistled over their heads. Knox was clearly unnerved by the shot that barely missed the yard arm above them. "So," Carleton casually turned to Knox and asked, "How do you like your first sea fight?" ("Dr. Knox's Journal," 148).

34. "Wigglesworth Journal," 358; *American Archives*, series 5, vol. 2, 1038, 1224.

35. NDAR, VI, 1275, IX, 49–51; *Hadden's Journal*, 24; *Pausch's Journal*, 84–85.

36. "Wigglesworth Journal," 358; "Journal of Jahiel Stewart," 92.

37. *American Archives*, series 5, vol. 2, 1038, 1079–1080, 1224; "The Diary of Pascal De Angelis," 198–199; "Wigglesworth Journal," 358.

38. "Dr. Knox's Journal," 148; *Hadden's Journal*, 24–29; NDAR, VI, 1274–1275.

39. "Wigglesworth Journal," 358; *American Archives*, series 5, vol. 2, 1079–1080, 1224; "The Diary of Pascal De Angelis," 199; "Journal of Jahiel Stewart," 94.

40. *American Archives*, series 5, vol. 2, 1079–1080; "Dr. Knox's Journal," 148.

41. *American Archives*, series 5, vol. 2, 1079–1080; NDAR, VI, 1275.

42. NDAR, VI, 1257–1258, 1274–1276, 1343–1344.

43. *Report on the Canadian Archives*, 1885, cxxxii–cxxxvi; NDAR, VI, 1336, VII, 784, 789–790; *Hadden's Journal*, 176–177.

44. *General Persifor Fraser*, II, 131.

CHAPTER 5: THE MASTERS OF THE LAKE

1. NDAR, VII, 830–831; *Hadden's Journal*, 52–53.

2. NDAR, VIII, 950–951, 1037; *Hadden's Journal*, 52–57; Burgoyne, *A State of the Expedition from Canada*, viii–ix; *Journal of Du Roi the Elder*, 90–91. "You will be amazed at the work going on at St John's which really almost equals the Dock Yards at home," Lutwidge wrote to a colleague of the naval preparations at St. Johns (NDAR, VIII, 951).

3. Burgoyne, *A State of the Expedition*, xiv–xvi; NDAR, IX, 212–213; *Hadden's Journal*, 82–84; *Digby's Journal*, 201; *Baldwin's Journal*, 108.

4. *Hadden's Journal*, 296–297.

5. Burgoyne, *A State of the Expedition*, xvi; Stone, *The Campaign of Lt. Gen. John Burgoyne*, 16–17; Ward, *The War of the American Revolution*, I, 410; *Hadden's Journal*, 84; Anburey, *Travels*, 319–320.

6. *Proceedings of a General Court Martial . . . of Major General St. Clair*, 11–12, 24–25, 30; Thacher, *Military Journal of the American Revolution*, 82.

7. *Proceedings of a General Court Martial . . . of Major General St. Clair*, 18, 35, 37; Thacher, *Military Journal*, 82–83.

8. Thacher, *Military Journal*, 80; Burgoyne, *A State of the Expedition*, xvi.

9. Thacher, *Military Journal*, 83–84; Burgoyne, *A State of the Expedition*, xvi–xvii; *Journal of Du Roi the Elder*, 96–98.

10. *Hadden's Journal*, 85, 88–89; Thacher, *Military Journal*, 83–84; "Lord Francis Napier's Journal," *Maryland Historical Magazine*, 57, no. 4 (Dec. 1962), 303–305; *Burgoyne's Orderly Book*, 32–33; Anburey, *Travels*, 346–348; *Documents and Records Relating to the State of New Hampshire*, VIII, 621–622; "A Journal of Carleton's and Burgoyne's Campaigns," FTMB, 9, no. 6, (Sept. 1965), 312, 321.

11. For more on the Battle of Hubbardton see Williams, *The Battle of Hubbardton*, and Ward, *The War of the American Revolution*, I, chap. 36.

12. NDAR, VIII, 135–136, 187–188, 1000, 1038, IX, 174, 331–333; Burgoyne, *A State of the Expedition*, xi, xix, xlii; *Hadden's Journal*, 90; *Pausch's Journal*, 268.

13. NDAR, IX, 176; *Hadden's Journal*, 103, 107. The existing schooner may have been one of the forty-foot flat-bottomed vessels that Arnold requested be built in late May 1775 to shuttle supplies over Lake George to Ticonderoga. *American Archives*, series 4, vol. 2, 847–848.

14. *Hadden's Journal*, 96, 100–103; Anburey, *Travels*, 385; *Riedesel's Memoirs*, 274–275.

15. "Col. John Brown's Attack of September, 1777, on Fort Ticonderoga," *FTMB*, 1, no. 1 (1927), 212–213; Hoyt, "The Pawlet Expedition, September 1777," *Vermont History*, 75, no. 2 (Summer–Fall 2007), 75–76; "The Journal of Ralph Cross," *Historical Magazine*, 7, no. 1 (Jan. 1870), 9–10.

16. Hoyt, 90–91; *NEHGR* 74 (1920), 292; *Memoirs of Captain Lemuel Roberts*, 54–55.

17. *NEHGR*, 74 (1920), 286–287; Ira Allen's "History of Vermont," in *Collections of the Vermont Historical Society*, vol. I, 389–390; *Memoirs of Captain Lemuel Roberts*, 55–60; *Hadden's Journal*, 321–324; NDAR, IX, 934–935; "Col. John Brown's Attack of September, 1777, on Fort Ticonderoga," 207–210; *Journal of Du Roi the Elder*, 102; *Hughes Journal*, 13.

18. *NEHGR* 74 (1920), 288–290; *Journal of Du Roi the Elder*, 103; *Memoirs of Captain Lemuel Roberts*, 62–63. Brown's captured warships consisted of a small sloop carrying three seven-pound guns, one gunboat armed with a brass eighteen-pounder, and another gunboat armed with a single seven-pound gun (*NEHGR* 74 [1920], 288). Captain Starke of the *Maria*, in his report on Brown's attack stated that the sloop was armed with three six-pound cannons and had a crew of 2 officers and 12 seamen. One seaman was killed and another wounded, while the rest were captured. ("Col. John Brown's Attack of September, 1777," 207–208.)

19. *Hadden's Journal*, 324–325; NDAR, IX, 957–958; *NEHGR* 74 (1920), 288–290; *Memoirs of Captain Lemuel Roberts*, 62–63; DeCosta, *The Fight at Diamond Island, Lake George*, 9.

20. NDAR, X, 392–393; "Clune's Letter" in *Pausch's Journal*, 149–151; *Journal of Du Roi the Elder*, 109–110.

21. Numerous details concerning British naval activity on Lake Champlain during this period can be found in Haldimand's correspondence with Provincial naval officers 1778–1784, listed and summarized in Breymner, *Report on the Canadian Archives 1887*. Haldimand issued the naval reduction order on August 14, 1783, and informed Captain Schank at St. Johns of the naval reductions in letters dated August 4, 14, September 15, and December 15 (ibid.).

22. For details behind Lake Champlain's early merchant fleet see Canfield, "Discovery, Navigation, and Navigators of Lake Champlain," *Vermont Historical Gazetteer*, 1, 668–670. The launching of the *Royal Edward* at a tense moment in Anglo-American relations caused some concern as the *Maria* was already stationed at Windmill Bay. One report of the launching in 1794 reads as follows; "By gentleman from St. John's we are informed that the British have just completed a

brig at that place, mounting 12 guns; the brig is every way completed and well manned, and is now stationed at Point-a-Fair, on Lake Champlain. Our informant adds that a very large roe [row] galley is now building at St. John's." (*Records of the Governor and Council of the State of Vermont*, VI, 468–469, 472–473.)

CHAPTER 6: THE BATTLE OF CUMBERLAND BAY

1. For Macdonough's service before his assignment to Lake Champlain, see Rodney Macdonough, *Life of Commodore Thomas Macdonough; Naval War of 1812*, I, 319–320.

2. Canfield, "Discovery, Navigation, and Navigators of Lake Champlain," *Vermont Historical Gazetteer*, I, 668–670.

3. *Naval War of 1812*, I, 325–327, 370–371, II, 424–425. The other purchased vessels were the *Juno, Jupiter, Champlain, Hunter*, and *Fox*. The *Hunter*, owned by Gideon King, would become the USS *Eagle*, and the *Fox*, also owned by King, would become the USS *Growler*. In fact, all the vessels with the exception of the *President* were purchased from Gideon King, who was known in the Champlain Valley as "The Admiral of the Lake" (Canfield, "Discovery, Navigation, and Navigators").

4. To confuse the issue there were also short long guns which employed shorter barrel lengths for the same sized shot. The reduced velocity made these weapons less effective in both range and striking power, which was partially offset in some instances by their reduced weight.

5. Chapelle, *The American Sailing Navy*, 89, 91–94, 133, 240, 318–319; James, *Naval Occurrences*, 4–9.

6. *Naval War of 1812*, II, 490.

7. James, *Naval Occurrences*, 12.

8. "Loomis Sailing Log," in Macdonough, *The Life of Commodore Thomas Macdonough*, 116–117; "H. B. Sawyer," *Vermont Historical Gazetteer*, I, 582–583; Lewis, *British Naval Activity*, 5–7; *Naval War of 1812*, II, 516. Macdonough later informed the secretary of the navy that the pilots on both vessels objected to entering the river because of the wind (*Naval War of 1812*, II, 516).

9. "Loomis Sailing Log," in Macdonough, *The Life of Commodore Thomas Macdonough*, 116–117.

10. "Loomis Sailing Log"; *Naval War of 1812*, II, 488–492, 516; Lewis, *British Naval Activity*, 7–8; Prevost, *Memoirs*, 84–86; Niles, *Weekly Register*, IV (Mar.–Sept., 1813), 263–264.

11. Wood, *British Documents of the Canadian War of 1812*, I, 240; Prevost, *Memoirs*, 86–87; *Public Life of the Late Lt. Gen. Sir George Prevost*, 23–24; Charbonneau, *The Fortifications of Ile aux Noix*, 130–145.

12. Malcomson, *Warships of the Great Lakes*, 120; *Naval War of 1812*, II, 516–517. The garrison at Ile aux Noix consisted of the battalion companies of the 13th reg-

iment, a company of the 10th Royal Veterans, and a battalion of militia as well as Marine and Royal artillery detachments.

13. Wood, *British Documents of the Canadian War of* 1812, II, 221–236, 516–520; *Naval War of 1812*, II, 516–520; Lewis, *British Naval Activity*, 10–12; *Records of the Governor and Council of the State of Vermont*, VI, 484; "The British Attack on Burlington," *Vermont History*, 29, no. 2 (April 1961), 82–83. One American account claimed that, "The water crafts which we have learned has fell into the possession of the enemy are, the Mars 34 tons, Enterprise 44, Essex 60 (laden with salt & burnt), Burlington 25, Lark, 15, William Maid 20, Federal Victory 20, Red Bird 10, and a Durham Boat laden with 80 barrels of flower" ("British Attack," 83).

14. Wood, *British Documents of the Canadian War of 1812*, II, 229–233.

15. *Naval War of 1812*, II, 490–491.

16. Ibid., 513.

17. "Discovery, Navigation, and Navigators of Lake Champlain," *Vermont Historical Gazetteer*, I, 669–672; *Naval War of 1812*, II, 512, 515–516, 518, 520, 604–606; Macdonough, *The Life of Commodore Thomas Macdonough*, 126–127. Both the *Francis* and the *Wasp* would serve with the fleet until Macdonough went to winter quarters at which point he declared both of them unfit for service and returned them to their previous owners.

18. Macdonough, *The Life of Commodore Thomas Macdonough*, 134–135; *Naval War of 1812*, II, 602–604, III, 426–427, 480.

19. Crisman, *The Eagle*, 14–16; *Naval War of 1812*, III, 393–395.

20. *Naval War of 1812*, III, 396–399, 424, 428–432; Crisman, *The Eagle*, 16–21. For more on the Lake Champlain Steamboat Company see "Discovery, Navigation, and Navigators of Lake Champlain." The first steamboat on Lake George, the *Caldwell*, was launched by this company in 1817.

21. *Naval War of 1812*, III, 479–480; *Records of the Governor and Council of the State of Vermont*, VI, 502; Macdonough, *The Life of Commodore Thomas Macdonough*, 139–141; "Otter Creek in History," *Vermont History* (for years 1913–1914), 139–142.

22. Lewis, *British Naval Activity*, 16–17; *Naval War of 1812*, III, 480–483; Brymner, *Report on the Canadian Archives for 1893*, 102; Malcomson, *Warships of the Great Lakes*, 124–125.

23. *Naval War of 1812*, III, 480–483; Lewis, *British Naval Activity*, 19–21.

24. "Otter Creek in History," 142–149; Lewis, *British Naval Activity*, 19–21; *Naval War of 1812*, III, 479–483, 505; *Niles Weekly Register*, 6 (May 26, 1814), 214; Hurd, *The History of Clinton and Franklin Counties*, 32–33.

25. *Naval War of 1812*, III, 505–508.

26. Ibid., 538–542; Crisman, *The Eagle*, 28–34.

27. Malcomson, *Warships of the Great Lakes*, 130–131; Wood, *British Documents of the Canadian War of 1812*, III part 1, 367, 411–412.

28. Lewis, *British Naval Activity*, 24–26; Prevost, *Memoirs*, 140; Holden, James, "The Battle of Plattsburgh," *The Centenary of the Battle of Plattsburgh*, 14–16; Wood,

British Documents of the Canadian War of 1812, III part 1, 350–351, 378, 410–411. Also see Appendix D.

29. Wood, *British Documents of the Canadian War of 1812*, III part 1, 350–351, 367, 377–385, 394–396, 402, 411–415, 440, 461–462.

30. *Naval War of 1812*, III, 596–597; *The Battle of Plattsburgh*, 11–13, map 22–23, 51; Macdonough, *Life of Commodore Thomas Macdonough*, 172–175.

31. Macdonough, *Life of Commodore Thomas Macdonough*, 174–175; Wood, *British Documents of the Canadian War of 1812*, III, part 1, 396, 412–413.

32. Wood, *British Documents of the Canadian War of 1812*, III, part 1, 369, 471–472; Lewis, *British Naval Activity*, 30–31.

33. Macdonough, *Life of Commodore Thomas Macdonough*, 171; Downie's comments in regards to his position on September 10, cast some doubt on his earlier statements. (Wood, *British Documents of the Canadian War of 1812*, III, part 1, 395.)

34. *Naval War of 1812*, III, 614; Macdonough, *Life of Commodore Thomas Macdonough*, 268; *The Battle of Plattsburgh*, 13–14; Holden, "The Battle of Plattsburgh," *The Centenary of the Battle of Plattsburgh*, 28–29.

35. Wood, *British Documents of the Canadian War of 1812*, III, part 1, 369, 411–412, 472.

36. *The Battle of Plattsburgh*, 14–15; Wood, *British Documents of the Canadian War of 1812*, III, part 1, 407–411, 417, 422–427, 436, 472–473, 497; *Naval War of 1812*, III , 610; Lewis, *British Naval Activity*, 33–34.

37. *Naval War of 1812*, III, 610; "Commandant Henley to Secretary of the Navy," in *Life of Commodore Thomas Macdonough*, 279–281.

38. Wood, *British Documents of the Canadian War of 1812*, III, part 1, 409, 429–435, 447–449, 482–483, 489–490.

39. "Lt. Budd to Macdonough," in *Life of Commodore Thomas Macdonough*, 282–284; *The Battle of Plattsburgh*, 39; Lewis, *British Naval Activity*, 37; Wood, *British Documents of the Canadian War of 1812*, III, part 1, 429–435, 442–456, 482–484.

40. Lewis, *British Naval Activity*, 33; *The Battle of Plattsburgh*, 17; "Midshipman Lea to his Brother," in *Life of Commodore Thomas Macdonough*, 293–295.

41. "Log of the United States Sloop or War Surprise (Eagle) on Lake Champlain, Aug 21–Sept. 28, 1814," National Archives, General Research Branch (NNRG–P), Record Group 45; "Commandant Henley to Secretary of the Navy," *Life of Commodore Thomas Macdonough*, 279–281; *Naval War of 1812*, III, 610–615.

42. *The Battle of Plattsburgh*, 17, 24–29; *Naval War of 1812*, III, 614–615.

43. *Naval War of 1812*, III, 609–615; Wood, *British Documents of the Canadian War of* 1812, III, part 1, 467–475.

44. *Naval War of 1812*, III, 610–611.

45. Wood, *British Documents of the Canadian War of* 1812, III, part 1, 482–484; *Naval War of 1812*, III, 614–615; Lewis, *British Naval Activity*, 37–39.

46. *The Battle of Plattsburgh*, 30–32; *Naval War of 1812*, III, 616; Prevost, *Memoirs*, 141–144.

47. *Life of Commodore Thomas Macdonough*, 267–276; Wood, *British Documents of the Canadian War of* 1812, III, part 1, 376; "Accounts of the Battle of Plattsburgh," *Vermont Antiquarian*, I, 3, (March 1903), 81–93; *Plattsburgh Republican* 3, Dec. 1814. The captured *Burlington Packet* was raised in November (*Niles Weekly Register*, VII, 192).

48. *The Battle of Plattsburgh*, 33.

CHAPTER 7: A NEW LAKE

1. *Naval War of 1812*, III, 642–644, 681–682.

2. *Naval War of 1812*, III, 681– 684; Malcomson, *Warships of the Great Lakes*, 136–137. Gourdie did finish the gunboats and the flat-bottomed transport *Champlain*, but the Peace of Paris, news of which reached North America in late February 1815, put an end to plans to build the other vessels. (Ibid.)

3. *Naval War of 1812*, III, 703–704.

4. Crisman, *The Eagle*, 97–110. The *Preble* sold for $2,340, the *President* $1,750, the *Montgomery* $1,900, the *Chub* (ex-*Growler*) and *Finch* (ex-*Eagle*) for $800 each, and the four small galleys for $259 (Emmons, *The Navy of the United States*, 20). Gideon King was reported to have purchased the *Finch* and the *Chub*, both of which had been owned by him before the war (*Vermont Historical Gazetteer*, I, 672).

5. Crisman, *The Eagle*, 105–107.

6. *American State Papers, Naval Affairs*, vol. I, 715, 907–908, 933, 1015; Crisman, *The Eagle*, 108–110.

7. *Niles Weekly Register*, VIII, June 24, 1815, 284. From 1809 to 1856 no less than 24 steam ships were built on Lake Champlain ranging in size from 107 tons to 881 tons in size. (*Vermont Historical Gazetteer*, I , 707).

8. Aske, Jerry, *From Steamboats to Subchasers*, 13–27. The subchasers constructed at the Shelburne ships yards measured 110 feet in length, 18 feet in beam, displaced 98 tons, and had a crew complement of 22 men. Besides antisubmarine duties these vessels were often used for minesweeping operations because of their wooden hulls. SC1029 and SC1030 were transferred to Free French forces in 1944, while SC1504, SC1505, and SC1506 were transferred to Russia under the Lend-Lease program. SC1029 participated in clearing minefields of the Normandy coast during D-Day operations. It was later damaged by an explosion while of the coast of southern France in August 1944. The subchasers were sailed to New York harbor via the Champlain Canal.

9. For the reader wishing to see the results of these archaeological surveys and current ones on the Lake Champlain waterway, I highly recommend the Lake Champlain Maritime Museum, and in particular, the gondola replica *Philadelphia II* built by the museum. Nothing ever brought me closer to understanding a small moment in time than standing on the deck of this vessel.

BIBLIOGRAPHY

MANUSCRIPT SOURCES

Canada, National Archives. (Ottawa)
Manuscript Division
    MG1: Fonds des Colonies
        C11A-Correspondance générale
    MG 8: Documents relatifs à la Nouvelle-France et au
        Québec
  A1: Documents généraux
    MG18: Pre-Conquest Papers
        K9-Bourlamaque Papers
    MG23: Late Eighteenth Century Papers
        A2-Chatham Papers
Great Britain, Public Record Office (London)
Colonial Office
    CO5, America and West Indies, Correspondence,
    originals on microfilm
War Office
    WO34, Amherst Papers, originals on microfilm
Admiralty Papers
Admiralty Papers, I, vol. 2046.
Lancaster Public Library (Lancaster, Mass.)
Col. John Whitcomb's Orderly Book for 1760

PRINTED SOURCES

Abbass, D. K. *Plan View of the Land Tortoise Radeau.* Land Tortoise
Underwater Preserve, State of New York.

"Accounts of the Battle of Plattsburgh." *Vermont Antiquarian*, 1, no.
3 (March 1903), 75–93.

Allen, Ira. "The Natural and Political History of the State of
Vermont." *Collections of the Vermont Historical Society*, vol. I,
319–468.

Anburey, Thomas. *Travels Through the Interior Parts of America.* Vol. I. London: William Lane, 1789.

Angelis, Pascal de. "The Diary of Pascal De Angelis." *Vermont History,* 42, no. 3 (Summer 1974), 195–200.

Aske, Jerry. *From Steamboats to Subchasers.* Shelburne, Vt.: Wind Ridge Publishing, 2002.

Baldwin, Thomas. (ed.). *The Revolutionary Journal of Colonel Jeduthan Baldwin,* 1775–1778. Bangor: De Burians, 1906.

The Battle of Plattsburgh: What Historians Say About It. Albany: J. B. Lyon Co., 1914.

Baxter, James. *The Campaigns of General's Carleton and Burgoyne with the Journal of Lieutenant William Digby.* Albany: Munsell's Sons, 1887.

Bougainville, Louis Antoine. *Adventure in the Wilderness: The American Journals of Louis Antoine de Bougainville, 1756–1760.* Trans. and ed. Edward P. Hamilton. Norman: University of Oklahoma Press, 1964.

Bouton, Nathaniel. *Documents and Records Relating to the State of New Hampshire,* VIII. Concord: Edward Jenks, 1874.

Brannan, John (ed.), *Official Letters of the Military and Naval Officers of the United States during the war with Great Britain in the Years 1812, 13, 14, & 15.* Washington, D.C.: Way & Gideon, 1823.

Bratten, John. "The Continental Gondola *Philadelphia.*" Ph.D. diss., Texas A&M University, 1997.

Bredenberg, Oscar. "The Royal Savage." *FTMB,* 12, no. 2 (1966): 128–149.

Brymner, Douglas. *Report on the Canadian Archives for* 1883, 1885, 1887, 1893. Ottawa: Maclean, Rogers, 1884–1894.

Burgoyne, John. *A State of the Expedition from Canada.* London: J. Almon, 1780.

Canfield, Thomas. "Discovery, Navigation, and Navigators of Lake Champlain." *Vermont Historical Gazetteer,* I (1867), 656–705.

Carrington, Henry. *Battles of the American Revolution, 1775–1776.* New York: Promontory Press, 1877 (reprint 1974).

Carter, Clarence (ed.). *The Correspondence of General Thomas Gage,* vol. I. New Haven: Yale University Press, 1931.

Casgrain, H. R. (ed.). *Collection des Manuscrits du Maréchal de Lévis.* 12 vols. Montreal and Quebec: C. O. Beauchemin & Fils and Demers & Frère, 1889–1895. The individual volumes used from this collection are: Vol. 1, Journal du Chevalier de Levis; Vol. 5, Lettres du M. de Bourlamaque; Vol. 7, Journal du Marquis de Montcalm; Vol. 8, Lettres du Marquis de Vaudreuil; Vol. 10, Lettres de Divers Particuliers.

Chapelle, Howard. *The History of the American Sailing Navy*. New York: Konecky & Konecky, 1949.

Charbonneau, André. *The Fortifications of Île Aux Noix*. Ottawa: Department of Canadian Heritage, 1994.

Choate, Isaac B. (ed.). "Journal of a Provincial Officer in the Campaign in Northern New York in 1758." *Historical Magazine*, 10, no. 8 (1871), 117–119.

Clark, William, Michael Crawford and others (eds.). *Naval Documents of the American Revolution*. 11 vols. Washington D.C.: Naval Historical Center, 1964–2005.

Clarke, William (ed.). "Col. John Brown's Expedition Against Ticonderoga and Diamond Island, 1777." *NEHGR*, 74 (1920), 284–293.

Cobb, Samuel. "The Journal of Captain Samuel Cobb, 21 May–29 October, 1758." *FTMB*, 14, no. 1 (1981), 12–31.

Cohn, Art. *Galley Congress Inspection Report*. Vergennes: Lake Champlain Maritime Museum, 2001.

Colden, Cadwallader. *The History of the Five Indian Nations Depending on the Province of New York in America*. 2 vols. New York: 1727, 1747. Ithaca, N.Y.: Cornell University Press, 1958.

Collections of the New-York Historical Society for the Year 1881: Montresor Journals. New York: New-York Historical Society, 1882.

Collections of the New-York Historical Society for the Year 1921: Cadwallader Colden Papers, V, 1755–1760. New York: New-York Historical Society, 1923.

Cometti, Elizabeth (ed.). *The American Journals of Lt. John Enys*. Syracuse: Syracuse University Press, 1976.

Crisman, Kevin. *The Eagle: An American Brig on Lake Champlain During the War of 1812*. Shelburne, Vt.: New England Press, 1987.

Cross, Ralph. "The Journal of Ralph Cross." *Historical Magazine*, 7, no. 1 (Jan. 1870), 8–11.

DeCosta, B. F. *The Fight at Diamond Island, Lake George*. New York: J. Sabin and Sons, 1872.

De Léry Chaussegros. "Journal at Carillon, 8 May–2 July, 1756." *FTMB*, 6, no. 4 (1942), 128–144.

Doblin, Helga (ed. & trans.). "Journal of Lt. Colonel Christian Julius Pratorius: 2 June – 17 July, 1777." *FTMB*, 15, no. 3 (Winter 1991): 57–68.

Doblin, Helga, and Mary C. Lynn (eds.). *An Eyewitness Account of the American Revolution and New England Life: The Journal of J. F. Wasmus, German Company Surgeon, 1776–1783.* Santa Barbara: Praeger, 1990.

Dudley, William (ed.). *The Naval War of 1812: A Documentary History.* 3 vols. Washington, D.C.: Naval Historical Center, 1985.

Emmons, George. *The Navy of the United States from the Commencement, 1775–1853.* Washington, D.C.: Gideon & Co., 1853.

Eping, Charlotte (trans.). *Journal of Du Roi the Elder.* New York: D. Appleton, 1911.

Force, Peter. *American Archives: A Documentary History of the United States of America,* series 4 and 5. Washington, D.C., 1837–1853.

Frazer, Persifor. *Notes and Papers of General Persifor Frazer.* 2 vols. Philadelphia: 1907.

Gabriel, Abbé Charles-Nicolas. *Le Maréchal de camp Desandrouins, 1729–1702.* 2 vols. Verdun: Renvé-Lallement, 1887.

Gellman, Virginia. "Vision and Division in a Frontier Community: Burlington, Vermont 1790–1810." Ph.D. diss., University of Vermont, 2007.

Glasier, Benjamin. "French and Indian War Diary of Benjamin Glasier of Ipswich, 1758–1760." *Essex Institute Historical Collections,* 86 (1950), 65–92.

Hadden, James. *A Journal Kept in Canada and Upon Burgoyne's Campaign in 1776 and 1777.* Albany: Munsell's Sons, 1884.

Hastings, Hugh (ed.). *Orderly Book and Journal of Major John Hawks.* New York: Society of Colonial Wars in the State of New York, 1911.

"H. B. Sawyer." *Vermont Historical Gazetteer,* I (1867), 582–584.

Hill, Henry. "Otter Creek in History." *Vermont History* (1913–1914), 125–148.

Holden, David. "Journal of Sergeant David Holden." *Proceedings of the Massachusetts Historical Society,* 4 (1889), 384–409.

Holden, James. "The Battle of Plattsburgh." *The Centenary of the Battle of Plattsburgh.* Albany: University of New York (1914), 11–40.

Hoyt, Edward. "The Pawlet Expedition, September 1777." *Vermont History,* 75, no. 2 (Summer–Fall 2007), 69–100.

Hughes, Thomas. *A Journal by Thos. Hughes.* Cambridge: University Press, 1947.

Hurd, Duane. *The History of Clinton and Franklin Counties.* Philadelphia: J. W. Lewis, 1880.

Irving, L. Homfrey. *Officers of the British Forces in Canada During the War 1812–15.* Kingston: Welland Tribune, 1908.

James, William. *An Inquiry into the Merits of the Principal Naval Actions Between Great Britain and the United States.* Halifax: Anthony Holland, 1816.

Jenks, Samuel. "Journal of Capt. Samuel Jenks." *Proceedings of the Massachusetts Historical Society,* 5 (1889), 353–390.

Johnstone, James Chevalier de. *Memoirs of the Chevalier de Johnstone.* Trans. Charles Winchester. 3 vols. Aberdeen: D. Wyllie & Sons, 1870–1871.

Jones, Charles. *History of the Campaign for the Conquest of Canada in 1776.* Philadelphia: Porter & Coate, 1882.

"A Journal Kept During the Siege of Fort William Henry, August 1757." *Proceedings of the American Philosophical Society,* 37 (1898), 143–150.

"A Journal of Carleton's and Burgoyne's Campaigns." *FTMB,* Part 1: 11, no. 5 (1964): 235–269, Part 2: 11, no. 6 (1965): 307–335, Part 3: 12, no. 1 (1966): 5–62.

Kalm, Peter. *Travels into North America.* Trans. John Reinold Forster. 3 vols. London: T. Lowndes, 1771.

Kimball, Gertrude Selwyn (ed.). *The Correspondence of William Pitt.* 2 vols. New York: Macmillan, 1906.

Knox, John. *An Historical Journal of the Campaigns in North America for the Years 1757, 1758, 1759, and 1760.* 2 vols. London: 1764. Edited by Arthur G. Doughty and reprinted in 3 vols. Freeport, N.Y.: Libraries Press, 1970.

Knox, Robert. "Dr. Robert Knox's Account of the Battle of Valcour Island." *Vermont History,* 46, no. 3 (Summer 1978), 141–150.

Lamb, R. *Journal of Occurrences During the Late American War.* Dublin: Wilkinson & Courtney, 1809.

La Pause. "Mémoire et Observations sur mon Voyage en Canada." *Rapport de l'Archiviste de la Quebec pour 1931–1932.* Quebec: Rédempti Paradis, 1932: 47–125

Lapham, William Berry. *Bradbury Memorial.* Portland, Me.: Brown Thurston & Co., 1890.

Letter from the Secretary of the Navy . . . Relating to the Capture of the British Fleet on Lake Champlain. Washington, D.C.: Roger C. Weightman, 1814.

Lewis, Dennis. *British Naval Activity on Lake Champlain during the War of 1812.* Plattsburgh, N.Y.: Clinton County Historical Assoc., 1994.

L'Incarnation, Marie de. *Word from New France: The Selected Letters of Marie de l'Incarnation.* Trans. and ed. Joyce Marshall. Toronto: Oxford University Press, 1967.

Livingston, Henry. "The Journal of Major Henry Livingston." *Pennsylvania Magazine of History and Biography,* 22 (1898), 9–33.

"Log of the United States Sloop of War Surprise (Eagle) on Lake Champlain, Aug. 21–Sept. 28, 1814." National Archives, General Research Branch (NNRG-P), Record Group 45, Washington, D.C.

"Lord Francis Napier's Journal." *Maryland Historical Magazine,* 57, no. 4 (Dec. 1962), 285–352.

Lowrie, Walter (ed.). *American State Papers, Class VI: Naval Affairs,* I. Washington, D.C.: Gales and Seaton, 1834.

Macdonough, Rodney. *Life of Commodore Thomas Macdonough; Naval War of 1812.* Boston: Fort Hill Press, 1909.

Malartic, Gabriel de Maurès, de. *Journal des campagnes au Canada de 1755 à 1760 par le comte de Maurès de Malartic.* Paris: Librairie Plon, 1890.

Malcomson, Robert. *Warships of the Great Lakes 1754–1834.* Dubai: Caxton Publishing, 2003.

Mann, James. *Medical Sketches of the Campaigns of 1812, 1813 & 1814.* Dedham: H. Mann Co., 1816.

McCully, Bruce T. "Catastrophe in the Wilderness: New Light on the Canada Expedition of 1709." *William and Mary Quarterly,* 3rd series, 11 (1954), 441–456.

McTeer, Frances, and Frederick Warner (eds.). "The British Attack on Burlington." *Vermont History,* 29, no. 2 (April 1961), 82–88.

Meech, Susan Spicer, and Susan Billings Meech. *History of the Descendants of Peter Spicer, a Landholder in New London, Connecticut, as Early as 1666.* Boston: Gilson, 1911.

Meloizes, Nicolas Renaud d'Avène des. "Journal de Nicolas Renaud d'Avène des Meloizes." *Rapport de l'Archiviste de la Quebec pour 1928-1929.* Quebec: Rédempti Paradis, 1929: 4–86.

"News from America." *London Magazine,* Dec. 1759, reprinted in *FTMB,* 6, no. 33 (Jan. 1942), 108–111.

O'Callaghan, E. B. (ed.). *Orderly Book of Lt. Gen. John Burgoyne.* Albany: J. Munsell, 1860.

———. *Documents Relative to the Colonial History of the State of New York.* 15 vols. Albany: Weed, Parsons & Co., 1856–1877.

Osler, Edward. *The Life of Admiral Viscount Exmouth.* London: Smith, Elder & Co., 1835.

Pargellis, Stanley M. *Lord Loudoun in North America.* New Haven: Yale Historical Publications, 1933.

Pell, Joshua. "Diary of Joshua Pell." *Magazine of American History,* II (1878), 43–47, 107–112.

Perley, Sidney ed.). "Diaries kept by Lemuel Wood, of Boxford." *Essex Institute Historical Collections,* 19 (1882), 61–74, 143–152, 183–192; 20 (1883), 156–160, 198–208, 289–296; 21 (1884), 63–68.

Pouchot, Pierre. *Memoirs on the Late War in North America between France and England.* 3 Vols. Yverdon: 1781. Trans. Michael Cardy and ed. Brian Leigh Dunnigan. Youngstown, N.Y.: Old Fort Niagara Association, 1994.

Poulariès. "Relation de Poulariès Envoyé à Marquis de Montcalm." *Rapport de l'Archiviste de la Quebec pour 1931-1932.* Quebec: Rédempti Paradis, 1932, 47–125.

Prevost, George. *Memoirs of the Administration of the Colonial Government of Lower Canada.* Quebec: Robert Christie, 1818.

Proceedings of a General Court Martial . . . of Major General St. Clair. Philadelphia: Hall and Sellers, 1778.

Randall, Willard. *Benedict Arnold.* New York: William Morrow, 1990.

"The Revenge (The Hull of the Duke of Cumberland)." *FTMB,* I, 4 (July 1928): 6–11.

Roberts, Lemuel. *Memoirs of Captain Lemuel Roberts.* Bennington: Anthony Haswell, 1809.

Rogers, Robert. *The Journals of Major Robert Rogers*. London: 1765. Ann Arbor, Mich.: University Microfilms, Inc., 1966.

Roy, Pierre-George. *Hommes et choses du Fort Saint-Fréderic*. Montreal: Les Editions Dix, 1946.

Sainsbury, W. Noel et al. (eds.). *Calendar of State Papers, Colonial Series, American and West Indies, Preserved in Her Majesty's Public Records Office*. 45 vols. London: His Majesty's Stationery Office, 1860–1964.

Samuel, Sigmund. *The Seven Years' War in Canada, 1756–1763*. Toronto: Ryerson Press, 1934.

Skene, Phil. "Philip Skene to Lt. Thomas Gamble, 26 April, 1771." *FTMB*, 6, no. 35 (Jan. 1943), 163.

Some Account of the Public Life of the Late Lt. Gen. Sir George Prevost. London: C. Cadell, 1823.

Starke, John. "Col. John Brown's Attack of September, 1777, on Fort Ticonderoga." *FTMB*, I, no. 1 (1927): 19–21.

"Statement of Noah Brown." *Journal of American History*, 8 (1914), 103–108.

Stewart, Jahiel. "The October 1776 Journal of Jahiel Stewart." *Vermont History*, 64, no. 2 (Spring 1996), 89–98.

Stone, William. *The Campaign of Lt. Gen. John Burgoyne*. Albany: J. Munsell, 1877.

Stone, William (ed.). *The Journal of Captain Pausch*. Albany: Munsell's Sons, 1886.

———. *Memoirs, Letters and Journals of Major General Riedesel*. Albany: J. Munsell, 1868.

Thacher, James. *Military Journal of the American Revolution*. Hartford: Hurlbut, Williams, 1862.

Thwaites, R. G. (ed.). *The Jesuit Relations and Allied Documents*. 73 vols. Cleveland: Burrow Bros., 1896–1901.

Trowbridge, Francis Bacon. *The Champion Genealogy*. New Haven: Private printing, 1891.

Trumbull, Benjamin. "Journal of the Principal Movements Towards St. John's." *Collections of the Connecticut Historical Society*, 7 (1899), 136–173.

Verney, Jack. *The Good Regiment*. Montreal: McGill-Queen's University Press, 1991.

Walton, E. P. (ed.). *Records of the Governor and Council of the State of Vermont*, VI. Montpelier: J. M. Poland, 1878.

Ward, Christopher. *The War of the Revolution.* 2 vols. New York: Macmillan, 1952.

Webster, Clarence J. (ed.). *The Journals of Jeffery Amherst.* Toronto: Ryerson Press, 1931.

Wells, Bayze. "The Journal of Bayze Wells of Farmington, in the Canadian Expedition, 1775–77. *Collections of the Connecticut Historical Society,* VII. Hartford: The Society (1889), 239–296.

Wells, Frederic P. *History of Newbury, Vermont.* St. Johnsbury, Vt.: Caledonian Co., 1902.

Whitehead, William A. *Contributions to the Early History of Perth Amboy.* New York: D. Appleton, 1856.

"Wigglesworth Journal." In Vale Smith, *The History of Newburyport.* Newburyport: Damrell & Moore (1854), 356–362.

Wilkinson, James. *Memoirs of My Own Times,* I. Philadelphia: Abraham Small, 1816.

Williams, John. *The Battle of Hubbardton.* Montpelier: Vermont Historic Preservation, 1988.

Wood, William. *Select British Documents of the Canadian War of 1812,* 3 vols. Toronto: Champlain Society, 1926.

Woodwell, P. M. (ed.). *The Diary of Thomas Moody.* Berwick, Me.: Chronicle Print Shop, 1976.

ACKNOWLEDGMENTS

First and foremost I must extend my thanks to my wife Pam, without whose support this, along with most other elements of my life, would collapse into chaos. My thanks also extend to my children for their patience and understanding of the odd hours I keep in pursuit of my writing endeavors. Without their support none of this would go anywhere.

Many libraries and institutions were extremely helpful in researching this work. The staffs at the University of Arizona, University of Vermont, Canadian Archives in Ottawa, Library of Congress, Vermont Historical Society, and American Naval Records Society were of immense help. My sincere thanks to these first-rate organizations.

There are a number of people, many my colleagues, who deserve recognition for their patience, and for not giving into the urge to tell me to shut up about the project. Ernie Botos, Paul Browne, and especially my old friend Dave Child are foremost among these individuals. Thanks guys. And I would also like to extend a special thanks to Art Cohn for writing the foreword. It was an extremely nice gesture, sir, and is greatly appreciated. Last, I would like to thank the historians and writers of the past and present. Without the works of the former I would have never been inspired to put pen to paper in such matters, and to those of the present, whose works continue to inspire me and expand my horizons, my thanks as well.

INDEX

Abenaki, 46

Abercromby, James, 21-24, 195

Aigle, 33

Allen, Ebenezer, 98-99

Allen, Ethan, xii

Allen, 147, 153, 220, 227

Alwyn, 220, 227

Amherst, Jeffery, 23-26, 28-32, 34-35,
    38, 41-42, 44, 51-52, 55, 57-
    58, 62, 89, 106, 151-152, 171,
    190, 194-200, 214, 245,
    248n2, 248n6, 248n12,
    249n14-16, 250n25, 250n27

Arnold, Benedict, xi-xiii, 53, 60-63,
    65-70, 72-77, 79-85, 92, 106,
    151-153, 155, 159, 161, 172,
    174-176, 178, 200, 203, 205,
    207, 216, 221, 251n10,
    252n21, 254n13

Ash Island, 110, 112, 123, 125, 231,
    234, 246n4

Auguste, 45

Baldwin, Jeduthan, 95, 206

Ballard, 220, 227

Barbary pirates, 104-105

Barque de Saintonge, 8

Barque du Roy, 8

Basin Harbor, 11, 107

Battle of Cumberland Bay, 117, 131,
    137, 163-165, 167, 169, 220-
    223, 225-227, 230-236

Battle of Plattsburgh, 139

Battle of Valcour Island, xii, 78, 155,
    158-162, 200, 202-207, 209,
    212-215, 218

Beauharnois, Charles, 7-8

Beckwith, 234

Beresford, 114, 136, 234

Betsy, 60, 189, 203

Blackburn, John, 188-189

Blucher, 139, 234

Bonaparte, Napoleon, 105, 126

Borer, 220, 227

Boscawen, 34-36, 38-40, 42, 44, 152,
    193, 197-199

Boston, 68, 71, 85, 200, 205, 219

Bougainville, Louis-Antoine, 42-47,
    50, 91, 186

Bourlamaque, Charles, 26, 31-32, 34,
    36, 38, 41-43, 51, 170-171,
    186-188, 191, 249n15-16

Bowman, Solomon, 66

Bradstreet, John, 30

Brochette, 29, 33, 40, 186, 188, 193

Brock, 114, 234

Broke, 116, 123, 231

Brown, Adam, 126

Brown, Johnathan, 60, 97-101, 203,
    211, 254n18

Brown, Noah, 120, 146-147, 221, 227

Bruyeres, Ralph, 114

Brydon, Robert, 134, 141, 232

Budd, Charles, 138-139, 146

Bull Dog, 230

Burgoyne, John, xiii, 54, 63, 86-87,
    89-90, 92-97, 101, 162, 177,
    201, 203-204, 206, 208, 210,
    214-215, 217-218

Burlington Packet, 144, 169, 219, 236

Burrows, 220, 227

Buttonmold Bay, 68, 83

Camel, 102, 210

Canada, 123, 131, 137, 235

Canadian Rebellion (1837), 149

Canceaux, 58

Carleton, Guy, 52-60, 62-64, 70, 72,
    81, 83-86, 90, 102, 106, 114,
    151, 175, 177-178, 201, 211-
    212, 215, 232, 250-251n2,
    252n33

Carleton, 52, 56-57, 71, 73, 75-79, 81-
    82, 86, 94, 99, 102-103, 158,
    160-161, 176-177, 209-213

Carter, John, 93-94

Casdrop, Thomas, 67

Cassin, Stephen, 226
Centipede, 220, 227
Chambers, William, 203
Champion, Henry, 194
Chimney Point, 4-6, 159, 246n5
Chippewas, 19
Chub, 123, 130, 133-135, 137, 139,
    144-145, 147, 163-164, 167,
    169, 181, 228-230, 258n4
Chudière River, 61
Cobb, Samuel, 22-23, 194-195
Cohn, Art, xi-xiv
Commodore Preble, 118
Confiance, 126-127, 130, 132-135, 137,
    139-141, 144-148, 163, 165,
    169, 179, 181-183, 228, 231-
    233
Congress, 67, 70-71, 74, 76-77, 79, 82-
    83, 159, 161, 169, 174-176,
    200, 207
Connecticut, 68, 71, 200, 205
Constellation, 106
Continental Congress, 61
Cooper, James F., 163, 167
Corbin, David, 8
Cox, Henry, 232
Crab Island, 39-40, 131-132, 138-139,
    142, 165, 182, 184
Crown Point, 4, 6-7, 9, 12, 25-26, 28,
    30-31, 34, 41, 44, 54-56, 62-
    63, 66-67, 79-81, 83-84, 87,
    126, 172-176, 178, 190, 197,
    199, 204, 208, 214-215,
    246n5, 249n15
Cumberland Bay, 39, 44, 72, 109,
    117, 124, 127-128, 130-132,
    137, 143, 146, 163-165, 167,
    169, 220-223, 225-227, 229-
    236

d'Olabaratz, Jean, 33-35, 38-40, 42-
    43, 170
Dacres, Richard, 75-76, 90, 176
Darby, John, 45, 48-50, 250n27
Dearborn, Henry, 107
de Champlain, Samuel, xi
de Lery, Chaussegros, 8
de Prouville, Alexandre, 1
de Rigaud, Pierre, 15, 18
Diamond Island, 96, 100-102

dit Laubaras, Jean d'Olabaratz, 33-35,
    38-40, 42-43, 170
Donovan Contracting Company,
    150, 236
Douglas, Charles, 56, 58, 209, 211-
    212
Douglas, James, 218
Downie, George, 127-130, 132-134,
    139, 143, 180-181, 183
Drew, William, 184
Duke of Cumberland, 30, 34-36, 39,
    42, 44, 47, 191, 193, 198-199
Dunham Bay, 101

Eagle, 107, 109-113, 115-116, 126,
    128, 130, 132-135, 137, 139-
    142, 144, 146-148, 153, 163,
    165, 179, 219-226, 229-231,
    233-234, 255n3, 258n4
Earl of Halifax, 22, 24, 28, 193-196
English Rangers, 16
Enterprise, 60, 67, 71, 79-80, 82, 84,
    91, 93, 104, 200-201, 203-
    204, 220, 256n13
Essex, 116, 219, 256n13
Esturgeon, 29, 33, 40, 186, 188, 193
Everand, Thomas, 116
Exmouth, Viscount, 77
Eyre, William, 17, 30

Faden, William, 155
Federal Victory, 235, 256n13
Ferris Bay, 83, 155, 161
Field Book of the War of 1812
    (Lossing), 163, 165
Finch, 123, 129, 132-133, 135-139,
    142, 144, 147, 163, 165, 167,
    169, 181-182, 228, 230-231,
    258n4
Fort Amherst, 26, 44, 62-63, 152,
    190, 199
Fort Carillon, 11-12, 15-16, 21, 23-
    24, 26, 28, 42, 195, 199
Fort Cassin Point, 124
Fort Chambly, 5, 10, 51, 54, 152
Fort Duquesne, 21
Fort Edward, 12, 44, 94-95, 149
Fort George, 63, 95-96, 100, 102,
    194-196
Fort Independence, 90-92, 94

Fort Lennox, 149
Fort Montgomery, 150
Fort Niagara, 42
Fort St. Frédéric, 6, 8-12, 14, 26, 42
Fort St. Jean, 10-11, 30, 48, 50-51,
    187-188, 190-191, 217
Fort St. Johns, 54-60, 64-65, 69, 85,
    86, 90, 94, 96, 101-103, 114,
    172, 187-191, 201-203, 205-
    206, 208, 217-218, 231,
    251n10
Fort Ticonderoga, xii-xiii, 26, 30-31,
    44, 60, 63, 87, 89, 91-93, 95,
    97, 99, 102, 152, 190, 202-
    203, 210-211, 215, 217, 245,
    249n16
Fort Vaudreuil, 11
Fort William Henry, 14-18, 20, 22-
    23, 192, 250n25
Forty-second Royal Highland
    Regiment, 38
Forty-seventh Regiment, 96, 100
Four Brothers, 38, 170
Fox, 230
Francis, 118, 256n17
Fraser, Simon, 94
French and Indian War, 98, 187-188,
    192

Gabare, 186
Gamble, Peter, 140, 180
Gates, Horatio, 62-63, 67-70, 172,
    174-175, 252n21
Gates, 67, 70, 84, 91, 93, 201, 207-208
George III, 155
Gleaner, 149
Goélette du Roy, 8
Goudie, John, 147, 235
Grand Diable, 43, 46, 48-51, 186,
    189-191, 250n25
Grand Island, 35-36, 40, 72, 103, 236
Grant, Alexander, 35-36, 39-42, 44-
    45, 50, 198, 249n16
Green Mountain Boys, xii
Growler, 107, 109-110, 112-113, 115-
    116, 146, 223-225, 230-231,
    234, 255n3, 258n4
Gulliver, 105

Hadden, James, 160-162, 216

Hamilton, Paul, 105-106
Haviland, William, 44-48, 50-51, 190,
    249-250n23, 250n25, 250n27
Hawley, Joseph, 74-76
Henley, Robert, 133, 135, 140, 179
Herrick, Oliver, 98-99, 111
Hertel, Joseph, 19
Hicks, William, 135-136, 138, 142-
    143, 181-183
Hinman, Benjamin, 61
History of the Navy of the United States
    (Cooper), 163, 167
Hocquart, Gilles, 8
Hopkins, Joseph, 30-31
Hospital Island, 112
Hudson River, 5, 12, 96, 149, 211
Hull, Isaac, 104

Icicle, 131-132, 163, 169, 228, 235
Ile aux Noix, 29-32, 35, 38, 41-42,
    44-45, 49-50, 54, 59, 87, 91,
    103, 110-112, 114-116, 118-
    119, 121-123, 125, 147, 149,
    186-188, 190-193, 197, 208,
    212, 215, 218, 222, 229, 231-
    232, 234-235, 250n27, 255n12
Iles aux Quatre Vents, 170
Inflexible, 58-60, 70-71, 73-75, 79, 81-
    82, 86-87, 101-102, 126, 158,
    160-161, 176, 209-211, 213,
    217-218
Invincible, 28-29, 193, 196
Iroquois Confederacy, 1
Isle La Motte, 1, 68, 129, 144, 171,
    181, 204
Isle of St. Michael, 39

Jacobs, 186, 191-192, 199, 250n27
"Jersey Blues", 18
Johnson, Samuel, 97
Johnson, William, 26
Jones, William, 117, 119-120, 125, 178
Justin, Joshua, 180

Kalm, Peter, 8, 10
Katherine, 60, 203
Kennebec River, 61
King, Gideon, 230
King William, 4
Knox, Robert, 72-73, 252n33

La Chute River, 18, 90, 96, 98-99,
    199
La Colle River, 59, 107
Lake Champlain
  American fleet (1814) and, 220
  Battle of Cumberland Bay, 117,
    131, 137, 163-165, 167, 169,
    220-223, 225-227, 230-236
  Battle of Plattsburgh, 139
  Battle of Valcour Island, xii, 78,
    155, 158-162, 200, 202-207,
    209, 212-215, 218
  British fleet (1814) and, 228
  list of American merchantmen and,
    219
  U.S. Navy vessels constructed on,
    236
Lake George, 2, 4-6, 12, 14-18, 20-
    22, 24, 28, 94-102, 152, 158,
    192-197, 211, 216, 240,
    254n13, 256n20
Lake Ontario, 14, 26
Lambert, Robert, 171-172, 198-199
Land Tortoise, 23-24, 152, 193-194,
    196
Langdale, Charles, 19
La Pointe à Margot, 32, 45
Laramie, Michael, xi, xiv
Lea, Robert, 140
Lee, 68, 71, 81, 84, 87, 102-103, 182,
    200, 205, 210
Leonard, James, 147-148
Levasseur, René-Nicolas, 11, 32, 187-
    188
Levis, François, 18, 20, 42, 46-47,
    170-171
Liberty, xii, 60, 65, 67, 84, 91, 93,
    200-203
Ligonier, 33, 35, 38-39, 44-45, 58, 82,
    193, 197, 249n14
Lincoln, Benjamin, 97, 99
Linnet, 123-124, 130, 133-135, 137,
    139-141, 144, 146-148, 163,
    165, 169, 181-182, 184, 228-
    229, 233
Little One, 186, 190
Livingston, Henry, 202, 204, 206
Lizard, 212
Long, Pierce, 91-92, 94
Loomis, Jairus, 112, 255n8

Loring, Joshua, 12, 14-15, 22, 24, 28-
    31, 34-36, 38-41, 152, 171-172,
    187, 194-199, 247n7, 248n6,
    248-249n12, 249n15, 250n25
Lossing, Benjamin, 163, 165
Loudoun, General, 16, 21, 247n14
Louis XIV, 1
Loyal Convert, 52, 57, 71, 75, 79, 86,
    158, 160, 209-210, 213-214
Ludlow, 220, 227
Lutwidge, Skeffington, 87, 102, 218,
    253n2

Macdonough, Thomas, xi-xii, 104-
    107, 109-110, 112, 116-120,
    122-126, 128-130, 133, 140-
    141, 143-144, 146, 178, 180,
    220-226, 229-231, 255n8,
    256n17
Macomb, Alexander, 128
Mahan, Alfred Thayer, 163
Maria, 52-53, 56-57, 71-73, 75, 81-83,
    86-87, 94, 99, 102-103, 176-
    177, 209-213, 219, 252n33,
    254n18, 254n22
Marquis de Montcalm, 16, 20-22, 42,
    192, 247n14
Marquis de Tracy, 1-3
Mars, 220, 235, 256n13
Martin, 212
Massachusetts Committee of Safety,
    61
Master, Bryden, 183
Menominee, 19
Missisquoi Bay, 36, 170-171
Mohawks, 1-4, 17-19, 26, 245n3
Monro, George, 16, 18
Montgomery, 118, 146-147, 220, 222-
    224, 258n4
Montgomery, Richard, 53, 55, 62,
    203
Montgomery's Highlanders, 35
Montressor, James, 195
Mount Defiance, 90-91, 97-99
Mount Independence, xiii, 63, 88-91,
    95, 97, 100, 102
Murray, 136, 234
Murray, James, 51
Murray, John, 115

Musquelongy, 29, 32, 40, 186, 188-
  189, 193, 203

Nelson, Lord, 140
Nettle, 220, 227
New Haven, 65, 71, 200, 205
New Jersey, 68, 71, 79, 81, 83, 200,
  205, 210
New Jersey Regiment, 18, 20
New York, 68, 71, 77, 79, 82, 84, 91,
  93, 173, 200-201, 205
Northern Army Department, 66

Ord, Thomas, 29-31, 34, 44-46, 52,
  58, 196-197, 214
Oswald, Eleazer, 60, 203
Ottawas, 19
Otter Creek, 12, 118-119, 122-123
Outarde, 33

Parker, John, 18-21, 247n14
Paulding, Harim, 138
Pausch, Georg, 161
Payant, Joseph, 8, 10, 32-33, 36, 39,
  46, 48, 50, 187, 250n27
Peace of Ghent, 147
Peace of Paris, 213, 258n2
Pellew, Edward, 77-78
Philadelphia, 77, 79, 173, 200, 205-
  206, 258n9
Phillips, William, 90
Plattsburg Bay, 117, 180-181
Point au Fer, 53, 59-60, 208
Popham, 114, 136, 234
Potawatomi, 19
Poultney River, 222
Powall, Henry, 99
Prairie de Boileau, 50
Preble, 118, 128, 130, 136-139, 144-
  147, 163, 165, 167, 220, 225,
  227, 258n4
President, 107, 110, 115, 131, 147,
  219-220, 224, 255n3, 258n4
Prevost, George, 114-115, 117, 122,
  126-127, 143, 145, 147, 181,
  232
Prevost, 139, 234
Prideaux, John, 26
Prince Frederick Regiment, 97
Pring, Daniel, 116, 122-126, 134-135,
  142, 180, 184, 232
Pringle, Thomas, 59, 70, 72-73, 76-
  77, 79-81, 83, 90, 106, 176,
  213, 252n32
Providence, 65, 70-71, 120, 200, 205,
  225-226

Queen Anne, 4

Reid, John, 38
Revenge, xii, 65, 67, 71, 82, 84, 91, 93,
  200-201, 206
Richelieu River, 4-5, 8, 12, 29, 51, 54,
  59, 106, 110-111, 113, 125,
  188-190, 192, 208, 216, 240,
  243, 245n3, 250n27
Rising Sun, 117, 219, 225
Rivière du Sud, 46, 48-49
Rogers, Robert, 11-12, 16, 18, 44, 49,
  98, 198, 248n6, 250n25
Roi du Nord, 34
Rouses Point, 111, 116, 149
Royal Artillery, 29, 44, 93-94, 96,
  114-115, 162, 192, 196-197,
  216, 233, 255-256n12
Royal Edward, 103, 113, 212, 254n22
Royal Engineers, 30, 90, 195
Royal George, 86-87, 101, 210, 217
Royal Highlanders, 38
Royal Marines, 114-115, 124, 233
Royal Navy, 12, 14, 53, 55-56, 58-59,
  87, 144, 213, 238, 240
Royal Savage, xii, 67, 71, 73-76, 79-80,
  159-160, 162, 172, 177, 200-
  202, 252n32

Sabbath Day Point, 18-19, 100
Saintonge, 8, 10-11, 51
Saranac River, 143
Saratoga, 120, 124-125, 128, 130,
  133-135, 137, 139-143, 146-
  148, 165, 178-180, 220-221,
  233
Saucy Fox, 219
Saunders, Charles, 26
Sayer, Robert, 158
Schank, John, 58-59, 90, 96, 254n21
Schuyler, Abraham, 4
Schuyler, Johannes, 4

Schuyler, Peter, 4
Schuyler, Phillip, 63-66, 70, 95, 174,
204-206
Schuyler's Island, 81, 83, 172, 174
Seaman, Isaac, 95
Shannon, 115-116, 123, 230
Sheaffe, Roger, 116
Shelburne Bay, 116
Shelburne Shipyards, 236
Shirley, William, 14
Simmons, William, 122-123, 229,
232
Skene, Philip, 60, 203
Smith, James, 204
Smith, Sidney, 110-113
Spitfire, xiii, 68, 71, 79, 81, 153, 200,
205
St. Amand Bay, 68
St. Clair, Arthur, 91, 95, 175
St. Lawrence River, 7, 16, 26, 29, 53,
55, 58, 62, 119, 127
St. Onge, Joseph Payant, 8, 10, 32-33,
36, 39, 46, 48, 50, 187,
250n27
subchasers, 151, 236
Surprize, 212

Taylor, George, 115
Third New York Continentals, 206
Thirty-ninth Regiment, 233
Three Mile Point, 87
Thunderer, 52, 57, 71, 75, 86, 94, 102,
158, 160, 209-210, 214-215
Ticonderoga, 120, 124, 128-130, 133,
135-139, 141-142, 144-148,
163, 165, 167, 179, 220, 224-
226, 233-235
Triton, 211, 218
Trumbull, 67, 69-71, 73, 79-80, 82, 84,
91, 93, 200-201, 207-208
Tsonnonthouans Cove, 170
Twiss, William, 90-91, 96
Two Brothers, 36

Valcour Island, xii-xiii, 69, 72-75, 78-
80, 85, 155, 158-163, 200,
202-207, 209, 212-216, 218
Valette, Jean, 46
Vanderford, Charles, 85
Vaudreuil, Philippe, 5

Vaudreuil, Pierre, 11, 15, 34, 42, 51,
171, 247n14
Victory, 14
Vigilante, 11, 29, 32, 35-36, 41, 43, 46,
48-50, 186-187, 250n25
Viper, 220, 227

Waggon, 51
Walters, Abraham, 112
Warner, Seth, 98-99
War of 1812, xii, 109, 113, 121, 150,
152, 163, 165, 220-226, 228-
231, 234-236, 255n3, 256n13,
258n2
War of Austrian Succession, 33
Washington, George, 61, 63, 65, 95,
173-174, 176
Washington, 67, 70-71, 77, 79, 81-82,
87, 173-174, 176, 178, 200,
207-208, 210
Wasp, 116, 118, 223-224, 256n17
Waterbury, David, 67, 69-70, 72-73,
81-82, 173, 175, 178
Webb, Daniel, 16, 20, 247n14
Wells, Bayze, 70
Whitcomb's Rangers, 98
White Mountains, 104
Wigglesworth, Edward, 73, 80, 82,
173
William Maid, 235, 256n13
Williams, Edward, 66
Wilmer, 220, 227
Windmill Point, 45, 111
Winooski Falls, 106
Winslow, John, 14
Winthrop, Fitz-John, 4
Wolfe, James, 26, 41
Woodbridge, Benjamin, 97
Wood Creek, 4, 64
Wooster, David, 62
Wyknoop, Jacobus, 67, 95-96

Yeo, 136, 180, 234
Yeo, James L., 180, 232